CISTERCIAN FATHERS SERIES: NUMBER SEVENTY

Ogier of Locedio

In Praise of God's Holy Mother
On Our Lord's Words to His Disciples at the Last Supper

CISTERCIAN FATHERS SERIES: NUMBER SEVENTY

Ogier of Locedio

In Praise of God's Holy Mother

On Our Lord's Words to His Disciples at the Last Supper

Translated and annotated by
D. Martin Jenni

CISTERCIAN PUBLICATIONS
Kalamazoo, Michigan

The work of Cistercian Publications is made possible in part by support from Western Michigan University to the Institute of Cistercian Studies.

Library of Congress: Cataloging-in-Publication Data

Ogier, of Locedio, Abbott of Locedio, d. 1214.
[Tractatus in laudibus Sancte Dei Genetricis. English]
Ogier of Locedio / translated and annotated by D. Martin Jenni.
v. cm. — (Cistercian Fathers series ; no. 70)
Includes index.
Contents: In praise of God's Holy Mother — On our Lord's words to his disciples at the Last Supper.
ISBN-13: 978-0-87907-570-5 (alk. paper)
ISBN-10: 0-87907-570-8 (alk. paper)
1. Mary, Blessed Virgin, Saint—Sermons. 2. Last Supper—Sermons. 3. Catholic Church—Sermons. 4. Sermons, Medieval. 5. Sermons, Latin—Translated into English. I. Jenni, Donald, 1937– . II. Ogier, of Locedio, Abbott of Locedio, d. 1214. Expositio super Evangelium in Cena Domini. English. III. Title. IV. Series.

BT608.O35 2006
232.91—dc22

2006009032

Printed in the United States of America

TABLE OF CONTENTS

Abbreviations

Ambrose	
De virg.	*De virginitate.* PL 16
Hom. in Lucam	*Expositio euangelii secundum Lucam.* PL 15.
Augustine [of Hippo]	
Contra Acad.	*Contra Academicos.* PL 32; CCL 29
Quaest.	*Quaestiones in Heptateuchum.* PL 34; CCL 33
Bernard	
In laud.	*Homelium super* Missus est *in laudibus virginis matris.* Homilies in Praise of the Blessed Virgin Mary. CF 18A.
Blaise, DAC	*Dictionnaire latin-français des auteurs chrétiens,* ed Albert Blaise. Turnhout: Brepols 1967.
Cassian	
Conf.	*Collationes. The Conferences.*
Inst.	*Institutiones. The Institutes.*
CCL	Corpus Christianorum Latinorum. Turnhout: Brepols
CF	Cistercian Fathers Series
CLS	Cistercian Liturgy Series
CS	Cistercian Studies Series
Ep(p)	Epistolae / Letters
GR	*Graduale Romanum.* Solesmes 1973.
Gregory the Great	
Hom. Evang.	*Homeliae xl in Euangelia.* PL 76; CCL 14; *Forty Gospel Homilies.* CS 123.

Innsbruck UB	Innsbruck (Austria), Univeritätsbibliothek
Jerome	
Heb. Nom	*Liber interpretationis hebraicorum nominum.* PL 23.
Heb Quaest in Gen.	*Liber quaestionum hebraicarum in Genesim.* PL 23.
LH	*Liber hymnarius.* Solesmes, 1983
Ogier	
Expositio	*On the Lord's Words to his Disciples at the Last Supper*
Tractatus	*In Praise of God's Holy Mother*
PL	J.-P. Migne, Patrologia Latina
RB	*Regula Benedicti;* The Rule of Saint Benedict. Benedict's Rule for Monasteries

Introduction

IT IS NONE TOO SURPRISING that we do not really know by what name to call a Cistercian Father who was for some four hundred years eclipsed by the shadow of Saint Bernard. The singular manuscript of his major writings, which may well have been produced before 1214, while our author was still alive, identifies him as *Ogerius* (or, more precisely, by the ablative and genitive forms of that name). He is so named as abbot in an official act, dated 19 December 1211, between his monastery, Locedio, and the diocese of Vercelli. Other documents, written after his death, refer to him as *Oglerus* and *Occlesius;* in a seventeenth-century cistercian menology, his name is given as *Oglerius*. This last is the form promoted by many scholars since that time, though several cistercian publications (e.g. *Pain de Cîteaux*) still refer to him by the earliest documented form of his name. Not so much to complicate matters further as to express gratitude for a colleague's help in locating a rare edition of the manuscript, I will call him, as David Bell does,[1] Ogier.

What we know of Ogier's life, sketchy at best, is owed chiefly to Giovanni-Battista Adriani, who gathered the meager evidence in his 1873 edition of the Staffarda manuscript.[2]

[1] In his 'Lists and Records of Books in English Cistercian Libraries', *Analecta Cisterciensia* 43 (1987) and *An Index of Authors and Works in Cistercian Libraries in Great Britain* (Kalamazoo 1992); cf. n. 10. The case for Oglerius is made by Canon J. Raviola in his proemium to Adriani's 1873 edition (pp. XLVII–VIII; see next note).

[2] *Beati Oglerii . . . Opera quæ supersunt . . . nunc primum descripta ac notis declarata cura et studio Joannis Baptistæ Adrianii* (Turin, 1873). I am indebted to David N. Bell

Indeed, the fate of our author became curiously intertwined with that of the earliest copy of his work. The monastery of Santa Maria di Staffarda, named after a dense forest in the marchisate and diocese of Saluzzo (Piemonte), was founded by order of Saint Bernard in 1122 and housed in the *castellum* of the ruling family. Staffarda's history comes to an abrupt halt in 1606, when, over an observance dispute, its monks were condemned, and the contents of its confiscated library found their way into the hands of the Duke of Turin. Thus the Ogerian manuscript came to be housed in the duke's Athenaeum, where it was discovered by a fellow Cistercian, Giovanni, Cardinal Bona (1609–1674). A year before Bona's death the manuscript was transferred to the library of the recently founded University of Turin; from there it passed to the Biblioteca Nazionale of that city, where it is catalogued as E.V. 4. Bona recognized in Ogier the author of the Last Supper discourses included in Mabillion's 1642 edition of the works of Saint Bernard, and he published that fact in his *Psallentis Ecclesiæ Harmonia* of 1653. In the definitive 1690 edition, the Maurist scholar Jean Mabillion, citing his indebtedness to Bona, reassigned the discourses to a supplement devoted to falsely attributed writings;[3] but by this time the work of the monk and abbot of Locedio had long and extensively traveled under another author's name. Translating two of the discourses 'into common German' in 1471, the Carthusian Heinrich Haller, of Cloister Allerengelberg in the southern Tyrol, confidently titles them *omelien des heiligen sant Wernharcz*.[4] The same pseudonymity befell the *Liber de Passione Christi et doloribus et planctibus Matris eius* (or, as it is perhaps better known, the

---

of Memorial University of Newfoundland for locating a copy of this edition for me.

[3] Thus also Migne, in PL 184.

[4] Erika Bauer, ed. *Zisterzienser-Predigten (Homiliæ 9 et 13 expositionis super Evangelium in Cena Domini Oglerii de Trino) in der Übertragung des Heinrich Haller O.Carth.* (München 1969) 39.

Planctus Marie),[5] aided in part by its having been excerpted from a larger work bearing the rather generic title of *In Laudibus Sancte Dei Genetricis* (cf. Bernard's *In Laudibus Virginis Matris*). Publication under a name of greater renown has, of course, a long christian history—already in evidence in the (canonical as well as apocryphal) New Testament. A later redactor of Ogier might well have recognized a distinctly bernardine mellifluousness in many a passage from the discourses; in the case of the tractate he would often have been confronted with Bernard's very words.[6]

Ogier's birth in Trino, just north of the Po some forty-five kilometers east of Turin, is well attested; so, too, are the year of his election to the abbacy of Locedio (1205) and the date of his death (10 September 1214). Just when he was born, however, is a matter of considerable confusion, over which looms, once again, the shadow of Bernard. Situated like Ogier's birthplace in the diocese of Vercelli, the former benedictine abbey of Saint Michael of Locedio (founded 1050) was reconstituted in 1124—*operante Sancto Bernardo* (according to a late-seventeenth-century archival record)—by Cistercians from La Ferté, and was thereafter, in good cistercian style, known as the Abbey of Saint Mary. The belief that Ogier was a near-contemporary of Bernard—an assumption maintained well into the seventeenth century—owes principally to mistaken identity and pious legend. The abbot of Clairvaux addressed four letters[7] to a certain Canon *Ogerius*. Their content and frankly reluctant manner—in one, the Canon is referred to Guerric of Igny—suggest that the correspondence was initiated and protracted by the recipient. Some time later Bernard commends him[8] to the bishop of Winchester—unless this is yet a third Ogerius. But not even the earliest conjecture of

[5] The 'Lament of Mary' is also known by its *incipit*, *Quis dabit;* see below, n. 12.

[6] See the discussion below, in the Introduction to *In laudibus Sancte Dei Genetricis,* of Ogier's use of Bernard's marian homilies.

[7] Epp 87–90.

[8] Ep 93.

our author's birth year fits these situations. In 1148 Bernard stopped in Trino during a visitation of Locedio Abbey; from this event sprang the legend of an encounter between the famed Cistercian and the 'youthful Oglerius' (so Canon Raviola's transmission of the story, citing an eighteenth-century account, in his foreword to Adriani's edition). By Bona's reckoning, Ogier had already become Locedio's abbot eight years earlier, in 1140; if this were true, his tenure in that office, which he held until his death in 1214, would therefore have lasted seventy-four years!

In 1720, the learned Cistercian Dom Andreas Irico of Locedio, attempting to correct Bona's patent error, proposed 1140 as the year Ogier entered monastic life at the (then) canonical age of 14, thus reckoning his birth as having occurred in 1126. This date, however, is contradicted by Irico himself, who gives Ogier's age at the time of his death as seventy-eight; he must then have been born in 1136, as Raviola asserts. It seems not to have occurred to Irico, or to Adriani, that 1140 held no particular biographical significance for Ogier. The *Dictionnaire de Spiritualité* offers that year as the earliest likely date of his birth.[9] The data are admirably summarized by Bauer;[10] 'the whole', she concludes, 'is wanting in probability'.

The records of Locedio indicate that the abbot elected in 1140 was Peter I, and that some time after 1184 his successor, Peter II, appointed our Ogier as his *vicarius* (second-in-charge). In this capacity Ogier accompanied Dom Peter II to Jerusalem as abbatial secretary. In 1205, when Peter's meteoric career took him first to Thessaloniki as archbishop and then to Antioch as patriarch, Ogier succeeded him as thirteenth abbot of Locedio, serving in that office until his death. Ogier appears to have been beatified in 1653, the very year of Bona's publication, though he had long before that been called *beatus;*

[9] *Dictionnaire de Spiritualité* 11:733-736 (Edmund Mikkers).

[10] Bauer, p. 11.

the cultus that sprang up almost immediately after Ogier's death was at long last officially approved in 1875 by Pius IX.

The Manuscript Tradition

The Staffarda manuscript preserves two works of ambitious length, each occupying seventy leaves; they bear the titles: *Tractatus in Laudibus Sancte Dei Genetricis* (here translated as *In Praise of God's Holy Mother*), and *Expositio super Evangelium in Cena Domini (On Our Lord's Words to His Disciples at the Last Supper).* The two compositions differ markedly in tone and technical skill, yet the same authorial *persona* speaks in both, over the considerable interval of a long and diligent monastic life. That interval—between the first drafts of what came to be the *Tractatus* and the last great Chapter sermons *In Cena Domini*—spans near-extremes in Ogier's community life at Locedio. The author of the marian tractate is identified by the Staffarda scribe as a monk of simple profession; the author of the *Expositio* is Locedio's shepherd. The extremes meet when *Ogerius Abbas* takes up once more (as senior redactor now) what appears to be a long-standing project begun by *Frater Ogerius*. There had been some gap in the undertaking: two decades of far-ranging travel and coadjutorial diplomacy have irrupted into the life of a cistercian monk who writes with undiminished longing for the Beatific Vision. Embracing the greater part of Ogier's spiritual journey at Locedio, the two documents offer seeds of contemplation whose power to bear fruit remains vital in our day; vital, too, is their inspiring testimony to this 'monk of Christ'. Yet it is tempting to suppose that the contents of Staffarda are not the whole of Ogier's output; in this one is both encouraged and cautioned by Bona: 'He is said to have written other things beyond [the two in Staffarda], but none, so far as I know, is extant.'[11]

[11] Adriani, p. 19. The *Cena* homilies are followed in PL 184 by a discourse titled *Item In Cœna Domini Sermo*. While the opulent-banquet imagery of its base

The four-century lag between the composition of the manuscript at Staffarda and its fortuitous discovery in Turin by Bona supports an argument for other early transmissions of these writings, as a pair or, more likely, in various parts. At least the segment of the tractate known as the *Planctus Marie* ('Our Lady's Lamentation') and broken or whole forms of the *Expositio* enjoyed an independent transmission as extensive as that of the earliest surviving witness. When, nearly two centuries before Bona discovered the Staffarda manuscript, Haller began his translation of a (non-adjacent) pair of two of the Last Supper Discourses, two markedly divergent latin editions had already been produced in his scriptorium near Innsbruck.[12] The transmission of the *Planctus* is quite another, as yet unwritten, tale.[13] In a signatory couplet, the scriptorium monk of Staffarda names himself. Given the shadow cast by Bernard (and Bernard's Canon Ogerius) over the author-abbot of Locedio, the identity of the scribe is delicious for its symmetry—it is Ogier's Bernard:

Finito libro sit laus et gloria Christo.
Descripto libro benedicat Deus Bernardo.[14]

text (Prov 23:1, 2) is suggestive of Ogier's opening *Paschalibus dapibus* theme, I do not recognize his voice in its argument. I have translated it for publication elsewhere in the Cistercian Fathers series.

[12] Innsbruck, UB Cod. 570 (E 40), cf. Bauer pp. 22-30; there is moreover a fragment of the *Expositio* in a manuscript of the Schottenkloster at Vienna (Cod. 192, dated 1443).

[13] 'Little attempt has been made to document the extent of its influence through a census of the surviving manuscripts or references in medieval texts.' C.W. Marx, 'The *Quis dabit* of Oglerius de Tridino, Monk and Abbot of Locedio', in *The Journal of Medieval Latin* 4 (1994) 118. David Bell has discovered a copy of the *Planctus* in the erstwhile library of Whalley Abbey, and a French translation formerly at Bordesley; cf. Bell (1992), p. 107.

[14] 'The book is ended: To Christ be the praise and glory! Now that I have written it down, may God grant his Bernard a blessing.' The graceless hexameters can hardly be ascribed to the abbot of Clairvaux.

The Works

In Praise of God's Holy Mother

The marian tractate identifies its author as a 'certain faithful lover of hers [named] Brother Ogier of Locedio'.[15] That it is a pre-abbatial composition is further evident from a comparison of its style and manner with that of the *Expositio*. In stark contrast to the internal unity and logic of the latter, the somewhat rambling composition, apparent shifts of plan, and wide stylistic range of the marian piece suggest a project returned to time and again over several decades. While Ogier's promotion to *abbas in secundis* might signal the year 1184 as the *terminus ad quem* for his being called a *frater,* the draft of the work the scribe of Staffarda had before him some three decades later bears distinct, if sporadic, signs of redaction; it is arguable that what I call its Prologue and Final Homily constitute a framing device intended to impose an overall shape to a rather diffuse argument. The work may well have been taken up anew with the intention of publication, especially during Ogier's rise to prominence in the 80s and 90s, but the duties of coadjutor appear to have permitted him little time for thorough revision. *Nec mirum*—as Ogier is wont to say: unifying a work in which youthful exuberance and rhetorical excess are met by the fruits of maturer reflection and study would have required a luxury of labor no shepherd of souls (or his *vicarius*) could afford.[16]

Though unified by a distinctively 'Cistercian devotion to the Virgin Mary',[17] the aptly named *tractatus* contains both private reflection and public instruction. Much of the work

[15] *Tractatus . . . a quodam fideli servo ac dilectore ipsius fratre Ogerio de Locedio* (f. 1).

[16] Bernard himself must snatch moments when he might otherwise sleep to pen 'what devotion demands but overwhelming duties prohibit' *(In laudibus Virginis Matris, Præfatio)*.

[17] Marx, p. 118.

seems written for the edification of *virgines sacræ,*[18] though Ogier makes a point of including his own community of monks eight times over the course of five discourses. The impact of Bernard is clearly reflected, though perhaps less as a youthful influence than as that of an *auctoritas* to be consulted at length.

The marked concentration of Ogier's bernardine inspiration in the central seven homilies of the tractate (IV through X), while owing in some measure to the Lucan source text the novice author is sharing with his practiced mentor, suggests that the period during which the core of the work was composed coincided with—and may well have been refired by—the arrival at Locedio of a copy of *In Laudibus Virginis Matris*. Within the first four of these homilies Ogier allows himself to cite Bernard *verbatim* nine times,[19] in addition to ten further paraphrases and direct influences. It is only in VII, in the midst of a sixty-word citation, that Ogier acknowledges the author (*ut dicit beatus Bernardus:* 'as Blessed Bernard says') of what has been for some time by this point his *vade mecum*—and from which he will name his *opusculum*. Thereafter, until a few allusions to this source appear for the last time in IX and X, the spirit and voice of Bernard have become thoroughly internalized.

The final form of the tractate as a Life of the Virgin—in part directly revealed to the author by his subject, in part a series of meditations—bears signs of having been imposed on a disparate collection of writings at a fairly advanced stage of composition. As biography, the scheme is both disproportionate and incomplete. Between its twin focus on early and

[18] Bauer (p. 11) describes the tractate as *Sermones, an Nonnen gerichtet, oft in Gesprächsform*. Ogier's intention, apparently formulated some time into the composition of the tractate, to address the work *virginibus sacris* may have been suggested to him by a phrase in Bernard's First Homily (*miramini etiam vos, sacræ virgines* I.9.).

[19] These are set off in the translation by font, like other cited sources; paraphrases are mentioned in the notes.

late events in the lives of Mary and Jesus yawns a span of decades (from the Presentation in the Temple to the Passion) either ignored altogether (the Flight into Egypt, the Wedding at Cana) or only scantily alluded to (the slaughter of the Innocents, the public ministry of Jesus). As the fruit of monastic *lectio,* the writing is naturally enough shot through with allusion to the Scriptures (above all, the Psalter recited at the Divine Office) and is further characterized by a completely internalized liturgical repertory (e.g. Mass antiphon texts, Office hymns and Lessons).[20] But Ogier's interests inevitably lead him far afield from the sacred canon: the plan of the tractate necessitates the flanking of its central gospel narratives (Mary's betrothal to Joseph, the Annunciation, the Nativity of Jesus, the Presentation, the Passion, Resurrection, and Ascension) with apocryphal material related to Mary's parentage, birth, and childhood, her espousal to a widower with grown children, and her Assumption.[21] Ogier not only embraces the legendary with a credulity the Abbot of Clairvaux would have deemed rash he treats such material in much the same way as his biblical sources, through word-play, invented or amplified direct speech, and dramatization.

The medieval passion for word derivation, particularly the hidden meaning of proper nouns, is well known.[22] While most of Ogier's etymology of hebrew names relies on Jerome,[23]

[20] The diffusion of Scripture throughout all such sources (including the contents of the monastic library), and the author's typical reliance on memory, often make primary source identification a matter of speculation.

[21] For the infancy legends, see n. 25 below; the assumption accounts are based ultimately on the coptic apocrypha (e.g. the *Book of John the Evangelist*) and the *Transitus Mariæ Virginis* of Pseudo-Melito.

[22] The Bible itself is studded with onomastic etymologies. Perhaps the most famous wordplay of the New Testament is made by Jesus himself *(Tu es* Petrus, *et super hanc* petram *ædificabo ecclesiam meam).* The subject is engagingly treated by Bernard Guenée in his *Histoire et culture historique dans l'Occident médiéval* (Paris 1980); see particularly, 'La passion de l'étymologie', pp. 184-191.

[23] *Liber interpretationis hebraicorum nominum,* ed. P. de Lagarde, CCL 72 (Turnholt, 1959) 57-161.

he indulges here and there in philological flights of fancy (such as his treatment of *Anna, Eva/ave,* and the Tetragrammaton).[24] Much in evidence also is the device of the exegetical *amplificatio* of direct speech ('as if to say').[25] Virtually every 'speaking role' is liberally amplified, and entire speeches are invented where no basis exists in the source. Ogier has no paucity of models on which to draw for such invention; in giving utterance to John the Baptist within the womb of Elizabeth, for example, Ogier is clearly following Chrysostom. Here and there, speakers are told what to say. Akin to such devices is the divining of the intention of his speakers, and the dramatic intensification of the occasions of their utterance. The latter reaches fever pitch in Ogier's depiction of the *Virgo perdolens.*

Although Ogier has been repeatedly cited as an early witness to the doctrine of the Immaculate Conception—in distinct contrast to Bernard—the reference occurs in the later *Expositio*, not in the tractate (see below). Ogier's earlier mariology is conventional enough for its time. The account of Mary's birth to Joachim and Anne—based ultimately, though not directly, on the *Protoevangelium of James*[26]—makes no par-

[24] Such inventiveness may have been locally inspired: Ogier's monastic home, variously spelled Locedio or Lucedio, was popularly interpreted as *locus Dei* ('God's place') and *luce Dei* ('in God's light'). A seventeenth-century archivist assumes a less fanciful origin in *lo seggio* ('the [ecclesiastical] see') cf. Adriani, pp. VII, XVIII-XIX. That there is scarcely any of this sort of thing in the *Expositio* is due both to greater focus of source and a relative paucity of interpretatively useful proper names; apart from the straightforward (and well-known) glosses on *pascha*, *Jesus*, and *Didymus,* the sole etymological note is to Simon Ischariot, Judas's father's name.

[25] The device is virtually as ancient as the latin exegetical tradition: in Ambrose, whose Lucan commentary Ogier cites verbatim, paraphrase immediately following direct quotation is often linked by *hoc est.*

[26] H. R. Smid's *Protoevangelium Jacobi: A Commentary* (translated G. E. van Baaren-Pape, Assen, 1966) provides the best modern edition of the greek text; for an english translation see M. R. James, *The Apocryphal New Testament* (Oxford, 1955) pp. 38-49. The work is also known (as early as the third century) as The Birth of Mary; cf. Michel Testuz, *Papyrus Bodmer V: Nativité de Marie* (Geneva, 1958). The narrative, on which Jacobus de Voragine's *Legenda aurea* relies, nearly

ticular case for the singularity of her conception, except that it came very late in the lives of her saintly parents—whose conjugality is utterly without lust. While much else has been trimmed from the second-century fable, the pious incongruity of her consecration as a Temple virgin is uncritically transmitted; indeed, Ogier (or his intermediate source) has Mary inhabiting the sacred precincts 'upon her being weaned from her mother's breast' (rather than at three years of age, as in the *Protoevangelium*). Still, one senses the author's desire to shift to the firmer ground of the Scriptures in his interlarding of this material with accommodated passages from the Gospels (e.g. '*she* will be great and shall be called the *Mother* of the Most High').

Once having arrived at Mary's betrothal to Joseph, Ogier can pursue the course of speculative exegesis that sustains most of what follows. The years between her consecration and espousal are devoted to Mary's practice of *lectio* (chiefly of the messianic prophecies) and her longing for the promised incarnation. This forms a lovely bridge, well suited to Ogier's presumed audience, but the inception of gospel material introduces the unintended dissonance of Mary's lifelong anticipation of the annunciation and her shock and misgivings —chiefly at what she assumes will entail the loss of her virginity—when it comes to pass. The latter serves our author's desire to play up the emotional impact of the scene for his hearers. Here his inspiration—the breathlessly awaited moment of Mary's *fiat*—is clearly Bernard himself (*In laudibus Virginis Matris*, homily 4). Similarly, Ogier responds with initial indignation to Mary's swaddling of the infant Jesus and his

---

a century after the composition of Ogier's *Tractatus*, has a long and complex latin transmission in the West, such that an immediate source here cannot be identified, short of the discovery of a library list for Locedio during Ogier's years there. Ogier's material differs most strikingly from the *Protoevangelium*—and from the *Legenda aurea*—by its inclusion of the youthful betrothal and marriage of Joachim and Anne, motivated by Joachim's dread that the 'curse' of not fathering a child will make him unfit to perform his priestly duties.

being laid in a manger, before extracting from it a well-reasoned *exemplum*.

My division of the tractate into fourteen sections—a prologue and thirteen homilies—is based on internal signs of closure, chiefly the doxology formulas in which all but section XI terminate. (The division of XI from XII at this point is admittedly arbitrary, though, I think, rhetorically satisfying.) The *Prologue*, addressed internally to 'all who may come upon these writings', contrasts with the *Introductory Homily* (I), which engages the *Theotokos* in dialogue reminiscent of both the apocryphal Questions of Mary tradition and passages in Bernard's *In laudibus Virginis Matris* of 1125. Well over half of Homily I is composed of Mary's direct address to the author. This terminates in a doxology, suggesting its origin in an earlier set-piece. What follows—appended by 'to these words I would add'—is too brief to constitute a section of its own; it forms the concluding member of a redactorial framework.[27] The dialogue device of I is thereafter abandoned until the end of section XI, where its resumption is triggered by an appeal to 'promises' of further direct revelation made to the author 'at the beginning of the work'.[28]

As if starting afresh, the *Second Homily* (II) embarks on an amplified account of Mary's birth and childhood, now addressed to 'consecrated virgins' of whom the author is 'reminded', towards the close of I: those who follow Our Lady's example of chastity and devotion. Once again a later redaction may be signaled here.

[27] Its own doxology comes soon enough after that of the Words of Mary to seem awkwardly redundant. The length of Homily I thus refashioned is comparable to that of II, III, IV, VI, and X. The remaining sections are considerably more expansive, from roughly twice (V, XI, XII, XIII) to three (VII) and four times in length (VIII).

[28] Dialogue (as distinct from interpolated utterances which the Virgin, like Gabriel, Elizabeth, Joseph, and other *personæ*, 'might have said') is central to the composition of XII, and is further invoked in XIII.

From this point onwards, through most of Homily XI, the tone and manner of discourse are those of readings intended for the refectory or the chapter room. The exegetical nature of these homilies harmonizes with the author's characterization of himself (in the *Prologue*) as one 'compelled by the love of discoursing on the Word of Life'.

In Homily V, Ogier offers an unusually personal account of a wayward sinner (presumably a layman), who 'some fourteen years ago' was reconciled to God through Mary's intercession. Although cast as the witness of an acquaintance, the account suggests an intimacy between narrator and subject that may well exceed the conventions of rhetoric; later references to the author's 'personal experience' and the sustaining charity of his fellow monastics are similar in tone to the conversion story. Like Aelred of Riveaux (1176), had the penitent of Locedio found a nurturing cistercian community—over which, in time, he too was to preside as abbot?

The admonitory tenor of Homilies VII and VIII suggest an author mature enough to address his community with the authority of a *vicarius*. While indeed reminiscent of the Rule of Saint Benedict, and in one instance clearly inspired by the abbot of Clairvaux, their condemnation of monastic shortcomings—and call to repentance and conversion—markedly anticipate the fuller development of these themes in the *Expositio*.

With similar maturity, Ogier embarks on an exegetical contemplation of the *Magnificat* midway in his account of the Visitation (VIII); the exegesis is continued in—indeed, occupies the whole of—IX. In these passages we are closer than anywhere else in the tractate to the style of the author of the *Expositio*. In X and XI Ogier returns to his Visitation narrative, to which he links, in language borrowed directly from Ambrose, the consequences of Mary's long stay with her kinsfolk, and the visible source of Joseph's dilemma upon her return to Nazareth. Having advanced his biographical plot to the point of the Presentation, our author is clearly impatient to lunge into the long postponed Passion account foretold in I.

Ogier's treatment of Mary's *compassio* reverts to extended dialogue, but with the abrupt intrusion of a narrative third person in addition to the author's *persona* to this point. Conspicuous throughout the long (eleven-leaf) discourse is the absence of direct address to monastics of either gender. Folio 56r of Staffarda, roughly the beginning of our XII, bears the marginal rubric *In parasceve ad collacionem* ('for [reading] at a monastic assembly on Good Friday'). The notation could refer as easily to an original occasion as to a later usage (at Staffarda, for example); whatever its particular significance, the independent function of the Passion dramatization is without doubt. As the so-called *Planctus Mariæ,* or *Lamentatio S. Bernardi de compassione Mariæ,* the set-piece took on a life of its own, becoming, in the estimation of a recent scholar,[29] 'the model of Low Country and German Marian laments'. Its formal peculiarities and at times hysterical pitch appear to indicate a very early independent composition by Ogier awkwardly incorporated into the tractate at an appropriate point in the chronological scheme. Whether Staffarda represents the onset of its independent career or its reintegration after such a process had already ensued cannot be determined from our present knowledge of the manuscript trail. Its attribution to Bernard throughout virtually all of its known transmission history leaves us with a missing link: who substituted *Sancti Bernardi* for *fratris Ogerii*—and where.[30] Further problematic

[29] K. Chr. J. W. de Vries, cited without source title by Bauer, p. 7.

[30] H. Barré, in his 'Le *Planctus Mariæ* attribué à Saint Bernard, *Revue d'ascétique et de mystique* 28 (1952), appears to have been the first to recognize the work as 'an extract from a larger text' (so Marx, p. 119). I have not seen Barré's article, nor the 'Codice delle opere del B. Oglerio de Lucedio' of Mario Capellino in the *Bollettino storico vercellese* 18 (1982) also noted by Marx. According to Sandro Sticca, *The* Planctus Mariæ *in the Dramatic Tradition of the Middle Ages* (translated J. R. Berrigan [Athens Georgia, 1988]), Barré argues that the marian lament came to be separated after the composition of the Tractatus, into which it '*s'insère parfaite-*

is the discrepancy of the point of *incipit* of the independent *Lament*, taking as its proemium nearly the whole of f.55 (beginning at *O quis dabit*), nearly three leaves before the Good Friday rubric. The *Planctus* thus spans our Homilies XI and XII (where, uniquely, no doxology intervenes).

The *Final Homily* (XIII) offers both a conclusion to the marian hagiography and a summary recapitulation that brings the long and at times rambling work to a cogent and moving cadence. Its technical assuredness bespeaks a later final redaction—perhaps for the scribe at Staffarda, who has received not a loose-leaf compendium, but a 'little book' *(libellus)*.[31]

On Our Lord's Words to His Disciples at the Last Supper

The *Expositio super Evangelium in Cena Domini* invites us to a 'paschal feast' of ineffable savor and richness: the food is the very Bread of Life himself. What our fatherly author will offer from his modest little board, *mensula,* are, in Ogier's exquisite trope, mere 'crumbs', but, as their ultimate source is 'the Lord's own table'. In them we will find refreshment far beyond the scraps that fell to the beggar Lazarus.[32] In the course of fourteen homilies,[33] the fruit of a lifetime of *lectio* will illumine

ment . . . et n'apparaisse pas comme une pièce rapportée après coupe' (p. 103). I find the judgment debatable.

[31] See the work's *explicit* (and n. 168 to *In Praise of God's Holy Mother*), which differs distinctly from the scribe's signatory couplet to the *Expositio.*

[32] Lk 16:21.

[33] Reckoning the number of these homilies has proved problematic since their first copying at Staffarda, where the rubricist, failing to note the doxology which closes VII, did not enter EXPLICIT and INCIPIT until the beginning of IX, which he numbered as VIII. The error, though noted, is preserved in Adriani; thus his total (and Bauer's, p. 11) of thirteen. In its transmission under Bernard's name, VII and VIII were correctly divided, but the final homily was split into two. While the latter error was recognized as such as early as Mabillon's incunabulum edition,

some seventy-eight verses of the johannine Last Supper discourses in a compelling and movingly personal way. Their author's voice is that of a seasoned exegete and homilist; it is, moreover, that of an exemplary monk, and the evidence of his beatitude.

The homilies' intended auditors are clearly Dom Ogier's spiritual sons, his 'dear brother Christians, monks of Benedict'. He bids them 'ponder what it means to be a monk' (XI). He corrects them gently—and also with stunning directness: 'Yes, brother, you!' (XIV); he instructs them on fine points of grammar and rhetoric, and he inspires in them tears of profound remorse, and of mystical joy. But others are addressed as well in the course of these outpourings. Echoing Benedict's admonition to abbots on the tempering of discipline with humble charity, Ogier rails against false monks who bear abbatial authority (II, III); 'better a swineherd' such a prelate 'than a shepherd of monks'. Three of the homilies (III, IV, XII) are incidentally addressed to a lector, indicating perhaps a refectory reader, or perhaps the later-imagined reader of a promulgated edition. As in the case of the tractate, we may read into this title the future beneficiaries of a draft gingerly redacted for the Staffarda scribe. (Alternatively, the term may be a scribal addition.)

The source text, John 13:1–15:14, is distributed variously among the homilies, where it is cited largely intact, with some narrative paraphrasing and a few omissions.[34] While there are themes aplenty in the rich ore of Ogier's source, the great

---

it persists in Migne's PL, and the tally is still conventionally given as being fifteen. That Haller began his translation of *die neunt omelia* at the correct division of IX from VIII—*Sequitur: Non relinquam vos orphanos*—suggests either a discerning reader or one in possession of an accurate manuscript source; indeed, the compiler of Innsbruch (UB Cod. 570, for whose role as *princeps* Bauer, pp. 22–23, cogently argues), though he misattributed the homilies as being *'beati Bernardi abbatis,'* got their count right at fourteen.

[34] I.13:1-2; II.13:3-19; III.13:20-30 (paraphrasing 22-24a and 25a); IV.13:31-33 (omitting 32a); V.13:34-35; VI.13:36-38, 14:1-4; VII.14:4-13 (omitting 12a); VIII.14:15-17; IX.14:18-26; X.14:27-31, 15:1-2 (omitting 1b); XI.15:3-6 (omit-

theme that occupies his discourse is that of the Commandment of Love (Jn 13:34, Homily V). Clearly a deep, and deeply experienced, love of Christ permeates these heart-felt meditations. Jesus is its sole cause (IX) and its incomparable reward. However imperfectly reflected in us, that love *is* Christ himself. 'O boundless love! O incalculable loving-kindness! O unfathomable affection!' (III). That love, Love himself, must possess us utterly, to the abandonment of every other consideration and desire. Intensely personal, it must be witnessed as the mutual bond of christian community. And it must generate in us an insatiable thirsting for the Word (XIII). Yet Ogier's response to the love of Christ is one of intense longing for the union with the Beloved that death alone will realize. This may well seem the imminent anticipation of an aged senior, but the sentiment is to be found as well in the junior author of the tractate.[35]

Many echoes of that earlier work can be heard in the *Expositio,* but here they attain the clear focus of maturity in the *schola charitatis* of cistercian monasticism.[36] Ogier's fondness in the tractate for poetical citation and rhetorical set-pieces is evidenced in the inclusion here of two verses from a compline hymn (IV), a couplet from the hymn for Prime (IX), and, remarkably, lines from the Bucolics of Vergil (XI) and the Satires of Persius (XIV); but whereas the set-pieces of the former composition (with the *sui generis* exception of the *Planctus*) are largely derivative, those of the *Expositio* are genuinely distilled *inventiones*. Several of them, such as 'A little while' (*Modicum*, IV) and 'I am the Way' (VII), linger long in their listeners' recollection.

---

ting 5, a fragment of which is taken up in VI); XII.15:7–9; XIII.15:9–11; XIV.15:12–14 (omitting 13). Omissions are noted in the text.

[35] For example, in IV, VI, VII, IX, X, and XIII; the longing for seeing 'face to face' embraces Christ's Mother here as well.

[36] Ogier's 'monks of Benedict' are cowled in white (*Expositio*, XII), and the Order is named *(religionis Cysterciensis)* in the Tractate (VIII).

A passage from the Thirteenth Homily has often been cited as a landmark in the late-medieval development of Mary's Immaculate Conception, particularly as Ogier's assertive language stands in contrast to Bernard's, at best concessive, response to the doctrine.[37] What is, however, remarkable about Ogier's formulation is its obliqueness to the argument at hand (Jn 15:9, 'remain in my love') and a mode of expression that has given more than one reader pause. The passage in question reads:

> *Non est in filiis hominum . . . qui non in peccatis fuerit conceptus vel in peccatis post fuerit conversatus preter matrem immaculati peccatum non facientis sed peccatum mundi tollentis*

> Among the children of men there is none who was not conceived in sin or, thereafter, did not live in sin save the Mother of the Immaculate One, who [himself] did not sin but bore the sin of the world.

This is straightforward enough; the unmarked gender of the two genitive participles is, by apposition to the clearly masculine *immaculati*, unambiguous. Yet Haller, in the main a reliable translator, gets the sense dead wrong:

> *Es ist kchain mensch geporen worden . . . da nicht enpfangen ist worden in den suenden oder darnach nicht gesuendet hab, denn ausgenamen die vnuermailiget junkchfrau Maria, die da nie gesuendet hat, aber sye hat auf gehebt die suenden der welt*

[37] In a letter (Ep 174) written shortly before 1140, Bernard censures the canons of Lyons for introducing the feast of Mary's Conception. That she was *ante sancta quam nata* ('holy before she was born') is undoubted, but from the fact that her conception preceded her holy birth it does not follow that her conception, too, was holy. What is to be added thereby to the honor of her sacred birth and sinless life? 'What I have said here', Bernard concludes, 'is nonetheless without prejudice to one of maturer wisdom, above all, to the authority of the Roman Church. Should my understanding differ from hers, I am prepared to emend my judgment.'

> *No* human has ever been born who was not conceived in sin or thereafter did not sin, excepting of course the Immaculate Virgin Mary, who never sinned, but *she* took up the sins of the world.

This would appear to make a case not merely for the Immaculate Conception, but for Mary's role as Co-Redemptrix as well. Even the scribe of Staffarda struggled with the passage: inserted after *immaculati*—as if in a moment of epiphany—is a quickly penned *Xristi*.

The homilies stop short, as formal exegesis, roughly midpoint (verse 15) in John 15; but much of what occupies in the remaining discourses (through Chapter 17) has already been foreshadowed, and their mystical summation—'[Father,] I have made your Name known to them and shall continue to make it known, so that the love with which You have loved me might be within them, and I within them' (Jn 17:26)—has been the heart of Ogier's contemplation from the start.

The Translation

The base text of my translation of Ogier's writings has been Staffarda, either directly *(Expositio)* or through the mediation of Adriani *(Tractatus)* and Marx (the *Quis dabit* or *Planctus Marie* excerpt). This is, so far as I have been able to determine, the first english translation of the whole of the tractate; it may well be the first translation of the entire work altogether. The *Planctus,* however, has, from the late Middle Ages on, undergone translation into numerous languages, though I have not examined any of these; this is, I believe, its first modern English rendering. In translating the *Expositio super Evangelium in Cena Domini* I follow in the small but not undistinguished company of the fifteenth-century Austrian Carthusian Heinrich Haller, the nineteenth-century Abbé Dion, the late Dom Anthony Chassagne, former abbot of Mepkin Abbey, and the contemporary French Trappist Robert Thomas.[38]

I have in particular taken Pater Heinrich as my guide with respect to the inescapable necessity of reducing some of the redundancies in Ogier's rhetorical style; verbatim reproduction would ill serve the original, which was, of course, intended to be delivered *viva voce* and grasped by ear, rather than read privately in silence. Scripture passages have in many cases been translated afresh from the Vulgate, particularly where specific vocabulary forms the basis of ensuing commentary. Ogier's penchant for immediate paraphrase of a cited source, generally signaled by 'as if to say' or some such tag, has led me, in cases of direct speech, to incorporate such amplification (distinguished typographically) within the citation itself. Again, this is a matter of auditory delivery transmuted into a read text. I have also given distinctive formatting to several of the set pieces, hoping thereby to effect the shift of voice a reciting reader would have given them. Scriptural and liturgical citations (where reasonably straightforward) are set off by font, and their sources noted in the apparatus. Indeed, all discovered sources have been noted. These represent most, though of course far from all, of Ogier's manifold (and typically unidentified) *fontes*. I welcome the assistance of readers to locate many others, such as miscellaneous metrical excerpts that are clearly taken from commonplace books and other items in the library of Locedio.

The translation of the *Expositio,* excepting the revisions of phrases and format in its final form here, precedes that of

[38] Haller, cf. Bauer (1969); Dion, *Les Quinze sermons sur le discours après la cène*, in *Œuvres de S. Bernard* (Paris, 1867); Homily XIII: Chassagne, Daily Readings from the Cistercian Fathers [typescript] (Mepkin Abbey, *c.* 1957), Thomas, *Pain de Cîteaux 19* (Chambarand, 1963).

the *Tractatus* by an interval of nearly three years. The labor chiefly took the form (and pace) of *lectio,* during morning work periods—but especially during the predawn hours between Vigils and Lauds—at the cistercian abbeys of New Melleray and Mepkin and the benedictine monastery of Christ in the Desert, where the voice of Blessed Abbot Ogier could penetrate and resonate most fittingly, and most tellingly. To these communities and their beloved shepherds I owe the fruits of this encounter.

Martin Jenni

Iowa City

In Praise of God's Holy Mother

PROLOGUE

MY LOVE OF DISCOURSING upon the Word of Life—despite my manifest unworthiness—began to draw me ever more avidly to that honeyed sweetness *the heavens dripped down from the face of the God of Sinai.* It was then that God's chosen vessel herself, the storehouse of every virtue, hastened to satisfy my desire. That vessel of choice, the salver of life and everlasting bliss, is the beauteous Virgin in whom *the fullness of the Godhead* was infused *in bodily form.* From that vessel of solid gold, bedecked with precious stones, there rises the fragrance of myrrh and aloes, of cinnamon and balsam, of scents that surpass the perfumer's art. Within that vessel of ivory, pricked with sapphires, lie contained the Alpha and Omega—the beginning and the end. Worthy is she who bore her own Maker to be praised by all on whose lips such praise is fitting![1]

Ps 67:9

Col 2:9

[1] The entire first paragraph here unpacks a dense opening sentence of ninety-seven words, in which the identity of the principal image is made explicit *(scilicet illa speciosa Virgo)* two clauses before its close. Ogier's *amor tractandi* is displayed in the maze of allusions: *vasculum electionis* feminizes the Pauline epithet of Act 9:15 (*vas electionis,* the continuation, *ut portet nomen meum coram gentibus et regibus et filiis Israel,* befits Mary's role) by substituting the diminutive as a reference to her womanliness (cf. 1 Pet 3:7 *vasculo muliebri*). The description of the 'vessel' echoes Job 28:17 *(vas auri),* Rev 21:19 *(lapide pretioso ornata),* Prov 7:17 *(myrrha et aloe),* Sir 24:20 *(cinnamomum, balsamum, myrrha),* Is 57:9 *(ornasti unguento, multiplicasti*

To all who come upon these writings I freely admit that I am little suited even to speak her name, let alone her praise. Yet, ineffective as I am, affection compels me to do so; I cannot—indeed I must not—refrain from praising her whom angels, archangels, and all the orders of heaven laud as Mother of Creation's Lord and Bearer of the Maker of all things. Drawn by loving-kindness and enticed by love, I would not forgo the bounty of our Lady. *May my tongue cleave to my palate if I do not keep* her *in mind, if I do not count* her, after

Ps 136:6 her most Holy Son, *the greatest of my joys.* May she be mindful of me on the day of Jerusalem.[2] May I find repose in her on the day of tribulation, there to join the people clothed in her Son. Thus shall I praise her ceaselessly throughout my life, singing her praises so long as I may live. May my words be pleasing to her in whom I delight, and may our Lord Jesus Christ, her Son, grant me the accomplishment of what he has inspired, according to his will: he who lives and reigns with the Father and the Holy Spirit, God throughout eternity. Amen.

---

pigmenta), Sg 5:14 *(eburneus distinctus sapphyris),* and Rev 1:8 (A *et* Ω, *principium et finem*). The figure of the 'salver' (*ferculum,* cf. the *fercula misericordiæ* of Peter Chrysologus, *Sermo* 30) appears prominently in the eucharistic symbolism of Aquinas (*Lauda Sion* and *Verbum supernum*); *ferculum* in the sense of 'palanquin', 'litter', occurs in Sg 3:9 (cf. n. 151 below).

[2] Perhaps an allusion to the Parousia; cf. Rev 3:12.

I. Introductory Homily

Mary Speaks with the Author

O MOST HOLY and immaculate Virgin, wholly comely and beautiful, ever kind and merciful, do not, I beg you, be repulsed at praise from me, but receive it kindly for the sake of your Son. Do not, I pray, shun discourse with a servant, but speak with your attendant. Teach this unskilled soul about yourself. Guide me in my artlessness to proclaim your mighty deeds—*for they are sweet in my throat, sweeter than honey and honey-comb to my lips.* Yours *Ps 18:11*
indeed is the delicious sweetness of honey and milk. O fair of face, fairer still of mind, the meadow's graceful comeliness, the desert's austere beauty: speak! In you the Son of God the Father was greatly pleased. Are you not, O Virgin, that branch of Aaron[3] which, without sap or moisture, brought forth foliage, flowers, and nutmeats? *Let your sweet voice resound in my ears* [Sg 2:14]! Your servant desires to see you and to hear you; may I prove to be a good servant, not a useless or an evil one! Let me hear your voice! Speak!

[3] *Virga* (emending Adriani's *Virgo*) *Aaronitica*, cf. Bernard's *Aaronica virga* (*In laud.* II.6) and Num 17:8; Mary's priestly lineage, implied through her kinship with Elizabeth (Lk 1:5), is claimed through Joachim in the *Protoevangelium of James*. *Sine succo vel humore flores protulit* embroiders Bernard's *florida nec humectata* (*In laud.* II.5), even as *procreavit nuces* simplifies the Biblical source *(foliis dilatatis in amigdalas)*.

Is 11:1 'I am of the Root of Jesse, the Virgin from whose root emerged the flower of life. I am that Virgin of whom Isaiah said: *Lo, a virgin shall conceive and bear a son, and she shall name him* Jesus [Is 7:14]. I am that Mosaic *plate of purest gold, upon which the artful hand of the engraver has engraved* the ineffable Holy Name of
Ex 28:36 the Lord;[4] for *lo the Name of the Lord is coming from far off, and his brightness fills the earth.*[5] That Name, composed of four Hebrew letters, is interpreted: "He is the beginning of life's suffering."[6] How much of suffering and of life this Name portends I have sensed deeply and with greatest grief; in answer to your tears I shall make known its full import.'

O loveliest among women, comely and sweet in such delights, whole and spotless
Lam 1:20 Virgin: *my soul is deeply troubled* to hear this,
Jer 23:9 and *all my bones tremble with fear.* What words of yours are these?

'In time I shall reveal them for you to ponder in the bitter grieving of your soul.[7]

[4] What is engraved on the gold-leaf adornment of the priestly turban is *SANCTUM DOMINO* ('consecrated to the Lord'), here either misremembered or deliberately refashioned so as to link the commentary that follows.

[5] Magnificat antiphon for the First Vespers of Advent I; the first period directly cites Is 30:27, the second is a paraphrase of Wis 1:7 *(Spiritus Domini replevit orbis terrarum).*

[6] Ogier's bizarre interpretation of the tetragrammaton (HE = *iste,* JOHT = *principium,* EHT = *passionis,* VAU = *vite*) bears little likeness to Jerome's treatment of the Hebrew alphabet in *Heb. Nom.* (IOTH = *principium, scientia, dominator,* HE = *ipsa, ista,* VAU = *ipse*). The HE occurs in the Holy Name twice, as its second and fourth letter; Ogier's substitution (HETH = *vita, vivacitas* in Jer., a sense Ogier assigns to VAU) somehow provides him with a reference to Christ's Passion. No less curious is the willful scrambling of the letters so as to produce this gloss; whether original or borrowed, it displays a sophomoric rashness quite uncharacteristic of our author.

[7] See Homily XII.

But meanwhile I would speak with you of other matters; weigh them carefully! You seek to know who I am and all that concerns me; this I shall reveal to you. I am Mary, born of David's line.[8] My father and mother were Joachim and Anne.[9] They consecrated me to the Lord and trained me to learn his ways, taught as I was by the Creator of all, whom he purified and sanctified while yet in my mother's womb. When I grew into womanhood it was God's will that I should be espoused to Joseph the just. Then God, who even in my mother's womb had set me apart, was pleased to accomplish in me the mystery of his Incarnation. Thus he sent to me his archangel Gabriel—mighty of fortitude and devout and lowly of mien—to announce to me that the author of all would take on flesh from me. But when I heard the angel say, *"Hail, greatly favored, the Lord is with you; you are blessed among women,"* I was troubled by *Lk 1:28*
his words; what manner of greeting was this? Seeing my perplexity, he began to speak these words of consolation: *"Fear not, Mary. You have found favor with the Lord. You will conceive and bear a son."* At this, I asked to know how these *Lk 1:30*
things might come to pass: had I not vowed to God my chaste virginity,[10] to keep it spotless

[8] So also Bernard: *Non tantum Ioseph, sed et Maria descendisse credenda est de domo David (In laud.* II. *16);* as such she is Isaiah's *virga Iesse,* despite the genealogical contradiction of her assumed Aaronic lineage (see n. 3).

[9] Mary's parentage is taken up afresh in Homily II; on the apocryphal bases of this account of her birth and girlhood, see the Introduction.

[10] Inferred by Augustine (*De sancta virginitate*, IV.) from Mary's questioning of the angel: 'she would not have said this [Lk 1:34] had she not vowed her virginal state to God beforehand'.

Lk 1:34 and undefiled? *"How can this be?"* I said. He
Lk 1:35 answered: *"The Holy Spirit shall come upon you."*
The mighty promise thus assured, I gleefully
rejoiced and said, *"Behold the Lord's handmaid;*
Lk 1:38 *let it be done to me according to your word!"* Thus
in accordance with the message of the angel,
I, a Virgin, conceived the Word of God, not
by a man, but by the Holy Spirit. I, a Virgin,
gave birth, not merely to a man of remarkable
merit, but to the author of our very well-being.

'At his birth the angel of the Lord—
indeed, the Lord to whom I gave birth—
appeared to certain shepherds, saying: *"I bring*
you good news of great joy to all people: the Saviour,
Christ the Lord, was born this day in the city of
David. You will find the infant wrapped in swad-
Lk 2:10, 12 *dling cloth and lying in a manger."* And then a
voice as of a million angels sang: *"Glory to God*
in the highest, and on earth peace to men of good
will!" And they came with haste and found every-
Lk 2:13, 16 *thing just as the angel had told them;* then they
went back with great joy and glorified God.
There also appeared at that time between
heaven and earth a great star of wondrous
brightness. It shone in the East to certain
Chaldeans, leading them to the birthplace of
my Lord and my God, the everlasting King,
my son. But as to what happened to them on
the way, the gifts they brought, and the atrocity
unleashed by wicked King Herod, you have
Mt 2 learned all this in the Gospels.

'I nursed my beloved infant son with virginal milk. I hugged him close to me with all godly dread, for this beloved son was my Creator, my God and my Lord! As a man he grew in years, and, wise before God and men, performed many marvels—many more than those recorded in the Gospels. He touched the blind and the lame; they saw, they walked. Lepers he cleansed; the dead he raised to life. Who could tally all the wonders he performed? Through these and other signs and powers he shone forth in the world, mighty in word and deed before God and humans. *Cf. Jn 20:30*

'A crowd of people wanted to make him king and called him so, with joyous applause. *"Hosanna,"* they cried, *"blessed is he who comes in the name of the Lord, Israel's King!"* Hearing this, the Scribes and Pharisees were blinded by jealousy and overcome with wickedness; *they conspired to find a way to kill him.*[11] They bribed one of his own disciples to betray him to them, and when he did, they bound my son and punished him dreadfully. They beat him with rods. They pummeled him with fists and clubs. They struck his head and crowned him with thorns. At length they hanged him on a tree to die. I know: I was there; I bear witness to the truth. I am that woman he entrusted to his apostle John as he—as Life itself—was dying on the cross. The grief that crushed me beggars human comprehension. But after three days my Lord and son quickly turned my woe to joy: he rose up from the dead and appeared, glorious and immortal, before me.[12] On the fortieth day many watched in amazement as he went up into heaven; *Jn 12:13* *Jn 11:53*

[11] The Passion summary is based on Jn 18–19.

[12] The apparition of the resurrected Christ to his mother may be founded on Coptic apocrypha such as the *Book of Bartholomew*.

there he sits at the right hand of the Father. He will come again to judge the living and the dead and the world by fire, rendering to each according to their works.

'So, now I have taught you a little about who and what I am, and who and what my only son is, my Lord and my God. I believe your love will not conceal what I have told you: then, from what your love believes, let your good works ensue. The reward is great: you shall have me as your lover, and you shall have Jesus, my son, as saviour: he who with the Father and the Holy Spirit lives and reigns, God for ever and ever. Amen.'

To these words I add: *Blessed be the Lord God of Israel who has brought to pass the redemption of his people.*[13] He created you such that *Lk 1:68* he should deign to be born of you, and that through you the devil should be vanquished, and humankind redeemed. To him your servants give great thanks, not as we ought, but to the extent we are able to endeavor. Your generous instruction has taught us what has been said about your birth. We have learned the truth of those ineffable graces granted you by the Holy Spirit of which Scripture tells. How you were ineffably infused with them by the Spirit Paraclete, we truly know and fully believe to our great comfort and rejoicing. Yet the love of my Lady and the loving-kindness of the Mother of my Lord—so redolent of the pomegranate and the fruit of the apple-tree—compels me to speak further. I would address those consecrated virgins who, following your

[13] Slightly refashioned and abridged.

example, have either vowed their virginity to the Lord or have strived to please him through their purity of body and heart. May your merits win me the grace to speak well and rightly of you, to your glory, and to the glory of the one who for the salvation of the world did not shrink from clothing himself in your flesh. Ever blessed be he who deemed it fitting to work such wonders through you!

To him be honor and glory for ever and ever. Amen.

II. Second Homily

Mary's Birth and Childhood

DEAR CONSECRATED VIRGINS, it is not Paula and Eustochium,[14] but the love and loving-kindness of the Mother of God, and my tender regard for you, that compel me to speak of your Mistress, recalling the abundance of her sweetness. To you I shall address whatever God in his generous kindness shall grant this poor servant to tell. Meanwhile pour forth to the Lord your prayers for this sinner, so that, supported by the merits of that most blessed Virgin, I may step forth to proclaim who and what she was, and what gifts the Lord conferred upon her.

This most holy Virgin Mary was of royal lineage: Joachim was her father, and Anne her mother.[15] She is that mighty woman presaged by the Lord when, at the time of Eve's undoing, he told the serpent, '*You shall lie in wait*
Gen 2:15 *for her heel, and she shall trample your head.*' She is that mighty Virgin who *trampled the head of*
Ps 73:14 *the dragon* by her power, and waged war against the powers of brass.[16] Through her the Lord

[14] Saints Paula (347–404) and Eustochium (*c.* 368–*c.* 419): Roman matron and daughter, friends and co-workers of Jerome, whom they joined, in 385, at his monastic community at Bethlehem. Jerome dedicated several Biblical commentaries to them.

[15] See Introduction, n. 25.

[16] Cf. Ps 106:16 *(contrivit portas æreas)*—in the light of the vision of Rev 12:4.

delivered our first parents, Adam and Eve, from everlasting death. She is that most wise Judith who in your wisdom slew Holofernes and freed the people of Israel. She is that most beautiful Virgin, for love of whose beauty that unicorn is captured who strikes down all his enemies with his horn (that is, with the power of his godhead).[17] She is that *valiant woman,* endowed with strength and choicest virtue, of whom Solomon spoke: *Who shall find a valiant woman? Hers is a prize far beyond all bounds.* Indeed, her prize was none other than the Son of God the Father, who from *far beyond all bounds* (that is, from the ineffable and incomprehensible bosom of God the Father) marvelously and ineffably entered the enclosure of the virginal womb.

Est 8:13

Prov 31:10

But before the time of that ineffable conception and birth arrived, the Son of God, wishing to be conceived and born of her, chose his most faithful servants, Joachim and Anne, as those from whom that Virgin should be born whose flesh he would take on, and, in whom, by dying he would redeem humankind. Rightly then our thanks are due to Joachim and Anne, to whom that child was born, who through her preparation and lofty virtue would be found worthy to conceive and bear her Maker.

The name Joachim means 'whom God prepares'.[18] Joachim indeed kept the tabernacle

[17] The 'one-horned beast' as a symbol of divine power is based on Num 23:22. The beast in that passage *(rinoceros)* is equated by Priscillian (Tract. 1:28) with the 'unicorn' of Ps 21:20; both are LXX misreadings of the Hebrew dual r^{e}*'em* ('two-horned', i.e. wild ox).

[18] Jerome, *Heb. Nom.*, with substitution of *Dei* for *Domini*.

of his heart a dwelling-place of the Holy Spirit through his tireless meditation and spiritual discipline. He was generous in his alms, devout in his obedience to God's commandments, a despiser of self, and a true worshipper of God. As a youth, though he shone forth with exceptional holiness, he feared he might incur the curse of the Law, namely: 'Cursed is the man who does not leave behind his seed in Israel.'[19] Thus he took as wife a certain young woman of charming mien named Anne, who was adorned with every virtue, and faithful in true worship. He wedded her, not out of lustful love, but solely for the procreation of an heir—as what came to pass then proved. Anne, whose name in the Greek means 'above', is justly said to have contemplated the sublime. In the Hebrew, moreover, the meaning is 'his (which is to say, God's) grace'.[20] Not that she herself was God's grace, but that the grace of God made her fruitful. Thus she was found worthy to conceive and bear a daughter of such holiness as was the Virgin, the very Bestower of grace, even as Isaiah foretold: *Behold, a virgin will conceive and bear a son whose name*
Is 7:14 *shall be Emanuel.*

For a very long time, however, Joachim and Anne remained childless. From the depths of their hearts they daily prayed to God with

[19] While childlessness was regarded by the Jews as cause for opprobrium (cf. n. 60 below), no such curse is recorded in the OT; in the *Protoevangelium*, Joachim is prevented for this reason by Reuben (or, in some versions, Issachar) from offering in the Temple, while Anne is similarly chided by her handmaid. Quite another legend has intervened in Ogier's account, however (see Introduction, n. 25).

[20] Jerome, *Heb. Nom.*; the Greek preposition (ανα) is not an etymon, but a mere pun, perhaps Ogier's own.

all their might, that he might grant them a child—any child, whether son or daughter—through whom the curse of the Law would be lifted from them, and who, in himself or herself, would loose the Law's curse. And the Lord favorably heard their prayer, for the wish, and the necessity of its fulfillment, were his as well: this was how he would save humankind by taking human nature. Thus one day, as Joachim was returning home from the Temple, where, having made offering to Almighty God, he had poured forth his whole being that God might deign to grant at last that long-desired offspring, the Lord's angel appeared before him on the path as he came, comforting him with these words: 'Be sad no longer, for the Lord has heard your prayers. He will give you a daughter, *whom you will call* Mary. She *will be great;* she *will be called* the Mother *of the Most High.*[21] *For she will bear a son* who is none other than her God. As a virgin she will conceive, and as a virgin bear, not from a man's seed, but through the power of the Holy Spirit, the Word of God the Father Most High. *He will save his people from their sins.*' Thus saying he left them in a flash of lightning. The angel also appeared to Anne, informing her in similar words of what had come to pass. The just and saintly Anne conceived a child of her just and saintly husband Joachim, giving birth to her first-born daughter, she who was holy, just, and spotless in the sight of her God.

Mt 1:21

[21] Lk 1:31b, 32, appropriated.

How greatly God's angels rejoiced when thus the restoration of humankind was secured! The whole world leapt for joy, heaven thundered with praise, the earth danced for delight, her song of joy soon joined by the skies above and the seas below. The skies more serene, the sun more bright, the moon more resplendent, every star more brightly twinkling, the earth teeming with flowers, the waters gushing with goodness: so the whole universe took on its pristine glory as that most blessed daughter was told: *Virgin Mother of God, your birth is news of joy to all the world!*[22] If therefore all the orders of angels rejoice in the birth of Mary the Mother of God, let all orders of monks rejoice therein as well. If heaven and earth rejoice, then all Christ's consecrated virgins also. Let every-
Phil 4:4 one rejoice—*and again I say, rejoice*—rejoice with great joy, for the birth of Mary the sacred Virgin spells joy for the whole of heaven and earth.

Thus Mary, the morning star that drives away all darkness, came forth from her mother's womb *beautiful as the moon, sought-out as the*
Sg 6:9 *sun, dreadful as a well-armed camp,* the glorious light that came forth from the darkness, within whose womb Light itself would shine. *From Jesse's root there came* the Virgin who *would bear*
Is 11:1 *the flower.*[23] It is she who says, *'I am the flower*
Sg 2:1 *of the field and the lily of the valleys'*. Before that

[22] The text occurs refrain-like in the Office for the Solemnity of the Nativity of Mary (8 Sept.): it forms the first period of the Magnificat antiphon (Vespers I) and the first Responsory at Vigils, as well as the whole of the Short Responsory at Vespers II.

[23] Cited in this connection by Bernard (*In laud.* II.5); the mingling of *Virgo* and *virga* is his as well: *virgam virginem, florem virginis partum intelligens.*

fragrant flower all other flowers lose the sweetness of their scent. From earth the Most High brought forth his healing remedy: the man of wisdom, namely the Lord Jesus, did not shrink from it, for to free the humankind he was to receive in nature, he did not disdain the womb of that most blessed Virgin. By means of Anna and Joachim God created that remedy whereby humankind would be freed from everlasting death. Through that healing remedy, blessed Mary, the Lord gives light to the blind, heals the sick, raises the dead, frees us from sin, justifies us through grace, and crowns us with his glory. Let therefore all the just rejoice at the birth of her through whom they have been justified. Let the blessed rejoice who through her have been made blessed.

Brides of Christ, rejoice at the birth of the Mother and Bride of Christ. Mothers, rejoice at the birth of God's chosen Virgin and Mother. Let all women rejoice, for this most blessed woman has delivered you from the curse of Eve. Indeed, let all rejoice for whom her birth is the cause of great joy. And you, virgin, who have vowed your virginity to God: rejoice in the birth of Christ's Virgin Mother! Let widows rejoice who seek the Lord as their sole husband; how great is their father-in-law! Let all my brothers who share the contemplative life rejoice as well, for the joy of such bliss is no less theirs. Let them approach the blessed child, the sublime Queen on high. Let them embrace her, let them cradle her in the arms of perfect love. Let them bear her in their hearts, her praises ever on their tongues, so as to possess her with their love. For this is no woman to be slighted, this is no ordinary mother: this is blessed Mary, wholly sweet and lovable, wholly delightful! She is the very beauty of delight, the fountain of gladness, the overflowing of glory, most beautiful, most loving, dearest, sweeter than all honey and every nectar, more precious than gold and jewels. Through her we are illumined; through her we contemplate the brightness of heavenly light.

She is called Star of the Sea: through her the darkness of our ignorance is expelled, the blight of our sins[24] is worn away, sinners are justified, and clouded consciences becalmed. She illumines the world, surrounding it in her splendor. She is the sweetness of myrrh, the absence of all bitterness. She who was never to dwell in the bitterness of sin is rightly named Mary.[25] She never sinned nor ever wished to sin, in thought or word or deed. Wholly beautiful, there was no blemish in her;[26] only thus could she become the Mother of the Lord, our Saviour and our God—and hers.

Throughout all ages blessed be the Virgin:
through our Lord Jesus Christ,
who with the Father and the Holy Spirit
lives and reigns,
God for ever and ever.
Amen.

[24] *Rubigo peccatorum:* Gregory the Great (*Hom. Evang.* 30).

[25] The passage elaborates several interpretations of *Maria:* Jerome (Liber interpretationis hebraicorum *Heb. Nom.*) is the direct source of *illuminans* and *zmyrna* ('myrrh'); *stella maris* is Isidor's reading of his *stilla maris* ('a drop of sea-water'); 'without bitterness' is derived from Jerome's reading of *Mara* as *amaritudo*, prefixed by the Greek privative (or perhaps the Latin preposition) *a*.

[26] Sg 4:7, also the text of a Marian antiphon *(Tota pulchra es).*

III. Third Homily

Mary's Longing for the Incarnation

IF, AS THE APOSTLE ATTESTS, *loving-kindness does not seek what is its own,* it none- 1 Cor 13:5
theless compels me to continue; for, by divine right, what by human right is denied to me (and rightly so) becomes my due. By human right, one thing is mine, another yours alone; but by divine right all things are accounted to all in common. That from which human right precludes me, not yet purged of dross and mire,[27] is by divine right incumbent not only on me, but on all living beings, whether in heaven, on earth, or in the sea: namely, to praise and bless the God of the universe, always and everywhere. If then, unlike the birds of the air, I do not deserve *to follow the Lamb* through
white fields of lilies *wherever he may lead,* yet Rev 14:4
like the beasts that creep and lumber on the Cf. Rom 1:23
ground, I shall follow his footsteps from afar, so long as I may be granted breath in this present life, praising him and, through him, his most blessed Mother. His name has poured
out an ointment to my soul; *my soul* thus *clings* Cf. Sg. 1:2
to him, and to her who bore him. He loves us Ps 62:9
not according to our due, but as he alone is

[27] *A fæce lutuosa non defæcatus ex toto,* cf. Ambrose, *caro ab omni defæcata labe vitiorum* (*Expos. evangelii secundum Lucam* 7:141).

able. And since the praise of God is also the praise of his mother, and the praise of the most blessed Virgin is that of her most beloved Son,[28] our God, I shall continue to sing the praises of her in whom God was truly well-pleased, whom *all generations from that time forward call*
Lk 1:48 *blessed.* For truly blessed she is, not only among women, not only among angels and archangels, but above all the Thrones, Powers, and Dominions of heaven: for she was worthy to bear her Maker in her virginal womb, and with her sacred breasts to give him milk who feeds the creatures of the air and all that creep on the earth and swim in the waters.

She set her heart to watch at daybreak for the God who made her, and ever guarded her steps
Sir 39:6 *in the sight of the Most High.* Thus the Holy Spirit, the Spirit of all that is holy, could say of her: *How comely are your sandaled steps, O daughter*
Sg 7:1 *of the Prince!*—and what follows in the Wedding Hymn of the bridegroom and the bride, Christ and the Church. For comely and wholly beautiful she was, when, weaned from her mother's breast, she was offered to the Temple by her parents and consecrated to bear the godhead.[29] There, day and night she poured out her soul in prayers and praise to God: she who was to bear him in her body already bore him fully in her heart. Even then there dwelled in her

[28] Cf. Bernard, *In laud.* IV.1: *Non est dubium, quidquid in laudibus Matris proferimus ad Filium pertinere, et rursum, cum Filium honoramus, a gloria Matris non recedimus* 'whatever praises we offer the Mother belong without doubt to the Son, and, similarly, when we honor the Son we do not diminish his Mother's glory'.

[29] At three years of age, according to the *Protoevangelium Jacobi,* although a considerably older maiden is pictured here. Sighing and groaning for the Presence denied until death in the Lord is an Ogerian common-place, adapted here to Mary's longing for the Incarnation.

most pure heart the one who owed his robe of flesh to her most chaste body. To him she sighed, to him she breathed her loving groans. How frequently her lovely gleaming cheeks—so hued with every charm—were bathed with overflowing tears: for with the veiled eyes of her flesh she could not glimpsed the one Isaiah had foretold, who would be born of a Virgin and share our lowly lot. How many sobs, how many groans she uttered, who could not yet behold her Creator in the flesh!

What do you suppose she prayed? What do you think she read? That blessed Virgin, wholly blessed of God the Father through the incarnation of his Son, may well have said: 'God and Father of us all, let, I beseech you, your Son come in the overshadowing of the Holy Spirit. *Let him kiss me!* Let him who *Sg 1:1* made me receive flesh from me! Let him be born of woman who created women and all things! Let him become man by being born of a mother who is God of God by being born of the Father.' This she said continuously, not merely crying out with her mouth but desiring as well with her heart. *'Send forth the Lamb, O Lord, the ruler of the earth, from the rock of the desert to the mountain of the Daughter of Zion. Come and free us, Lord God of might; show* *Is 16:1* *us your face and we shall be saved. You who govern Israel, attend! You who shepherd Joseph and are seated above the cherubim, manifest yourself before Ephraim, Benjamin, and Manasse. Stir up your power and come to save us!'*[30] This was her prayer *Ps 79:20, 2-3*

[30] The order of the verses suggests a direct source in the gradual texts for the final days of Advent; they are furthermore introduced here by a phrase from the Magnificat antiphon for December 19 *(O radix Iesse)*.

and supplication; this she spoke in tears, weeping as she spoke. How often she read, how often she meditated in her heart, those words
Is 7:14 of Isaiah: *Behold a virgin shall conceive and bear a son whose name shall be called Emanuel,* God with us. Blessed indeed that Virgin, and rightly deemed as favored who, radiant with the prerogatives of her merits, would worthily conceive and bear her Maker!

And so it came to pass. Dear virgins, let us thank God together that our Lady is that most blessed Virgin who vowed her virginity to the Most High in a way unlike that of any other woman we have read or heard tell of. For this and many other virtues far beyond all other women, she rightly deserved to be most favored. During her childhood she was visited by angels who guarded and preserved her. They consoled and strengthened her; they instructed her and taught her. The angels attended her, ministering to her; and so she
Lk 2:52 *grew in years and in wisdom before God and men.*[31] She was loved and cherished by all who knew her or had heard of her holiness. In sublime humility she transcended human bounds. Such was her chaste purity, such the blush of virginal modesty upon her cheeks, that she who was accustomed to the sight of angels' faces would not—could not—look upon the face of a man. Instead she kept the chaste gaze of her mind fixed upon her Creator, sighing blissfully for his embrace. With love she swooned for him: how often the tears streamed down her cheeks! With mournful voice and

[31] Appropriated, with some reordering of elements.

chaste and upright heart she would cry out to him, saying: *'Ah, why are you not my brother, nursed at my mother's breast! Then if I met you out of doors I could kiss you.'* *Sg 8:1*

O Virgin Mary, Virgin undefiled, immaculate Virgin, Star of the Sea, splendor of the world, joy of Paradise and gladness of all the blessed,[32] second only to Jesus your beloved Son and God and the Creator of all: well might you have said to the Lord your God, your Maker and Creator: 'Ah, that you might be my son, nursed at my breast! *Then if I met you out of doors,* clothed in my flesh, you whom the Catholic faith teaches to be the one true God with the Father and the Holy Spirit, I could embrace you in my arms and *kiss you with the kiss of my mouth!* I would embrace you with all my love and kiss you with all the cherishing love of my mind!' Well might you have said this; for doubtless it was granted to you. From the beginning of time it was appointed that he who made you would be born of you. Blessed be he who chose you for his mother! Whatever may befall us, whatever our lot, may he who was born of you be ever blessed.

Amen.

[32] The litany of Mary's titles derives in part from interpretations of her name (cf. n. 25); the figure of *paradisus* embraces both the pleasure-garden of the Song of Songs and Eden itself (cf. Theodotus of Ancyra, Sermon before the Council of Ephesus, 432).

IV. Fourth Homily

The Annunciation

Ps 144:10

LET ALL YOUR CREATURES *thank you, and your faithful bless you!* Come, virgins of Christ, bless God with us and confess him before all living beings, for he has worked mercy through our Virgin. But before he was born, before the time of his incarnation and our reconciliation drew nigh, it was his will that our Lady, his future mother, should wed Joseph the holy and just man, so that the mystery might be concealed from the devil and the wickedness of the Jews might not bring about his Virgin mother's death.[33]

Thus Mary was betrothed to Joseph, not in matrimonial familiarity (ordinary conjugality), but rather so that he might be of service to her, attend to her and care for her: that, as a husband, he might be a most faithful guardian of her absolute virginity. Now a young woman, she who from girlhood had consecrated her fertility to the Lord God is betrothed to the just man, Joseph. She who was to be the Mother of God becomes the promised bride of a Jewish man.

[33] The function, in the divine scheme of the Incarnation, of Mary's betrothal to Joseph as a means of concealing the mystery from the devil is argued by Bernard (*In laud.* II.12-13) in similar language.

But what does this mean for you, Joseph, just and good and holy as you are? Could any man be more fortunate, more blessed, than you, to whom so priceless a treasure is entrusted, so indescribable a pearl, so utterly beautiful a woman as God's chosen mother? Was ever anyone so honored among the sons of men? Was ever a man so privileged with the responsibility that elevates you? How is it, then, for you? Well may you be struck with dread and wonder to be entrusted with the Temple of the Holy Spirit, the Mother of the Son of God! Be subject to her, be wholly devoted to her: she is not merely your wife, but your sovereign lady. And though she is your spouse, as you are hers, she is nonetheless your mistress, and you are her servant, for she is the chosen mother of your God and Lord, the Creator and Saviour of all. Pause and reflect a while, Joseph, and see the marvels of God. He who was promised by the patriarchs and foretold by the prophets, the Holy of Holies, the God of all, shall quickly come and will not delay; he shall sojourn within the womb of your spouse—your mistress—to take on her flesh, to be born of her!

Thus the time arrived when *the angel was sent by God to the city of Nazareth,* to that Virgin betrothed to Joseph, *of the house* and lineage *of David, and the Virgin's name was Mary.*[34] In *Lk 1:26-27*
this verse are named the Messenger who was sent, the Lord who sends him, the Virgin's

[34] Partially paraphrased. This is the source text of Homily I of Bernard's *In laud.;* what follows cites him in varying degrees of literalness (cf. Leclercq & Rochais edd., *Sancti Bernardi Opera* IV [1966] pp. 13-16, 24).

betrothed, the blessed Virgin herself, and the city where she resided. All is filled with heavenly mystery, all overflows with divine abundance and blessed sweetness for those *who have drawn honey from the rock and oil from the steely*
Deut 32:13 *stone.*[35] 'Gabriel' is interpreted as 'God's strength'.[36] Rightly then is Gabriel, mightiest of the archangels, sent to the valiant woman whose prize comes from afar. To her he bears, from the royal thrones of heaven, the message that the Lord who casts down the mighty from their sees and raises up the lowly is to be born of Mary.[37] Be humble, then, bride of Christ, and all who would be reckoned a Christian, whoever you are, that through Christ you have raised to such lofty heights! Otherwise he will come to you in his strength
Ex 32:20 and in his great power will *grind you to dust*
Jer 11:19 and *uproot you from the land of the living.*[38] *He is the Lord, mighty and powerful, the Lord, mighty*
Ps 23:8 *in battle.* It is he who says: *'I shall strike you down and heal you, for none can escape from my hand. When I have sharpened my sword like lightning, when my hands have seized in judgment, I shall avenge my enemies and pay back those who hate me. I shall make my arrows drunk with blood,*
Deut 32:39, 41 *and with my sword I shall hew away the flesh.'* But hope in him and belong to him, *for he*
Mt 1:21 *shall save his people.*

[35] Ogier's *lapide adamantino* is a variant reading of the Vulgate *saxo durissimo* cited by Bernard (I.1.).

[36] Jerome *Heb. Nom.,* as in Bernard (*In laud.* I.2.).

[37] The 'valiant woman' theme [Prov 31:10, cited in II] is linked to the Magnificat verse [Lk 1:52] by reference to Wis 18:15 (the descent of the angels from heavens' *regalibus sedibus*); cf. the introit antiphon *Dum medium silentium,* formerly for the Sunday within the Octave of Christmas.

[38] Ogier appears to have misremembered the verb *(eradere)* as *eradicare.*

Therefore the mighty angel Gabriel is sent by Almighty God to announce to the valiant woman that to her is to be born the Lord of might, the warrior against the gates of brass and the prince of darkness, the deliverer of souls whose necks once bent beneath the yoke of the devil's service.[39] Mightily armed, he guards his courtyard in peace; mightier than the foe, whose might he overcomes, he snatches in his might the apparatus of captivity.[40] An archangel is sent, comely with every beauty and charm, verdant in flower, burnished with grace, shining in splendor. From the realm of sweetness and comeliness he is sent by the very maker of lightning, the author of every grace and charm, whose beauty amazes the sun and moon, whose sweetness intoxicates the angels (but is yet hidden from his mortal lovers). To Mary, beloved of God and mortals, whose most blessed beauty the Daughters of Jerusalem foretold and queens and consorts praised, beauty himself sends his beautiful messenger to announce his coming—he *of all the sons of man the comeliest of form*. He sends *Ps 44:3*
him, not to a simple maid but to a betrothed Virgin, so that the great sacrament of love might be hidden from the devil, and lest the Virgin herself be charged with adultery and stoned by the hands of the wicked.[41]

[39] Like the burial responsory, *Libera me Domine de viis inferni,* which may have been a direct source, the symbolic language here unites images from Ps 106 and the *Gospel of Nicodemus*.

[40] Bernard's paraphrase (slightly reworked) of Lk 11:21-22 (cf. *Opera* IV, p. 15, 12-14).

[41] So also Bernard (*In laud.* II.13.).

The blessed Virgin was betrothed to Joseph the just, of David's line, so that he might provide for her needs with all husbandly solace, and nurture the Most Holy Son entrusted to him in his human form. *And the Virgin's name*
Lk 1:27 *was Mary*. How that Son responded to that lovely name we shall take up later. She who is worthy of all blessing and honor was living at that time in Nazareth, which name means 'flower'.[42] And rightly is the city called in which the Virgin Mary dwelt, the rose of roses, flower of flowers, and fragrance of all fragrances. She is that flower of every flower and fragrance of every spice: she who is pressed round with flowers and restored by every virtue would bear the fruit of life and everlasting bliss.[43] To this *Queen, robed in gold*
Ps 44:10 *and adorned with* virtues' *gems,* God the Father sent his messenger to announce that his Son was to be born of her. When at length the angel, performing the will of the Father Almighty, arrived and, with all humility and due deference gazed at her, he worshipped her as the Queen of Heaven and Mistress of the Angels, the Mother of the Son of God, saying: *Hail, full of grace! The Lord is with you: you are*
Lk 1:28 *blessed among women.*

Thus humbly he came to the humble maid, sublimely to the sublime queen, heaven-sent to the heavenly one, virginally to the Virgin, radiant to the resplendent, as wedding attendant to the bride, indeed as servant to his Mistress, the royal page to the Queen of the

[42] Nazareth means 'The flower of Galilee'; Jerome, *Ep. ad Marcellam,* 13.
[43] A loose paraphrase of Sg 2:5.

World. He found her alone on her couch in her bedroom, alone without a companion, with no one else present; and yet she was not alone: she was with her God. He who would put on the garment of her flesh had already prepared the bridal-chamber of her mind. He who was about to clothe himself in her most holy flesh clung to her with all his heart and hers.

How good it is to cling to him, *how delightful* and sweet *to dwell* with Christ! Nothing is better, more pleasant, more delightful, than to dwell with God. That is the supreme good, the ultimate delight, the utmost sweetness! Anyone who lacks it is bitter, sad, and mournful; thus Christ's virgins mourn, the brides of the Son of God who have vowed their virginity or their chasteness to him; they groan to see their Lord at last. Unable to see their bridegroom, the Savior of the world, nothing they see delights them. How happy are they! How blessed such monks and nuns! But whoever you are, maid or man, as you desire the coming of your Lord, so you must languish for love of him. Through love you receive him, through love you possess him: *do what you will, and love* him![44] For if your love for him is complete, you can only do what pertains to that bond of love. Love is that sure and certain guide, upright and perfect, that lets no traveler stray. Therefore, virgins of Christ, if you are drawn to Christ's intimate chamber, let his beatific love burn in your hearts, so that, robed in cloth of gold and arrayed in sapphires and

Cf. Ps 132:1

[44] Augustine, *Hom. in 1 Ioann.*

jasper, you may be found worthy of him. Then the holy angels, your bridal attendants, will lead you rejoicing and gladsome into the Temple of the King whom the Virgin Mary bore. To her be ever glory and honor, and may it ever be well with us through her:

so grant this Jesus Christ her Son,
who with the Father and the Holy Spirit
lives and reigns, God,
blessed for ever and ever.
Amen.

V. Fifth Homily

Mary's Response

RIGHTLY WOULD I LAUD the Virgin Mary's most chaste womb, the seal of her motherhood and the promise of grace, had I but worthy words. We have heard, from Gabriel's lips, the mighty proclamation of her praise. Such words I lack; even so, my breast heaves for love of her, in whose praise I could not be silent. She is, next to her only-born Son, all my hope and refuge, my life, my every desire. Thus I shall offer her heartfelt praise, not that which is due her but such as my soul can muster.

Let us picture the scene.[45] The archangel Gabriel, that mightiest of warriors against the spirits of wickedness, has been commissioned by the Lord to be the wedding attendant of his sublime Queen. Securely he enters that glorious bridal-chamber, worthy of extraordinary veneration. There, behind closed doors, cloistered from the gaze of men, the most blessed Virgin—worthiest of all praise—is

[45] The scene has been pictured beforehand by Bernard (*In laud.* III.1., direct citation italicized): *Puto in* secretarium pudici *cubiculi ubi* fortassis illa *clauso* super se *ostio orabat Patrem suum* in abscondito. . . . Marie autem orationes quantum placuerint *in conspectu Altissimi,* angelus indicavit qui ingressus ad eam *tam* reverenter salutavit ('*I reckon* it was *in* the inner chamber of *the cubicle* of her modesty *that,* the *door being closed, she prayed to her Father* in secrecy; that Mary's prayers were pleasing *to the Most High* was shown by the reverence with which the angel entered unto her').

praying in the secret chamber of her heart to her Father. Alone, before the Most High, she pours out in tears her soul's entire chaste and reverent love, languishing in love for him who was about to descend to earth from his Father's bosom, for him with whom it was her sole and constant goal to dwell in heaven. For her
Phil 1:21 *to live* was *Christ.* Daily she sighed for him, daily for him she yearned. Might he sojourn soon within in her most blessed womb! But rejoice with me, virgins of Christ, devoted brides: Mary, the wholly beautiful one, has been found worthy to become the Royal Virgin. Of her even now he was waiting to be born, so to vouchsafe his people from the thrall of the devil.

Thus unto Mary, so sublimely blessed, accorded all glory and praise, wreathed with all beauty and comeliness, abounding in grace and honor, the mighty Gabriel enters. Elected from the myriad hosts of heaven, replete with every grace, that noble archangel comes, blithely and joyously, humbly and devoutly, with these words of greeting: 'Rejoice, you who are greatly favored: the Lord is with you, and thus you are blessed among women.'

Ave gratia plena! The angel's salutation is the imperative of the incomplete Latin verb, *aveo,* the meaning of which is equivalent to 'I am glad'. But a much greater gladness is indicated here: this gladness is true jubilation. Let us hear in *ave* the subliminal meaning of Gabriel's greeting, pregnant with grace and praise: "Be hale indeed, you who are *without woe.*"[46] Thus

[46] Ogier's (?) invention appears to be based on a gloss that attempts to reconcile the Latin greeting with the Greek χαιρε 'rejoice', encouraged perhaps by the

Gabriel's greeting transformed our first mother's name, in which two expressions of grief[47] are entwined. The first grief is the death of the soul; the second the death of the body, for through Eve's fault we have fallen into the death of both body and soul. It is the grief of Eve, advancing[48] from generation to generation, from father to son and mother to daughter, to which our parents' tombs bear witness, where dust returns to dust, and all returns to nothingness. But even as in Mary *Eva* is transformed into *Ave,* so through the grace of Mary Eve's fault is destroyed; thus we are delivered from the double and everlasting death of body and spirit, and enter that life of consummate bliss which knows no end. Eve's curse has become Mary's blessing. *"Ave gratia plena!* You are full of grace, for Eve dies in you, and grief with her. You are the beginning of glory and life, for through you death is destroyed and life restored.

---

similarity of the Marian antiphon incipits, *Ave Maria* and *Gaude Maria.* I omit his oddly pedantic digression: "The verb *ave*, according to some, has but two persons, namely first and second, and these exist in the imperative mood: *ave* (sg.), *avete* (pl.). We maintain, however, that it is a verb of the second conjugation and is declined thus: *aveo, aves, avet* etc. It lacks a past tense, and the forms derived therefrom, such that we have only *aveo, aves*—as is also the case with *gaudeo, gaudes*." The argument—confusing number with person and equating the deponent perfective system of *gaudeo* with the absence of a *tempus præteritum*—is remarkably muddled. To it is adduced a fanciful etymological analysis of *ave* as *a væ* 'without woe': etymology by phonetic component, the examination, not of a word "as a word, but as a joining of letters *(conglutinatio litterarum)* revealing the secret message of the greeting."

[47] The interjections *hei* and *vah;* the latter, signaling pain or dismay in the classical language, is found twice in the Vulgate (Job 39:25, Mt 27:40) as an expression of contempt. A ready source of the symbolic palindrome *(Eva: ave)* is the 8th-c. hymn, *Ave Maris stella (sumens illud Ave . . . mutans Evæ nomen);* I have rearranged and simplified Ogier's somewhat awkward argument.

[48] The interpretation rests on the sense of the syllables *hei va[dat]* 'woe (lit. 'alas') advances'.

'*You are full of grace*—indeed, you are filled with the author of grace, the granter of virtue, the bestower of all good things. *You are full of grace* because, Virgin as you are, you are at once Mother as well. Like fragrant *spikenard* you *have wafted your scent; the King on his couch,*
Ps 44:12 *desiring your beauty,*[49] comes down into you to be born of you. Thus: *The Lord is with you,* in your heart and womb, in your soul and flesh. *The Lord* your God *is with you:* the Lord your son, *with you* when he created you, *with you* in being born of you. And therefore: *You are blessed among women,* for you alone escaped the general curse of Eve and her daughters, as it is written: *In intense pain you shall bear*
Gen 3:16 *children.*[50] In exultation you are to bear your Maker. *Blessed are you among women,* for you have escaped the curse that befell the barren in Israel.[51] You have obtained a singular blessing, neither remaining barren nor bearing a child in pain.'[52]

The noble and sacred Virgin Mary, immaculate, gracious and wholly beautiful, upon hearing these words was troubled by them,
Lk 1:29 wondering *what manner of greeting this was.* Let us not be amazed, for response of true virginity is to fear any man's entering, and to feel shame by any man's address, and unsafe in the

[49] Cited by Bernard (*In laud.* III.2.).

[50] The argument is closely modeled on Bernard (III.7.): *Benedicta inquam tu in mulieribus que illam generalem maledictionem evasisti qua dictum est: In tristitia paries filios.*

[51] Cf. Deut 7:14: 'You will be the most blessed of all peoples. None of you, man or woman, shall be sterile, no male or female of your beasts infertile.' The negative formulation *(Maledicta sterilis in Israel)* is Bernard's (*In laud.* III.7.).

[52] Bernard, *In Laud.* III.7., slightly retouched by Ogier: *singularem consecuta es benedictionem ut nec sterilis maneas* [O: *permanes*] *nec cum dolore parturias [parias].*

presence of men, even when there is nothing to be feared. This is especially true of all virgins who know that they bear a priceless treasure within their vessel of clay: on earth they dwell among the heavenly and in their flesh they lead a life of celibacy.[53] Such is the virginity we would wish. Never let Christ's virgin fix her gaze on the face of any man; let her rather be modest and chaste, let her keep her gaze directed downwards, speaking rarely if at all. Let her be steadfast in prayer and constant in meditation, fervent and devout in praise of her Spouse, and languishing for love of him.

Such a virgin was Mary. Struck with dread at the entrance of the angel, at the lightning flash of his brightness, she is troubled by his words. The sight of him is sudden and unexpected; his unheard-of greeting has filled her with fear and unsettled her. But then she notes his distinctive holiness, his pious and mild-mannered visage, his sublime presence humble and devout before her. In that fragrance of angelic sweetness, she recognizes him as an angel of God. Yet, in her chaste modesty, although she is thus assured of his identity, she is nonetheless perplexed by his words. Never has she heard such a greeting; never has she read it in the pages of her *lectio*. What can be the import of such words? Silently she turns them in her mind, disturbed, uncomprehending.

Seeing her there, chastely avoiding his gaze, the angel comforts her and seeks to enlighten her doubt.[54] He calls her by name: '*Do*

[53] Bernard (*In laud.* III.9), begun here in paraphrase and continued verbatim.
[54] Bernard (III.10).

not be afraid, Mary, for you have found favor in
Lk 1:30 *God's sight.* Star of the Sea, splendor of the world, ransomer of captives, saving grace of the lost, Queen of Heaven, the glory of the elect, do not be frightened of me. I am no man but an angel, an angel of light, not of darkness,[55] a wedding attendant, God's servant and yours. Do not dread my coming; do not take fright at my words. I am no purloiner of chastity nor predator of virginity. Chastity I praise; virginity I love. Trust me with all certainty: from high Olympus I, God's messenger, bear you tidings of great joy. He who made you will be born of you. Therefore, hail! Rejoice and be glad, for salvation is sent to you by the Lord: through you what long ago was promised is now granted to the sickly world. *You are* indeed *full of grace,* that grace of which all grace has its source, the grace that created heaven and earth, the sea and all therein. *Full of grace* are you who have found the favor you have deserved. *You have found favor with God* and have merited God himself: to have with you in your womb the son who is your Lord and God. *You shall conceive and bear a Son whose*
Lk 1:31 *name you shall call Jesus. He himself will save his*
Mt 1:21 *people from their sins.'*[56]

Behold, most sacred Virgin, our glory, our hope, and our refuge in the Most High God: the God who has done good things for you

[55] Bernard (III.10); the passage continues in paraphrase, the whole reading: *Non sum homo sed* spiritus et Dei *angelus,* non Satane: 'I am no man but a spirit, an angel of God, not of Satan.'

[56] Ogier is fond of linking this codicil to the preceding verse from Luke 1; he may well have linked them in his mind—they are easily fused—as coming from the same Gospel source.

has granted you understanding, through the words of the angel, of what great favor you have found with the Lord. *Full of grace* and *blessed among women* are you alone: you shall conceive and bear a Son who shall save his people from their sins. O noble Virgin, venerable woman! O wondrous grace that fills our fortunate blessed Mary! O glory of virgins and grace of women, their comeliness and their beauty! O Mary ever-blessed! You are the most fortunate and blessed of women. *"You shall conceive and bear a Son whose name you shall call Jesus; he himself shall save his people from their sins."* Who is this son of yours? He is the Lord your God.[57] *Blessed the nation whose Lord God* is your Son! *Blessed the people whom* your Son my *Lord has chosen as his inheritance.* *Ps 32:12*

O Lord Jesus, life that never dies, who will grant it to me to be of that people? *Who will grant me the wings of the dove that I might fly* to *Ps 54:7*
that people girded by the Lord, there to be found worthy to rejoice for ever in your inheritance? Who will grant it to me to love you with my whole being, my God? Lord Jesus, Truth incarnate, I do not doubt the truth of what you promised when you said, *'Whoever loves me shall be loved by my Father, and I shall love him and make myself known to him.'*[58] *Jn 14:21*
But who shall grant it to me to love you, my Lord and my God, as you have loved me? Who could grant this but you, my Jesus, my

[57] Perhaps a reflection of Bernard (*In laud.* III.8.): *Qualem filium? Illius eris mater cuius Deus est pater* 'What manner of son? One whose mother is you and whose Father is God'.

[58] The verse is taken up in Homily IX of the *Expositio*.

Lady's Son, she who is the salvation and redemptress of my soul?

He shall save his people from their sins. Jesus so loved us that he washed away our sins in his blood. Alas, how many there are who hope to be of the people of the Lord, to be chosen as his inheritance, who are bound to slip into the inheritance of the devil. As the Psalmist says: *A thousand shall fall at your side, ten thou-*
Ps 90:7 *sand at your right hand.* They fall from his side who disregard his commandments, those whom the Lord shall condemn to suffer eternal death; for surely those whom Christ judges to have fallen from his side shall perish eternally. Let us then truly dread falling from his side. May my soul ever cling to you, Lord Jesus, lest you permit me to fall. Let your right hand uphold me and lead me in the path of your will. In your glory receive me through your Virgin mother.

Do you wish to be of the people of Christ? Do what Christ has commanded and you shall be his. *'Learn from me'*, he says to his disciples,
Mt 11:29 *'for I am meek and humble of heart.*[59] Be meek and humble of heart and body and you will be one of his own, whom the Lord blessed saying: *You are the work of my hands, Israel, and*
Is 19:25 *my inheritance.*[60] If you would be of his people,

[59] Twice alluded to by Bernard, in *In laud.* II.1. and III.14.

[60] Virtually all of Ogier's argument here owes to Bernard (III.11.), including the personal appeal for grace *(utinam et me peccatorem dignetur Dominus Iesus annumerare populo suo)* and the rejoinder against the presumption of unworthy religious to count themselves among 'the Lord's people'. Ogier's hearer-directed moral *(Vis esse de populo Christi? Fac quod percepit Christus et eris de populo eius)* verges on direct citation *(Vis scire an pertineas ad populum eius vel potius vis esse do populo eius? Fac que iubet in evangelio Dominus Iesus . . . et eris de beato populo eius).*

seek the aid of the Lord's own mother to free you from sin and reconcile you to Jesus her blessed Son. One who seeks it with all his heart when trial and struggle beset shall not be denied that aid.

I knew a man, some fourteen years ago, who was beset with a multitude of ills. Vexed by disease, his skin was scabby, his flesh all leprous sores.[61] Death everlasting threatened him daily. With every effort he struggled to stand up, but sickness weighed him down; or, if he rose at all, he would soon fall again to the ground worse off than before. Unable to find a cure for his wounds, he stared at the ground. Then he gazed into heaven, seeking there to find the Physician of souls—but he dared not open his mouth, so often had he offended him who saved his people from their sins. Seeking but not finding the remedy of salvation, at length, he poured out his soul to the Mother of grace and mercy. She, he had heard, came swiftly to the aid of all who called upon her in truth for deliverance; she, he dared hope, would hasten with merciful kindness to help and strengthen one who cried out to her in tribulation. Thus that poor wretch groaned and, from the depths of his heart, called out to her in words like these: 'O glorious Virgin Mary! You see that I can neither rise up from my sin nor prevail against the wiles of the devil. By your Most Holy Son I implore you now: deign to help me, so that through your aid I may never fall again into this or any other sin! Deliver me from this sin,

[61] See the *Expositio,* n. 28.

and do not let me fall into any other!' And so the hope of salvation was restored to him. Then he began to mourn: awash with tears he fell to the ground, beating his head and breast and tearing out the hairs of his head. None could console him for the loss of the great treasure he now bewailed—except the Lord Jesus Christ! He ran to the church to confess to the priests, and he was healed. From then on the blessed Virgin saw to his care. I do not say that after this he did not sin, but rather that he no longer willed to sin, except where his human frailty could not fully avoid it. In such a one as this, Love—God himself—does not disdain to dwell.

Your gifts, O Virgin Mary, I confess before you: they are your favors, no merits of my own. The mercy you have shown your servant I celebrate here with the stylus of grace, for your honor and glory and for the usefulness of my hearers. Let those who do not love you love you, and let those who love you love you more and more. Let them not despair of salvation who hoped for that beyond which they had. Hear me, then, Christ's virgins: hear this servant, blessed ones, and do not disdain good counsel.[62] If wrathfulness or the desires of the flesh wrack your minds, call upon your Mistress, the Mother of mercy! Those of you perturbed by the enormity of your crimes, confounded by the rankness of your conscience, terrified by the dread of judgment,

[62] The 'good counsel' is Bernard's: namely, the great *Voca Mariam* peroration in which the Second Homily of *In laudibus Virginis Matris* concludes. Like every reader of the passage since, Ogier cannot but have been profoundly moved by it; his extensive borrowing (nearly eighty words) is largely transparent.

whose abyss of sadness engulfs you: fly to Mary! In your perils and your anguish run always to the Mother of mercy, the Most Holy Mother of our Lord Jesus Christ. Call upon Mary, our Queen, our Advocate, our Lady! She will not draw back from your cry; she will not recede from your heart. And, if you would seek to obtain her favor, do not shrink from the example of her life.[63] In her footsteps we cannot go astray; beseeching her we cannot despair; mindful of her we cannot err. In her grasp we shall not fall; in her protection we do not dread. With her guidance we do not grow weary; from her treasury of good we ever profit the better. This I know personally[64] and have written it for your exemplification. Let the Virgin Mary be glorified in her Son, to whom she commits her soul:

who reigns in the glory of her Son,
blessed for ever and ever.
Amen.

[63] *Conversationis exemplum:* a phrase of particular significance for monastics, for whom *conversatio* is synonymous with the life of the cloistered contemplative.

[64] Even this doubtless sincere confession *(hoc in me ipso expertus sum)* is inspired by Bernard (*In laud.* II.17.): *et sic in temetipso experiris.*

VI. Sixth Homily

The House of Jacob

1 Cor 7:29 TIME IS BRIEF and all things come to
nothing. Thus each of us, clothed in this
robe of flesh,[65] must not neglect to do the work
that readies us for the life to come, always and
everywhere to praise and bless God, proclaim-
ing him who sent his Only-begotten Son into
this world to save his people. For so the angel
said to Mary: *He shall be great and shall be called*
Lk 1:32 *the Son of the Most High. He shall be great* than
whom no one is greater nor indeed so great.
Cf. Mt 11:11 John was great, but he is greater. Great is he
of whom the Prophet said: *The Lord is great*
and greatly to be praised, and his greatness knows
Ps 144:3 *no end. Great is he who holds the seas in his hand*
and weighs heaven and earth in his palm: he who
holds in place the mass of the world between his
thumb and two fingers, who reckons the bulk of
Is 40:12 *mountains and balances the hills and plains. He*
shall be great as a man in the womb of his dear-
est mother who is great as God in the bosom
of his Father. The great God of God shall in-
deed be great made man, of rational soul and
the flesh of the Virgin. He is the Lord God,
Ps 94:3 *the great King above all gods*. He indeed is great
who shall be called the Son of the Most High.

[65] *Trabea carnis induitus:* the phrase is found in St. Fulgentius's *Sermo* 3 on Saint Stephen.

He is the light of light, the Word of the Most
High Father, of whose birth in time the
Prophet sang: *A light for the upright has arisen
in the darkness, compassionate, tender-hearted, and
just: cheerful* he comes in mercy to grant to
mortals everlasting life.[66] He shall be great: a *Ps 111:4-5a*
great Teacher and Prophet; for so we find it
written in the Gospel: *A great prophet has arisen
among us, for the Lord has visited his people.*[67] And *Lk 7:16*
elsewhere we read of this Prophet: *Behold a
great Prophet shall come, and he shall renew Jeru-
salem. He shall be great,* for God *declared his
magnificence in the sight of kings;*[68] therefore *let* *Sir 45:3*
*all the tribes of earth adore him, all nations serve
him.* He shall deliver the poor from the power- *Ps 71:11*
ful, the poor who have none to help them.
He shall spare the poor and the destitute: the
souls of his poor ones—those who for love of
him desire poverty—he shall vouchsafe. *Of
such is the Kingdom of Heaven.* *Mt 5:3*

O blessed poverty, to whom the Kingdom of Heaven is owing! Blessed are the poor who out of love possess nothing of this world, who see nothing that delights them; for them the trappings of the world are joyless. Sadness is their daily lot, for they are still deprived of the sight of the Son of the Most High, the Virgin's Son. Let them rejoice when Christ appears: Christ, the wealth of his poor and the comfort

[66] Verse 5 *(iucundus homo qui miseretur et commodat)* is paraphrased and extended: *homo iocundus qui venit misereri et vitam mortalibus donare perpetuam.*

[67] Cited by Bernard (*In laud.* III.13) in the context paraphrased here *(Hic erit magnus: magnus homo, magnus doctor, magnus propheta).*

[68] Substituting *magnificabit* for *glorificavit* (*magnificavit* occurs in v. 2), either from faulty recollection or in anticipation of the Magnificat commentary to follow.

of mourners, the desire of monks who yearn for him like deer desiring springs of water, Christ our life! They will appear with him in glory and be filled with the abundance of sweetness that flows forth from the face of the Lord who sits on David's throne.

His reign is everlasting, the angel tells Mary concerning her Son: *The Lord will give him the see of David his father, and he shall reign for ever over the House of Jacob, and his kingdom will never*
Lk 1:32b-33 *end.* The see of David to be given him is not figural but actual, not temporal but eternal, not terrestrial but heavenly. It is said to be of David because the temporal throne on which David sat bore the likeness of the eternal,[69] that is, the Heavenly Jerusalem, our mother. He is that King established by his Father who,
Ps 2:6-7 in the words of the Prophet, says of himself: *'Upon Zion his holy mountain God the Father established me King* [as man] *to proclaim his precepts.* He *said to me: You are my Son whom,* of my nature, *I have begotten today,* before all time. For the salvation of the world you took on flesh; therefore *ask it of me and I shall give you the nations for your inheritance, and the ends of the*
Ps 2:8 *earth for your possession.'* The Son of the Most High is called the Son of David because he was the offspring of the Virgin Mary, of Davidic lineage. The Lord therefore shall give him the kingdom of his father David, not the temporal and passing kingdom that was David's to use but fleetingly, but rather the Kingdom of Heaven that it symbolizes.

[69] Bernard (*In laud.* IV.1.), cited at length.

He shall reign for ever over the House of Jacob. The House of Jacob signifies Jerusalem, for there he shall reign, *and his kingship shall know no end*. But there is another 'House of Jacob' over which Christ the Lord will reign. The name Jacob means 'he who casts down and supplants'.[70] Blessed is that Jacob who has learned to cast down not only the devil but himself. Rightly can we be called a *Jacob* when we wrestle with our vices and desires, lest sin reign in our mortal bodies; when in this flesh it is not we who live, but he who for our salvation gave himself up to suffering and death and rose again from the dead to be seated at the right hand of God's power. We are truly Jacobs when we are crucified to the world and the world to us, for whom to live is Christ and to die is gain. We are Jacobs when, denying ourselves through vigils and penance and the works of our hands, we follow and embrace the Lord Jesus Christ in this life through grace, and in glory in the next. Over this House of Jacob, as over a beloved family, the Lord Jesus will reign for ever and beyond.

Would you be a strong athlete[71] against the devil? Believe me, you will not be able to withstand him unless for love of Christ you yourself despise yourself within yourself. Those who truly know the struggle of self against self and enter the contest bravely, not lazily or half-heartedly, will repel the inordinate appetite of the flesh and the mind, and so will triumph over the foe. Having won at

[70] Jerome; cf. Gen 27:36, cited and developed by Bernard (IV.2).

[71] Cf. Cassian, *Inst.* 5. The figure occurs as well in the *Expositio* (VII, see n. 99).

last the contest, they will reign in everlasting glory with Christ. Let Christ's virgins and widows learn in all humility to despise themselves, fleeing the desires of the flesh, hating the world and the things of the world, loving chastity, and fleeing boastfulness. Let them preserve their virginity unstained and incontaminate. Let them obey one another in Christ, and with their tears and prayers knock ceaselessly at the Gate of Paradise, our Holy Virgin Mary. She is the gate that opens to those who come to her and, seeking her and loving her, meet her on the way. She rewards all who seek her and guides all who love her to her Son, with whom they shall reign for ever: he who for our sake emptied himself and washed us from our sins in his own blood.[72]

Oh that her Son and Lord—may he ever be my Lord as well!—might grant me through her to be found worthy to enter and see the King of glory in his comeliness, to rejoice in the gladness of the nation of his inheritance, and to behold his mother, the Queen of the world, the second joy of Paradise, *adorned with*
Is 61:10 *jewels,* arrayed with precious stones! Might I merit to see her in her delightfulness, in the beauty of her countenance! Might the desire for her that I have from her be sated! My Lady, Mother of glory, Mother of everlasting gladness, glory of the world, my glory, shall I ever be sated with your presence? Shall I see you? Shall I know you with your Son as my sole love, whom now I cannot see? If I am to see

[72] Phil 2:7, Rev 1:5; the latter serves as a refrain in the *Expositio,* occurring once in Homily II, X, and XIV, and twice in V and XII.

sometime, why not now? What is a wretched man like me to do? Unless my Lady reveal herself, where shall I go? Where shall I seek you? Where shall I find you? To you I shall go, and you I shall seek; perhaps I shall find you. You sought me and you came to me and found me. But how and where you found me, you know, and I know; and, as you are witness, it shames me sorely to remember it. Thus I beg you, through him whom you bore, not to desert me, not to abandon me. I know I have sinned—but I have not denied your Son; and though I do not love you as I ought, yet through you I have loved, and indeed still love, those who love you. With all my being I desire you, bless you, praise you, adore you, and thank you, because through your Son you sought me as I wandered, you found me hiding in the brambles, you healed me as I languished, you cured my ailing soul, you called me back from error and gave me strength and comfort when I lost hope. Through you I have been reconciled with my Christ, my God, your Son. Take my hand and lead me according to your will. Never let me stray from the path that is the Way himself, but holding and guiding me, let me come with gladsome step to that same Son of yours who is to be seen in the goodness of his chosen ones.

To him and to you
be honor and glory for ever and ever.
Amen.

VII. Seventh Homily

The Word becomes Flesh

As TREES SPREAD out their branches, which, profuse with flowers, bear fruit for all who would pick it, so there is a Tree that bears the fruit of grace. Let anyone pluck there who would. It is that Tree by which the Lord raised me up from the dead. In its shade I rested, weary from toil, and it revived my spirit when I was well-nigh dead. Of that Tree I ate the

Cf. Gen 3:12

fruit. Its taste was sweet; to eat it was sweeter than feeding on honey and honeycomb. From the brink of eternal death this fruit brings back to life all who eat it worthily; to them it grants an everlasting life of bliss. For thus in blessing speaks the fruit of our blessed Tree: *'I am the resurrection and the life; anyone who believes in me, even if dead, shall live, and all who*

Jn 11:25

live and believe in me will never die.'[73] Blessed be that noble tree in root, more blessed still in trunk, most blessed in fruit and flower;[74] in its shade the human race is saved, and, eating that fruit, for ever lives. This is the Tree that gave

[73] Thanks to the feminine gender of *arbor*, the sustained image of Mary as the tree is more transparent in the Latin, as also the identity of its (masculine) 'fruit' (see also n. 98).

[74] An allusion to the Passion poem *(Pange lingua gloriosi prœlium certaminis)* of Venantius Fortunatus: *Nulla silva talem profert flore, fronde, germine* ('no other tree bears such a flower, bough, or bud').

us to eat from its very flesh, the manna of salvation that reached down to us as food the bread of angels. Through the mediation of this Tree, we have eaten the Bread of Angels: for the Lord of angels, taking flesh from her, became a man, gave us his own flesh to eat, and his blood for the forgiveness of all sins. It is to this Tree the angel says: *'Fear not, Mary: you have found favor with God. You shall conceive and bear a Son, whom you will name Jesus. He will be great; he will be called the Son of the Most High'.* *Lk 1:30-32a*

O wondrous Virgin, worthy of every honor, above all women singularly to be revered, admired, and blessed: you are the restorer and reviver of the lost and dead of this world! Prefigured by the Patriarchs and promised by the Prophets, you were chosen and foreknown by the Most High God who prepared you for himself and bid his angels keep you safe.[75] To you, Virgin in intention and profession, Gabriel is sent; are you then frightened at his coming? Why are you afraid, when there is nothing to fear? Why are you fearful where nothing is frightful? Gabriel is a lover of virginity and chastity. He announces to you the King of Ages who is to be born of you—he who can have neither beginning nor end—and you are frightened? Listen to him carefully; take pains to understand him! What he speaks is the truth: what he says about him will be accomplished in you. Be comforted and strengthened; banish fear, be joyful, maintain your modesty, and tell archangel Gabriel, your wedding attendant, 'I do not doubt that

[75] Bernard (*In laud*. II.3, 4), with several interpolations.

it be done, but I am ignorant of how it may be. I do not ask whether it will be, since you have been sent to me as God's truthful messenger, but I ask by what manner or design it is to come to pass. As the Lord bears witness to my conscience, his handmaid has ever kept her vow never to violate her virginity. By what law, what order of things, is it to come to pass that I conceive a son without losing my modesty? How am I to have a child and remain a virgin, become a mother without losing my virginity? Tell me, I beg you, *how*
Lk 1:34 *this can be, since I have not known a man?* I have known no man, nor do I intend to do so. I have a husband, but I have not known him. I have known none but the Lord. He is my husband and spouse. To him I was betrothed; to him I vowed my virginity; to him I was wed. In this I persist and intend to persist for ever. Explain to me, pray, how it shall come to pass that I am mother and virgin? I believe what you said, but how can I conceive and bear a child while remaining a virgin? I have read the passage in Isaiah, but I have not heard by what design this is to be accomplished. In what manner does it please the Most High that I, who would not exist except for his having created me, should come to be that Virgin? It cannot be through any merit of my own, but entirely through the abundance of his goodness. If I am to be she, it must needs be his will. Tell me, then, how I shall conceive and, bearing a child, remain a virgin?'

In answer, the angel tells her: '*The Holy Spirit,* who filled you with his grace and power, *will come upon you,* infusing you with

the power of the Most High, such that as a virgin you will conceive, and as a virgin bear, the Word of the Most High Father, the Son of the living God, true God of true God, born, not made, through whom all things were made, and in whom all matter has its substance. *You shall conceive* in your womb, not of man's seed but of a mystical inbreathing; you will be both mother untouched and child-bearing virgin. *You will bring forth* God the Savior who through his blood *will save his people from their sins. The Holy Spirit,* who is in *Mt 1:21b*
you, *will come upon you:* he who sanctified your mind will sanctify your flesh, such that the Son of God whom you conceived in your mind you might also conceive in your flesh. The same Spirit who sanctified you through grace will so elevate you in glory that you become mother without losing your virginity: a virginal mother, not through any man's worth save that of the author of salvation. You will become the mother not of patriarchs or prophets, but of God, the Lord of all the patriarchs and prophets, the Creator and fashioner of all. *The Holy Spirit will come upon you* that by him you might conceive and give birth to the Son of God. *And the power of the Most High shall overshadow you.* Just how this *Lk 1:35a*
will occur he will make clear to you alone; how, through the working of the Holy Spirit, you are as a virgin to conceive and bear a child is veiled and inscrutable to us all: to you alone he will reveal how he intends to be born of you. Christ, God's power and wisdom, will so betake you that you will conceive without the heat of passion and bear a child

without the pain of childbirth. In that conception there shall be no lust; and in that childbirth your virginity will remain whole. The Most High will cause the shadow of his power to extinguish in you any tinder of sin. So chaste and holy will you be that you may neither sin nor will to sin. He who sanctified you in your mother's womb will cleanse you with such grace that no sin may be in you. He will make you fruitful with such grace that as a virgin you will conceive, not of any man, but of the Holy Spirit. As a virgin you shall bear not only man, but God and man: not the son of any husband, but the Son of the living God. *Therefore that which is holy to*
Lk 1:35b *be born of you will be called the Son of God.* That holy one will be the Holy of Holies who is and will be the Son of God, who not only comes from his Father's bosom into your womb, but who joins to his soul your flesh. God's Son and your son will be one, not two: God's Son before all time, yours in the unfolding of time; God's Son according to his divinity; yours according to his humanity; God of God, your God made man.'

O wondrous and unfathomable union! O novel and unheard-of commingling! The Creator becomes a creature: the God who is before all time is born of a woman! Who has ever heard of the like? A virgin conceives, a virgin gives birth: the Word becomes flesh, God becomes man, the Lord a servant, the Immortal a mortal! O wondrous exchange! O ineffable cementing! Taking to himself an animated body, the Creator of humankind is born of a Virgin and, without human seed, comes forth a man to bestow his godhead on us![76] God becomes man so that man might become God. The Creator becomes a creature, the Maker something made, so that rational creation might be reconciled with its author, and, through the mediation of Mary, be reunited with the Maker. O fortunate, O so blessed Mary! There never was nor ever will be such as you! Mary, earth's glory and heaven's splendor, Mother of Life and begetter of glory, loveliest of the Daughters of Jerusalem![77] How does it come that the Creator should become your Son? *You are wholly beautiful: in you there is no blemish.* You are womanhood's beauty, the *Sg 4:7* beauty and loveliness of the roses that blossom along the waterway, or that are planted in the field of Jericho. You are a pleasure-garden of *Sir 39:17, 24:18* pomegranates and the fruit of other fruit trees. You are the fragrance of all spices, the scent of all aromas. Your beauty is beyond esteem, your holiness beyond telling—yet how do you come by this? Who could tell, who could possibly probe the great works of God accomplished in you? In your womb the Father's Word became flesh, God of God became man. In your womb the Son of the Most High came to ransom us from the thrall of the devil and adopt us as his children. O utterly blissful and blessed Mary, tell us how this can be!

[76] Cassian (*De Incarnatione* 7.28) and the antiphon at Vespers for the Octave of the Nativity *(O admirabile commercium)* are Ogier's principal sources here, which he interlards with imitative variants; *O glutinum ineffabile* may echo Cassian's *glutino caritatis* (*Conf.* 24).

[77] Cf. Ps 44:3, which is applied to the Royal Bridegroom; many such masculine references in the psalm have been transferred to Mary in the liturgy of the Blessed Virgin. The feminine *speciosa* alludes as well to Sg 2:13.

'It is not by me but by him from whom and in whom I am. What or who am I? Am
Cf. Job 33:6 I not miry clay made human? Exalt my magnificence as you will; to God alone, who brought me into being, such praise is due. I am his servant, his handmaid, the creature he fashioned. He made me such as I am; whatever in me is holy, just, upright, and worthy of admiration, is his. *Every good thing is from above, coming down from the Father of lights, in*
Ja 1:17 *whom there is no shadow of change or variation.*'

Forever blessed be that Virgin who deigned to speak so freely with her servant! Most beautiful of women, you surpass the angels in holiness and far exceed the universe in worth! Most certainly you were not mindless of your condition nor forgetful of your heritage; for this we rejoice. Gazing on your lowliness, the Most High leaned down from heaven and, for our salvation's sake, descended into your womb, there to take flesh of your flesh, so that he might through the flesh deliver flesh, lest anyone he formed be lost. This was the angel's wondrous message, that in your womb you would conceive and bear a Son whom you would name Jesus. Then, pausing a moment, the angel went on to say: *'Now Elizabeth, your kinswoman, has also conceived a son in her old age; she who was called barren is already in her sixth*
Lk 1:36 *month of pregnancy.'*

The Virgin, as blessed Bernard says, is told the news of her barren kinswoman's conceiving so that joy might be heaped upon joy, even as the miraculous is added to the miraculous. Moreover, Elizabeth's conceiving is announced to Mary since, inasmuch as it is soon to be generally known, the news should first be revealed to the Virgin by an angel than come to her knowledge through human means, lest she seem uninformed of the Son's counsel on earth.[78] Or perhaps the news of Mary's kinswoman has this import: 'What I tell you is great and may well seem impossible to human intelligence, that any virgin should conceive and bear a child and yet maintain intact her virginity. Yet this is to be accomplished in you, for as virgin you will conceive and bear the King of Ages who will save his people from their sins. That is why I tell you that Elizabeth, your relative, whom you have always known to be barren, has conceived a child in her old age. It seems indeed impossible that a woman so long infertile, and now so advanced in age, should be able to conceive and bear a child of such an elderly husband. And yet this is not impossible with the God who will accomplish in you everything that you have been told, so that through you the Scriptures concerning the incarnation of the Son of God should be fulfilled. Therefore make ready to receive the Word: prepare your womb to receive your Creator. Adorn the bridal chamber to receive the Son of God![79] I was sent by God to announce this to you. You will become pregnant and be a mother without defilement. *With God, nothing is impossible.*' *Lk 1:37*

[78] Bernard (*In laud.*, IV.6.), cited literally. Two further reasons proposed there, which have to do with Mary's service to Elizabeth during the Visitation, are absorbed into the argument of Homily VIII.

[79] *Extende sinum, prepara ventrem, adorna thalamum uteri tui*, paraphrasing Bernard (*In laud.* III.8.) *Aperi Virgo sinum, expande gremium, prepara uterum.*

You have heard it, ever-blessed Virgin! You have heard the deed and the manner, both of them good, both of them delightful.[80] Delight then, Mistress of the world, Mother of Zion! Rejoice exceedingly, Jerusalem's glorious Queen! for you have been given exceedingly much for rejoicing. And even as you rejoiced and exulted at the hearing of these words, let your servants and attendants hear from you your answer of joy and exultation: let them delight and rejoice in your words, teeming with the fragrances of Paradise and with such delicious sweetness for the sons of men and the daughters of God. You have heard the remedy for our grieving sickness, our hope and the refuge of our salvation: you will conceive and bear the offspring, not of some man, but of the Spirit Paraclete. We wait with the angel to hear your response: it is time that he return to the one who sent him! And deservedly so, since upon your virginal response depends the solace of the wretched, the ransom of captives, the liberation of the damned, the health and well-being of the ill, and the restitution of the lost. Your servants are listening: let us hear your voice! Let us hear the honey-sweet voice of the cooing turtle-dove, so that rejoicing we might sing that canticle of joy, of love, of loving dedication; and with heart's jubilee might sing out praise to the Most High, and say: *The cooing of the turtle-dove has been heard in our land, our fig tree has borne fruit,*
Sg 2:12b-13a *the flowering vine has wafted its scent.* Hasten,

[80] Bernard (*In laud.* IV.8.); the continuation of the passage is extensively paraphrased in what follows here, including the verse from Zach. 9.

Queen of the world, Garden of delight, humble Virgin: bear forth the Word of human life, and through your humility let the Son of God be incarnate of the Holy Spirit! Let the devil's haughtiness be unnerved, so that through you, Mother of life, we might return to the joys of the Garden from which through the mother of death we were driven, and where we may be found worthy to rejoice for ever with the Lord of glory!

Meanwhile, my brothers, and brides of our Lord Jesus Christ, God's Son, listen attentively with the ears of your hearts, not of your heads, those of the mind, not of the flesh. Then with all your hearts take heed of Mary's response, the words of our sublime Queen, Mother of the Maker of the world! Tell us, O radiant Mother of God, what did you say? We *wait patiently*[81] to hear that word of yours that is our well-being and salvation. Open your mouth and announce our joy. To the archangel Gabriel, your wedding attendant, say this:

'Behold the Lord's handmaid: as you have spoken, so let it be done with me. Great are the *Lk 1:38*
things you speak of, unspeakable the things you promise; but I know for a fact what I believe in my heart and confess with my mouth: I, a virgin, am not worthy to conceive and bear a child. I am not worthy that my Lord and my God should be born of me, his maid-servant. Yet if it is God's will that I conceive an offspring without the loss of my modesty, and that my Lord and my God become my Son,

[81] *Expectantes expectamus,* in imitation of Ps 39:1.

I thank him who sent you to announce this
unspeakable joy to his handmaid. It is my will
as well, the whole of my desire: *Let it be done
with me as you have spoken. Let it be done with
me* as concerning the Word: let *the Word that*
Jn 1:1 *in the beginning was with God* now enter my
womb to take on flesh from me. Let the Word
Jn 1:3 *by which all things were made* become flesh of
my flesh. Let him *who fashioned man from the*
Gen 2:7 *mud of the earth* become man in my womb for
the salvation of the world. Let him come to
deliver his people from their sins. God in
peace, messenger of the Most High: *let it be
with me as you have spoken.'*

Dearest brothers, you have heard it; brides
of the beloved Beloved, hear it as well. Found
worthy of the Son of the Most High, the lover
and spouse of consecrated virgins, the Creator
and Maker of all, who distributes the spoils of
his beauty to each according to their merit,
the Virgin responds with wondrous humility.
In answer to the angelic bearer of sublime
tidings the sublime Queen of Heaven says: *'I
am the Lord's maid-servant; let it be done with me
as you have spoken'*. Where are the proud, the
puffed-up?[82] *Let them be confounded and* quickly
Ps 118:78 *put to shame*. Here, as if mindless of her wor-
thiness (but mindful of her state) she would
rather call herself her Lord's handmaid than
his mother. She did not say (though in truth
she could have), 'Behold a woman who has
known no man, a virgin who has vowed to
God to live in the state of virginity, a woman

[82] Cf. Bernard (*In laud.* I.6): *Quid dicis, virgo superbe? Maria virginem se oblita gloriatur de humilitate et tu negligendo humilitatem blandiris tibi de virginitate?*

of royal lineage, to whom the slightest stain
of sin is foreign'" What she maintained in her
heart and observed in her action was this (per-
haps she had read it): *the greater you are, the more*
you must humble yourself to all. She knew that *Sir 3:20*
God resists the proud. She knew that the Holy *Prov 3:4*
Spirit does not come to rest except upon the
lowly, the meek, those who deny themselves
for love of him. This Prophetess of ours could
say with her forebear the Prophet David: *'My*
heart is not lifted up, nor my eyes raised on high;
I have not walked among the mighty, nor set my
mind on wonders beyond my scope. I have ever *Ps 130:1*
regarded myself humbly and have never exalted
myself. Because of this humility *let Israel hope*
in the Lord from the time forward and for ever, for *Ps 130:3*
it shall *be done to me according to* God's *word*.'

Then he *who ruled Israel* came down from
heaven into the Virgin's womb to rule human-
kind on earth, and he *who sat above the Cherubim*
of equality with his Father, emptying himself,
sought hospice in a Virgin mother. He *stirred*
up his power and came to save the powerless, and
he *appeared before Ephraim, Benjamin, and Manasse*. *Ps 79:2-3*
Oh that we might some day be an Ephraim,
a Benjamin, a Manasse, before whom the Lord
would appear! Might we be found worthy to
behold the beauty of his face, at whose beauty
sun and moon stand in awe, upon whom the
angels ever gaze with insatiable desire! Might
the sublimity of a life of contemplation and
self-denial make of us tall trees that raise their
boughs to heaven, where, before God and the
angels, they leaf and flower and bear fruit, and
so with other fruitful trees live with the Lord
for ever, even as the Lord spoke to his holy

angels concerning the valiant woman: *Give her the fruits of her hands, and let her works praise her*
Prov 31:31 *in the gates.*

Alas, how many trees planted in the Lord's orchard neither leaf nor flower nor spread out their branches, but are useless trunks to be devoured by the whirlwind of fiery flames! They neither love God nor in any way keep his precepts. Why do they take up the ground? Let them be rooted out and cast in the fire! Others leaf and flower, but then the harsh
Cf. Prov 25:23 north wind blows and they lose their flowers and so do not bear fruit. I am speaking here of those who live in monasteries and lead a merely physical monastic life: they wear the tonsure and cowl, they take their food and drink in common, they are to be seen in and out of chapter and church. They cincture themselves in the garb of their order; they fortify themselves with the trappings of worship. Inwardly empty, they are barren of good works and morals, prompt to anger and ready for revenge, quick to insult and indifferent at prayer. Tardy to *lectio,* lazy at work, negligent in the Work of God, they are swift to utter idle words. Weeds in the grass, prattling pulse,[83] they are more concerned with the look of their habits than their habits of living. Though they have boughs and leaves (their cowls and tonsures), they lose their flowers (the honor of their orders) and do not bear the fruit of virtue through true conversion. Their fate is

[83] *Legumina murmurantes,* cf. Dan 1:12, where pulse is reckoned inferior food; 'murmurers' are singled out several times in the *RB* as menaces to the community. Ogier's descriptive catalog of false monasticism recurs in the Exposition (II, XII).

certain and fearful: unless they repent and reform, they will be cut down and cast into the fire; the Lord will indeed appear, not before them, but against them in judgment.

Let us then strive to be a Benjamin or a Manasse, before whom he *who sits above the Cherubim* might deign to appear. The name Benjamin means 'son of my right hand', while Manasse means 'forgetfulness of the passing'.[84] It is incumbent on us to strive with all our might to forget all that is transitory, and ever to be mindful of that which neither perishes nor passes away, that which is eternal and of eternal permanence. Let us be sons of his right hand, not of his left; children of the light, not of the darkness. Let us be children of God, not sons of the devil; children of humility and long-suffering, not of pride and conceit. Let us therefore imitate our Lady, the Queen of Queens and the glory of young women, the confidence of sinners and the hope of the fallen-away, sins' pardon, the grace of the revived, and the bliss of the blessed, with Jesus, her Son, the author of all good things. She who was found worthy to become the mother of her Creator wished rather to call herself his handmaid.

And so the angel's tidings to Mary came to pass, and Virgin she conceived, and Virgin she bore a child. You, then, sister, who for Christ have shorn your hair and taken the habit of a religious: cleanse your heart and there receive Christ; purify your mind and

[84] Jerome *Heb.Nom.* The etymology of Manasseh (*obliviosus* 'forgetful', *quid oblitus est* 'what has he forgotten?') is glossed here as *oblivio transeuntium*.

there receive your Creator. If you are a virgin, be glad, for this is a great gift—so long as you maintain the standard of humility. Virginity and humility: how perfectly they agree, how they wound with love the Bridegroom of souls! Virginity is noble, but nobler by far is humility.[85] Without humility, virginity cannot enter that wine-cellar that is the house of eternal bliss. Like the rejected bride, virginity cries out '*Lord! Lord! open the gates* to me!' weeping and knocking at the gates of Paradise—and is answered, 'I do not hear you, I do not recognize you, *I do not know you; depart from me, cursed, into everlasting fire!*' But humility, even without virginity, is pleasing in the sight of the Most High; humility alone, without accompanying virginity, finds the gates of Jerusalem. There she enters and hastens to the site of the wondrous Dwelling; into the House of the Lord she hastens with gleeful song. There the angels rejoice and say to her: 'Come, bride of Christ,[86] the armament of humility has defended you with fear of every vice and sin.'

Sg 2:4

Mt 25:11-12

Be humble in word and deed. Bear insults patiently and give none yourself. *Let you not do to another but that which you would have done to you.* If someone does something to you that is unjust in your opinion, see that you do not

Tob 4:16

[85] Cf. Bernard (*In laud.* I.5.)—*laudabilis virtus virginitas, sed magis humilitas necessaria; illa consulitur, ista precipitur* 'the virtue of virginity is much to be praised, but humility is indispensable; the one is counseled, the other enjoined'—on whom much of the comparison of the relative merits of virginity and humility is founded. Both, however, are indebted to Ambrose and Augustine (see n. 104).

[86] Antiphon for the investiture of nuns; also the incipit of the tract from the Common of Virgins.

take up the arms of rage against that person; instead, let humility constrain you. Remember always that *it is the humble to whom God gives his grace* [Prov 3:34]. As the Lord tells us in the Gospel: *Unless you humble yourself like this little one, you will not enter the Kingdom of Heaven.*[87] *Mt 18:3-4*
Do not abandon the chasteness of your body; do not neglect the cleanliness of your mind. It behooves you, who have wedded yourself to that *most comely among the sons of men,* to maintain every suitable virtue. *Do not wash your face* with wine, nor *with soda or soap;* you *Jer 2:22*
would only reek in the presence of the Most High. Do not bathe in tubs of perfumed water, but in a font of tears. *Drench your bed every night with your tears; pour forth your tears where you lie.* Weep throughout the day; pour out *Ps 6:7*
your tears through the night: only then will you find and possess whom you seek and desire. If for a time the tears cease from your eyes, let them not cease in your heart. Let the night of your sighing and groaning know no rest until true day dawns: until you see the Morning Star that never sets. Perhaps someone negligent and slothful will say, 'I cannot weep for Christ'. I answer: If you do not mourn and weep for love of Christ, you do not, I assure you, love him completely; for if you did, you would not be able to hold back your weeping and your tears, but would cry out wailing and weeping: *'Daughters of Jerusalem, inform my beloved that I am swooning with*

[87] Similarly reordered in Bernard (*In laud.* I.5.): *nisi quis efficiatur* [O: *se humiliaverit*] *sicut parvulus iste non intrabit in regnum celorum,* for *nisi conversi fueritis et efficiamini sicut parvuli non intrabitis in regnum cælorum; quicumque ergo humiliaverit se sicut parvulus iste, hic est maior in regno cælorum.*

Sg 5:8 *love!'*[88] Ah, if ever they might tell the Beloved that I, too, wretched sinner that I am, begin at last to swoon with love of him!

You consecrated virgins and widows, whose only spouse is the Lord Jesus, to whom the world and its desires are dead, and through whose vouchsafed virginity or long-kept chastity you strive to please him: I beg your earnest prayers that I, too, corrupt as I am in body and mind, may prove worthy of his love. Then might I join my mourning wail to yours, until we find him whom our souls love. May he lead us into his eternal dwelling-place, there to feed us with the abundance of his sweetness. In this vale of corruption, that sweetness is hidden from those who strive to live honorably and chastely for love of him. Theirs is the sweet wound of his loving sweetness, the sought-for lance of his sweet love. For him alone they sigh through the night with godly desire. They cannot speak—indeed they will not hear or think—of anything but him; no other desire or wish or hope can satisfy them. Like these you too must be, you consecrated widows and virgins, whose husband is not earthly but celestial. Swoon with love for Christ. Adorn with flowers the bridal-chamber of your minds, not with roses or any other fading flower, but with the flowers of charity and all the other virtues. Then, like the *queen in golden garments* [Ps 44:10] damasked with precious stones and brocaded with pearls, you may take your place beside the Son

[88] Weeping as proof of love for Christ is similarly put forth in the *Expositio* (Homily IX).

of God, whom, as announced by the angel,
the Ever-Virgin Mary conceived and bore.
May she be blessed for ever,

and to Jesus Christ her Son,
with the Father and the Holy Spirit,
be honor and glory throughout endless ages.
Amen.

VIII. Eighth Homily

The Visitation;
Initial Reflections on the Magnificat

HOW SWEET AND PLEASANT it is to think and speak of the Mother of the eternal King, we know from experience: our love of all that concerns her cannot be sated. Once having begun to drink from the spring of her love, there breathes so delightful a fragrance of that loving-kindness that, throughout this sorrowful life, our thirst can never again be quenched. Through her we have received honey and milk from the Lord's hand; it is fitting, then, that her memory should sweeten our lips, more delightful than music
Sir 31:41 at a wine feast. We should ever quicken the memory of her sweetness, and so rejoice in glory, recounting the great works the Lord performed in her.

The Virgin Mary believed what Gabriel told her, and in her virginal womb she conceived of the Holy Spirit the Son of God the Father. The blessed Virgin, heavy with that noble burden, bore in her womb the One who created everything from nothing. She believed the word, and the Word impregnated her womb. As the heavens dropped down dew,[89] there came down from his Father's bosom that

[89] Cf. Is 45:8; the text occurs prominently in the Advent liturgy.

plenitude of sweetness that wondrously, ineffably infused the Virgin's womb. The glory of Paradise descended upon her, not violating her virginity, but making it bear fruit.

Having performed his delegated office, Gabriel hastens to return to heaven; while Mary, bearing the Heaven of Heaven in her womb, goes up with haste into the hill country and enters the house of Elizabeth, not doubtful of the miracle but certain of its promise. She goes to the house of the once barren and unfruitful Elizabeth, joyous at the news of her child. The youthful virgin, knowing no human husband, comes to the aid of her elderly kinswoman, the wife of the Prophet Zechariah. Having received the Virgin's consent, the angel seeks the heavenly realms; going forth into the hill country, the Virgin pursues his course below. The soul that has conceived the Word of God ascends the peaks of virtue with steps of love, so as to attain the city of Judah (that is, 'of affirmation')[90] and, scaling the heights of faith, hope, and loving-kindness, she enters the fortress of praise.

Not extolling her own singular merit, but mindful of her state, she calls herself the handmaid of him who has chosen her as mother, and with utter devoutness wishes the accomplishment of the angel's promise. Thus, not incredulous or uncertain of that promise, not doubting its example, but glad in her vow and religious in her office, she hastens with joy to visit Elizabeth, taking pains to show before men the same humility she had shown the

[90] *Confessionis,* cf. Jerome (*Heb. Nom.*).

angel. The roughness of the journey did not delay her; its toil did not weary her: *she went into the hill country with haste into the city of Judah, entered the house of Zechariah, and greeted*
Lk 1:39-40 *Elizabeth.*

How fortunate that blessed woman, in whose service the Queen of the world, God's chosen mother, makes haste! Bearing in her womb the world's salvation, the blessed Virgin greets her! Truly blessed is she who was worthy to be visited by so beautiful a virgin guest, to be greeted by the Mother of God, to be assisted by the Bearer of Christ! What woman has been more greatly blessed? Who worthier than Elizabeth? One alone: she whom *all gen-*
Lk 1:48 *erations shall call blessed*. Oh might that health-bringing Virgin,[91] through whom salvation was restored to the world, deign in her love to visit my soul! Might she, from whom the world's true well-being arose, speak at last to me those words of greeting! Come to me, Mother of my Lord who *saves his people from their sins,* come to me with that salvation of soul and body whom you conceived and bore without the need of any human husband!

Virgin of Christ, monk of God, so strive to please the Virgin's Son, the Son of God the Father, that you can no longer love or prefer anything to him who loved you and who washed away your sins in his blood. Love him with all your heart, for it is he who said, *'I love*
Prov 8:17 *those who love me'*. And you, virgin and widow, who through your religious vows are wed to

[91] *Virgo salutifera,* cf. Leo the Great *ipsum partum salutiferæ Virginis adoramus* (*Sermo* 29.2).

him, wed yourself to him in the bonds of love. If he, who created everything from nothing, loves you, what greater treasure could there be? What could be lacking? What could be harmful to anyone whom Jesus and his mother love? Love Christ as much! May this alone befall me, that my Lord and Mary his mother ever hold me in their love. Might I love him completely! May he manifest himself to me! If you love the Virgin's Son with all your heart, he will surely love you, and Mary will greet you in her Son, the Saviour of all.

Our blessed Mary entered the house of Zechariah and greeted Elizabeth, delighting with her in the gift she had received, as told her by the angel. She greets her first, as is fitting, for whoever is greater ought to be the more humble.[92] The greater nobility is made delightful by the sweetness of humility, for every excellence and dignity is confounded unless held in humility. Maintaining the standard of humility, the sublime Virgin greets Elizabeth first. *And it came to pass that as Elizabeth heard Mary's greeting, the child in her womb leapt for joy.* *Lk 1:41*
Elizabeth first heard the word, according to the natural order; but in response to the mystery it was John who first rejoiced, since his was the grace, like that of Mary, first to sense the coming of the Lord. He rejoiced in spirit, unable to do so in words; thus his office of forerunner began.

[92] This and much of what follows owes substantially to Ambrose (*Hom. in Lucam,* II); the passage in question supplies Lessons IX and X of the Vigils of the Visitation.

Happy the Prophet who while yet in his mother's womb recognized the advent of heaven's Lord in the bridal-chamber of the Virgin's womb: before emerging from his mother, he began to prophesy Christ's coming! He did not prophesy in speech, bound as he was in the darkness of the womb, but he exulted with all the joy of his heart, openly proclaiming that the one whose coming was foretold by patriarchs and prophets was present within Mary. With all his might he worshipped from the womb the Lord within the womb of the Virgin. When within the womb he heard Mary's greeting, his mind was filled with wondrous exultation, and to the extent he could he bowed down in utter subjection before the Lord whom the Virgin carried in her womb. It was as if to say mentally what he could not utter vocally: 'Welcome, my Lord! Welcome, Lady Mary, my Lord's mother! You are my Creator, I am your creature; you are my Lord, I am your servant; I your prophet, you the Lord of the Prophets. I am but a man, but you are God and man. I was conceived by human seed, but you by the Holy Spirit. My mother is a wife and mother, yours is a Virgin Mother. I thank you for having made me such as I am, and for having conferred such grace upon me, while yet in my mother's womb, as to sense in her coming the presence of your majesty! For what you created me to do, I am ready. I shall now emerge from the womb as a prophesying seer, to point to you not as who is to come, but as present in the flesh, as the Lamb that takes away the sins of the world. To you be ever honor and glory in heaven and on earth, in the sea and in the depths of the abyss, and in the womb of the most holy Virgin where now you are cloistered.'[93]

Elizabeth was filled by the Holy Spirit and cried out aloud, 'Blessed are you among women!' *Lk 1:41b-42a* Not that the mother was filled with the Holy Spirit before her son, but that the son, filled, fills his mother. Mary was filled before her conceiving, Elizabeth after hers. *She cried out mightily,*[94] because she recognized God's mighty gifts; not in a whisper, because she understood. Thus she said: *'Blessed are you among women, and blessed is the fruit of your womb!'* *Lk 1:42b* How well the words of the Gospel match those of the psalm in which David is promised: *From the fruit of your womb I shall set him upon your throne.* *Ps 131:11* Mark how Elizabeth's blessing echoes Gabriel's greeting to Mary: she is to be revered by angels and humans alike, and to be preferred before all other women. *Blessed are you,* not only *among women:* among all *blessed women* you shine with far greater blessing. *And blessed is the fruit of your womb:* God, for ever blessed above all. *Blessed is the fruit of your womb,* through whom the children of Adam are blessed for ever. Blessed be the field of your womb that, neither tilled by mattock or plowshare nor sown with any seed, has borne us the bread of life and resurrection.

Of this bread *no one who serves the Temple can partake*. *Heb 13:10* I speak here of the temple of the

[93] The paragraph is evidently inspired by Chrysostom's animated 'interview' of John the Baptist *in utero (Apud Metaphr. mense Iulio);* cf. Lessons V-VIII of the Visitation Vigils.

[94] *Magna voce* ('aloud', lit. 'with great voice'), a lexical link with the *Magnificat.*

flesh: how miserable and wretched are those who serve it! Well may their hearts mourn with bitter sobbing, for they do not deserve to partake of the bread the Virgin bore, the Bread of Life and of eternal bliss. Cultivating their flesh they fail to tend the field of their minds. They wash the dirt from their bodies, but not the filth of wantonness. They nourish their bodies with mounds of food,[95] but poison their souls with shafts of vice; thus they hand themselves over to everlasting flames. Such as these shall not profit from the fruit of the Virgin's womb, the Son of God the Father, unless they reform themselves altogether, *casting off the old man and clothing themselves in the*
Col 3:9 *new,* created by God in justice and the holiness
of truth. Such as these shall not be blessed by
the blessed fruit of Mary's womb, by whom
Ps 71:17 *all the tribes of the earth shall be blessed. Amen.*

This is the Virgin's Son to whom the people
of Jerusalem cried, *'Hosanna! Blessed is he who*
Mk 11:9b-10a *comes in the name of the Lord',* the blessed one
of whom the prophet said, *God shall give his*
power to the people: the Lord shall bless his people in
Ps 28:11 *peace.* May God the Father's Son, Mary's Son, grant us that power and bless us in peace! *In peace*—in himself, who is that true peace that came down from heaven to make peace between men and angels, to reconcile sinners to God, and to grant mortals everlasting life. May he grant the same to me, so that with consecrated virgins I might sing: *I lie down in peace,*
Ps 4:9 *and sleep comes at once.*

[95] *Stromis* [sic] *ciborum,* perhaps the mistaken ablative pl. of *stroma, –tis* ('[motley] tapestry', 'mélange').

O bride of Christ, and you, monk of the Mother of the Most High, you who have come to partake in the Order of Our Lady and consecrated yourself as a Cistercian religious: say, together with every people and tribe and tongue, with the angel Gabriel and with Elizabeth the mother of the Prophet of the Most High, *Hail Mary, full of grace; the Lord is with you. Blessed are you among women, and blessed is the fruit of your womb.* For if you so bless the blessed fruit of Mary's womb, with pure heart and conscience, you will surely be blessed by him on the day of his coming in peace. Nothing is more gracious to his virgin mother than to bless the blessed fruit of her womb. If then you wish to be loved by Mary, the Mother of your Savior, say this prayer often with your lips and ever in your heart. Believe me, you cannot be cursed by Christ if you bless him and his blessed Mother with all your being. Thus you join your voice to that of Elizabeth's benediction: *Blessed are you among women, and blessed is the fruit of your womb.*

Then she said: *'How is it that the mother of my Lord should come to me?* What a boon befalls *Lk 1:43* me that the mother of my Lord comes to me! But what have I done to merit it? Surely I do not deserve to be visited by the Handmaid of the Lord, the Queen of the world: the Mother of God, through whom humankind is returned to Paradise and human nature is reformed to angelic state. I am unworthy to receive the one of whom he who has ever existed is now to be born, and, in being born of her, takes on a new beginning—he who is the beginning of all things and knows no beginning himself.

How is it then?' O truly blessed Elizabeth, how great, how ineffable are the gifts bestowed on you! To you comes Mary, *adorned with necklaces, bedecked in topaz, clothed in royal purple and fine*
Ez 16:10-13 *Egyptian cotton,* the whole dyed scarlet woven
Sg 6:9 with gold, *fair as the moon, resplendent as the sun.*
Heavy with the noble burden of divine offspring, she brings to you the wondrous gift God the in heaven commanded: God himself, the Lord of all, the King of endless ages. She bears him, not in a common vessel but in her own most chaste womb, not openly in public but hidden within her sacred body. To you, and to John within, she makes him known through the Holy Spirit who, even as Mary greets you, speaks within your heart of hearts. For the Spirit has enlightened you, and not only you but John as well, and thus you have recognized the treasure the maiden bears in her womb, and rejoice in the coming of the Queen of Heaven. For behold—as you yourself declare—the child in your womb leapt for joy, the very moment her greeting resounded
Lk 1:44 in your ears.

The Holy Spirit, filling Elizabeth with himself, reveals to her the import of her child's rejoicing: the mother of him has come whose forerunner he shall be. She who at first blushed to see her young kinswoman with child (not knowing the fulfillment of promised mercy) now blesses her. And she who had hidden the conception of a son, now proclaims that she is to bear a prophet. What she knew in secret she now openly makes known to all who had been present and had heard the good news: *'Blessed are you who have believed, for that which*

was spoken by the Lord shall be accomplished in you'. Blessed indeed: raised to such great Lk 1:45
heights of excellence as to become a mother while retaining her virginity, and so conceive and bear the God of all, through whom all things were made, to whom the universe is subject, to speak of whom no one is worthy, neither angel, archangel, nor any other creature in heaven or on earth—save Mary herself, whose beauty vanquishes the sun, the moon, the stars! She surpasses the archangels in the purity of her holiness. None but God is more beautiful than she; none better than the one she bore. She gave birth to her Maker, the author of all good, the King of all ages, from whom and through whom and in whom everything comes. Rightly indeed is she called blessed and exalted above every blessing of Paradise.

On hearing Elizabeth's response—calling her blessed, the mother of her Lord, valiant in faith—our blessed Mary, all glory's crown and hope of our salvation, the defense of our virtue, the splendor and beauty of virgins and of all the faithful of Christ, will not conceal in silence the ineffable gifts God has showered upon her. She had, in her virginal modesty, received them in silence, but now the time has come for her to speak aloud: *'My soul proclaims the Lord's magnificence.'*[96] O wondrous joy, Lk 1:46
O great and solemn dance:[97] the world's bright

[96] Given as an incipit, the verse introduces the canticle that occupies the *Tractatus* to the end of Homily IX.

[97] *Tripudium* (cf. Est 8:16), see also n.112 below; the figure occurs as well in the *Expositio: On the Lord's Words to His Disciples at the Last Supper* (Homily IX, n. 87).

star, the chosen Mother of God sings out her heart's emotion and, ecstatic for joy, opens her mellifluous milky lips to intone her melodious hymn of praise. *'My soul proclaims the Lord's magnificence!'*

She first acknowledges the special gifts she has received, then the general benefice God has ever bestowed on humankind. Proclaiming the Lord's magnificence, she enumerates the merits the Lord has conferred on her, as if to say: 'No words could describe how the Lord has elevated me; I offer but the full affection of my innermost soul in due praise and thanks. All that is my life, all that I feel and discern, I give to the contemplation of his grandeur and to the keeping of his precepts.'

The Lord's magnificence is proclaimed, not by mere human speech, but when our souls, created in God's image, conform themselves in righteousness to Christ, the image of the Father. Just as by imitating Christ they proclaim his magnificence, and by sharing in his grandeur they are raised still higher; so by emulating his virtues they are seen to express that image of Christ in the rainbow of his blessed works. Thus in justice and in holiness did Mary conform herself to God, and so could say: *'My soul declares the magnificence of the Lord*—the God and Creator of all—for with devoutness and loving affection he is revered in the comeliness of my virtues.'

Truly the Lord's magnificence is proclaimed in you, morning star outshining all the galaxy, most holy of all mortals, more glorious than the angels in the sight of the eternal splendor:

since through you the God of all is known in
this realm of ignorance and blindness, this
abyss of firmly-rooted confusion and corrupt
mortality. Once it was known in Judea alone;
through you it thunders forth throughout the
world. *From the rising of the sun until its setting,*
through you *the Lord's name is praised,* which *Ps 112:3a, 2a*
once only the Jews revered. The whole world
now cries out with one voice: *The Lord's is the*
earth and its fullness. The universe rounds with *Ps 23:1*
applause: *O Lord, our Lord, how wondrous is your*
name in all the earth! Through you *he possesses* *Ps 8:2*
all nations and lands, and *all kings worship him,* *Ps 2:8*
every people and tribe and tongue pay him service. *Ps 71:11*
Not that you of yourself conferred these gifts
on him, but that being born of you he acquired
them for himself; for in dying, rising again,
and ascending to heaven he accepted these
gifts among humankind, dwelling as Lord and
God among unbelievers. *Blessed be the Lord—*
proclaim it daily—the God of our salvation, who *Ps 67:20*
for himself chose such a mother, that through
her those who walked in darkness beheld the
great Light of the Nations, and through whom
true Light, Christ our Lord and God, was
born to those who dwelled in the realm of
the shadow of death. You are the gate of life
through whom true Life and eternal Light
came forth *to enlighten those who were in dark-*
ness and sat in the shadow of death. You are the *Lk 1:79*
doorway to Paradise; *there the tribes of God go*
up, and *the princes of the people gather* daily *with* *Ps 121:4*
the God of Abraham, where the mighty gods of
earth are mightily lifted up. Through you God is *Ps 46:10*
forgiving of all our *sins and heals* us *of all* our
infirmities; through you *he ransoms* our *life from*

the *destruction* of everlasting death, *and crowns* us *in his mercy and compassion.*

Ps 102:3, 4

Blessed be she through whom such good things have come to us, she who so proclaims the Lord's magnificence that people and kings may gather together to serve him, and that those who did not know him might now become obedient to his voice, even to the shedding of their blood. She is the pleasure-garden of delights, from whom the fountain of glory, the Lord Jesus Christ, sprang forth to water the surface of the earth. To these waters he invites us: *'Let anyone who thirsts come to me and drink.'* The fountain of salvation was hidden from all, until that living water flowed forth from the Maiden's womb to water the earth of our bodies and souls in its flood, moistening and fructifying us with constancy of virtue. She is the House of the Lord from which there issued a spring of saving water to cleanse us of our sins and impurities. In that saving font our minds are washed of filth, our power of reason made whiter than snow.[98] She is that lofty ladder,[99] the excellence of whose virtues stretches forth to heaven, by which the Lord of heaven descends to earth to bring the earthbound with him to heaven. There in the company of angels we are to dwell in our everlasting home, praising throughout endless ages the author of the ages.

Jn 7:37

Cf. Ez 47:1ff.

The King of heaven, the Lord of all, is greatly magnified by our Queen, through

[98] *Hominem rationis cum suo iumento super nivem dealbat* (cf. Ps 50:9); the movement from mens to ratio recalls Augustine (*De ordine* II). I read *iumento* here as the syncopated form of *iuvamento* ('aid').

[99] cf. Gen 28:12, the connection being Jacob (see above).

whom the heavenly Jerusalem is daily built up and increased. Thus (though she could not have understood it then) God is magnified through her: not that she was the final cause of God's magnificence, but its material cause. The final cause of every good is Christ the Lord, but from Mary he received as it were the form of our salvation when he took on flesh from her for our redemption. When, *like a bridegroom from his bridal-chamber,*[100] the *Ps 18:6*
Saviour of the world came forth from our most blessed Virgin's womb, she thus became the formal or material cause of our salvation. By means of her he came to gather together the children of God, who had been scattered, and through his blood save both humankind and beasts of burden, even as God multiplied his mercy. By right, therefore, the Lord's *Ps 35:7-8a*
mother, the Virgin Mary, proclaimed the Lord's magnificence, for she had pleased him like none other. O most fortunate and supremely virtuous Virgin Mary, who without staining her snow-white modesty conceived and bore Christ! Well may our Lady say: *My soul declares the Lord's magnificence, and my spirit rejoices in God my Saviour.* *Lk 1:46-47*

The human soul and spirit are the same;[101] in us the one may stand for the other, though this is not so among the angels, for every Catholic professes that the cherubim and seraphim and all the other orders of angels are

[100] Augustine (Serm. 192) interprets this verse to mean *de utero virginali, ubi Verbum Dei creaturæ humanæ quodam ineffabili coniugio copulatum est* ('from the Virgin's womb, where God's Word was coupled to humankind by a certain ineffable bonding').

[101] Augustine *(In Evangelium Ioannis): spiritum dico, quæ anima vocatur.*

spirits, not souls. In the beginning God created all spirits, but every day he creates new souls and infuses them in new bodies; as these new creatures live and have wisdom and discernment, they may rightly be said to possess spirits. Thus the soul and spirit of Mary most blessed are one and the same. *'My spirit rejoices in God my Saviour',* she says, 'since I have no regard for earthly things—indeed, I count them vile as dung. Prosperity does not enfeeble me, adversity does not break me, for I am nourished solely by remembrance of him from whom eternal salvation is hoped for. I rejoice solely in the divinity of him who took on flesh in being conceived by me. Now my soul magnifies him in whom my spirit ever rejoices. I magnify and glorify him, I bless him and worship him in whom my spirit has ever rejoiced: God my Saviour.'

O truly blessed Virgin, blessed beyond all reckoning, the God of all is your God and Saviour; yet your relationship with your God and Saviour is other than ours, for he is our God and our Lord, but he is your God and your Son. He is our God and we are his servants, but you are his mother and he is your son. Deservedly your soul declares his magnificence, for by him you were granted such grace as to become his mother without losing the lily of your virginity. He chose his handmaid, his maid-servant, to be his mother. Let such a Son be for ever blessed, and also his mother, Mary. Let my soul magnify him whose magnificence Mary's soul proclaims, and let my spirit rejoice in him in whom her spirit rejoices!

He who saves his people, he who created you as his little servant, will also be your Savior if you proclaim his magnificence at every hour, ever rejoicing because of him and through him and in him. You will not fear adversity if your hope is Christ. Let your hope be Christ God, with Mary his mother. Let your soul depend on him; let your glory be in him. *Let all who glory glory in the Lord.* Bride *1 Cor 1:31* of Christ, glory not in the world, but in your God, your bridegroom, your Savior Jesus Christ. Glory not in the glow of your skin, but in the gleaming of your mind, not in nobility of family, but in the honorable humility of servanthood, for true nobility is proved in one's service for Christ. If you have been Christ's lowly handmaid, you will be the sublime bride of your Lord and God. If however you have been proud and haughty, you will not be his lover or his bride; you will be the devil's harlot and his mate.[102] If you desire to please the Bridegroom of virgins, the Virgin's Son, seek first *wool to spin and linen to weave,* *Prov 31:13* to be chaste in body and pure in mind. Then the clothing of your flesh will not reek of fetid lust, and the garment of your mind will not be stained by lewdness. A virgin in body whose mind is unchaste will be reckoned, not among the number of virgins, but among the whores of the brothel. Keep altogether clean the garment of your mind. Since by its very nature our flesh is corrupt, we must through vigilance and unflagging resolve seek to be

[102] *Bandesa:* apparently vernacular (cf. Ital. *banda*, 'gang'), the word, as Adriani notes (p. 52, n. 1), is unknown in the standard glossaries.

cleansed of every uncleanness, and to lavish every care to keep our honor spotless.

And since by neglect and inattention chastity cannot be maintained, let us strictly guard our sight and hearing, reining in our speech and restraining our thoughts from harmful wandering. In observing chastity of the eyes, let us be instructed by the example of Job, to whom much holiness was accounted: *'I kept a pact with my eyes not to linger upon any*
Job 31:1 *virgin'*. Anyone who carelessly looks outward through the windows of the eyes falls often into sin even without wishing to. Thus the mind of David, so often elevated by inner mysteries, was destroyed when he looked incautiously on another's wife, and, thus beclouded, sought illicitly to wed her to himself. On the careful management of the ears Solomon admonishes
Prov 4:24 us: *Keep your distance from a wicked mouth.* Likewise the Apostle tells us: *Evil talk spoils*
1 Cor 15:33 *good morals*. As to the custody of the mouth, heed his advice as well: *Banish obscenities from*
Col 3:8 *your speech*. Those whose modesty is dashed by dishonorable speech soon pass from word to deed. As to the careful concern we owe our thoughts, the voice of Solomon once again
Prov 4:23 instructs us: *Guard your heart with watchfulness.* For the evil of wantonness is renewed in us whenever our secret thoughts are those for which our foe, the devil, was cast out; thus it often happens that those whom he is unable to corrupt in their actions he pollutes nonetheless in their thoughts. Therefore, beloved virgins and brides of God, and you, beloved servants of Christ Jesus, insofar as you have withdrawn from the turmoil of this world and

seek to prove fit warriors for God, lead an angelic life on earth, and magnify the Lord Jesus, glorifying him in soul and spirit. Taste nothing in your hearts but him whose magnificence the soul of Mary proclaimed.

As to the soul and its powers, a few remarks here will be profitable, provided my labor prove worthy and acceptable to God and of such usefulness and necessity to my readers as Christ himself shall grant. The soul is that invisible substance that forms our principal part, and of which, with our bodies, we are composed. Its powers are three.[103] First is that power by which our bodies enjoy the life of the senses, by which the body waxes, perceiving and discerning what is outside it through the senses. The second reveals itself, not only with regard to that which pertains to the senses; it examines and analyzes higher matters, concerning which its inquiries touch upon much that is beyond the sensory. It is this aspect of the soul that, when developed, contemplates God himself. It observes not only what lies hidden in nature, but what truly befits human virtue as well. This is called reason; reasoning is its function, as, for example, in the investigation of mysteries. When it has finished its quest and arrives at a conclusion, the result is understanding or intelligence. The third power of

[103] Cf. the *De spiritu et anima* of Alcher of Clairvaux (also known as Pseudo-Augustine): the soul's three powers *(vires)* commingle elements of the Aristotelian sensory, vegetative, and locomotive faculties (1.); the rational faculty is divided into intellect and reason (2.) and appetite (3.), which appears here to include the consenting will. See Alcher, *On the Nature of the Body and the Soul,* translated Erasmo Leiva and Benedicta Ward, *Three Treatises on Man. A Cistercian Anthropology,* CF 24 (1977) 181–288.

the soul is the appetite, by which the soul is seized by a certain desire, for things discerned either through the senses or by the light of knowledge and the beauty of wisdom. This is the faculty by which certain physical pleasures are enjoyed, while other allurements of the flesh are despised; through appetite we strive to attain virtue and lead honorable lives. Of these three powers of the soul it is written:
You shall love the Lord your God with all your heart,
Deut 6:5 *with all your soul, and with all your mind. With*
your heart, so that the affection of the soul may be directed toward God. *With the soul,* so that what lives in the body and through the body senses the works of God may advance in praising and loving him. *With your mind,* so that human thought, memory, and reason may serve to contemplate and know God. To this end all three powers of the soul should strive, as the Evangelist briefly concludes, *with all your might.* 'Soul' in this sense comprises the sensorial, the rational, and the appetitive; but the word is also used to mean, not incorporeal substance, but rather its weakened state in and
Gen 2:7 through the body. Thus: *man became a living soul;*
Mt 16:25 and, *whoever loses his soul for my sake will find it.*
With all of her soul's three powers—indeed, with all her being—the blessed Virgin magnified the Lord and ever rejoiced in him, her God, Creator, and Saviour.

Thus rightly did she receive from him those precious gifts she goes on to enumerate:
'He has regarded the lowliness of his handmaid:
Lk 1:48 *henceforth all generations shall call me blessed. My*
soul thus *proclaims the Lord's magnificence,* because
Lk 1:49a he saw fit to do *great things for me.* I attribute

my greatness, such as it is, to no merits of my own; I refer to him to whom I commit myself in utter devotion, humility, and subjection, as his servant and handmaid.' She thinks but little of herself, attributing everything to God's grace. In her judgment she is lowly, but with respect to the grace that elevates her, all nations' voices will declare her blessed—and rightly so! For even as death entered the world through Eve's pride, so through Mary's humility the gates of life are flung open; and she whose lowliness the world's Creator regarded is rightly to be hailed by all as blessed.

O blessed humility, so loved by the Most High King of all the ages that he set his royal throne upon it! The King of Kings regarded and loved that blessed Virgin in her humility, and so desired his beloved as to be *ravished by a single glance and a lock of her hair.* She was *Sg 4:9*
wholly beautiful; in her there was no blemish. Beauty adorned her in bodily form; comelier still the gracefulness of her mind. Outwardly she was graced with the beauty of roses and lilies, comely in her virginity, but in the lightning flash of her humility she shone with a glory beyond all human measure. Virginity is greatly praised; humility is even more to be commended.[104] Virginity adorns a woman; humility saves her. Virginity is precious in the sight of the Most High; more precious yet is humility in the presence of God. Many a virgin, whether maiden or man, is betrayed by the ravages of hell, but none who are

[104] Cf. Ambrose, *De virginitate* (esp. II:2), and (especially) Augustine, *De sancta virginitate* (XXXI–XXXVII).

humble is estranged from God. As the Gospel
Mt 25:10 attests, five virgins were turned away from the door of the heavenly kingdom and shut out. But on the day of judgment every humble person will swiftly enter into the joy of the Lord, there to enjoy the best of all. Let all in whom the flower of virginity blooms keep to the path of humility, for all will be consigned to the savage pit who do not turn again their steps to that narrow way. Humility enjoys the highest rank among the virtues, for there he is seated who *casts down the mighty from their*
Lk 1:52 *thrones and elevates the lowly* in his glory. Humility is the intention of the mind directed toward God, the contempt of self and the love of God. Such was ever the intention of the blessed Virgin who held herself in contempt and loved God with all her might. To that humility the power and splendor of heaven came down to make himself a home in the humility's Queen; for so it is written in the Book of Wisdom: *Wisdom has built herself a*
Prov 9:1 *home and has hewn seven pillars*. In the most blessed valley, Mary, the God of Wisdom, the Son of the Most High Father built himself a home of matchless humility; for none is greater or more sublime than she who by her
Deut 33:29 own virtue *trampled the necks of her foes*. He conquered the proud through the shedding of his blood, and made his followers whiter than with snowy waters, bidding them enter the treasury of his everlasting glory.

Rejoice then, Mary, vale of virtue, temple of the Holy Spirit: in you the sublime mountain of mountains, the Word of God the Father, descended to be joined to the human flesh of our first parents, and to be anointed with the oil of the Holy Spirit for all who take part in him. He is the mountain of strength upon which it was pleasing to God to dwell, and in whom he dwells for ever. All who fly to this mountain shall be saved and live a life without end. Into the valley, redolent with the sweetness of honey, this mountain descended. There in her essential innocence the Virgin flowered, and of blossom of her beauty God clothed himself. He regarded her lowliness and took on her virginal flesh. Her beauty was not darkened, nor her virginal modesty diminished, because her God fell in love with her and the Holy Spirit impregnated her. Thus rightly is she to be hailed by every tongue and blessed by every descendant, even as she bears witness: *Henceforth all generations shall call me blessed*. Gazing on her, the daughters of Zion *Lk 1:48b* declare her most blessed, and queens and concubines together praise her. All the orders of heaven regard her radiant in comeliness and pay heed to her adornment. And thus they make a joyful noise to God with shouts of jubilee; choirs of angels rejoice to see her elevated above them as Mother of the King of Ages; they call her blessed, revere her, and gleefully adore her. For all are redeemed through her, especially consecrated virgins and nuns who join themselves in love to the eternal King, her Son, not neglecting steadfastly to praise her. She is indeed worthy of all praise who as Virgin was found worthy to conceive the Word of the Father through the Holy Spirit, in whom there is the forgiveness of sin, the resurrection of the dead, the life of the living, the glory of the saints, the bliss of the blessed, the delight of the delightful, the pleasure of joys, and everlasting eternity:

Christ, with the Father and the Holy Spirit,
blessed God for ever and ever.
Amen.

IX. Ninth Homily

Further reflections on the Magnificat

HOW SWEET AND DELIGHTFUL it is, ever to call to mind our heavenly mother, that fragrant spikenard, about whom roses waft the scent of Paradise! Young maidens steeped in that fragrance trace her course with the swift footsteps of desire. All who have eagerly drunk of the springs of the Christ she bore well know that fragrance! Let us then run to that spring of living waters, Jesus, her son, who from the Lebanon of his Father leapt forth into the field of Mary's virginal womb. And let us drink there with the same love with which he himself drank from the torrent of our mortality during his pilgrimage on earth. Since for us the blessed Virgin Mary distilled the honey of the honeycomb, let us then, with jubilant hearts and joyous voices, exalt and bless her for ever and ever.

Henceforth all generations shall call me blessed. From generation to generation let her works be praised, her powers be recounted, and the grandeur of her glory be proclaimed. To think of her is sweet; to meditate on her is great delight. Let us then sing to her a litany of praise: O blessed woman, immaculate Virgin, fragrance of the fruitful fields, delight of Paradise, the comeliness of virgins, the splendor of the saints, the glory of the elect, the bliss of the blessed, the hope of the dying, and the life of the living! *All generations*—yes, and every individual as well: let all declare you blessed, praise and bless you with heart and mind, and in every act and utterance!

Alas, how few, how rare are those who call you blessed and seek to bless you! As for us, unworthy as we are to speak your name, still we ever seek to call you blessed and sing your benediction. But to do so well we need to know—you ought to teach us—why you are to be blessed by humankind. Whence and why are all generations to call you blessed? Tell us, Mother of Truth; from you we wait to hear the truth! She answers: *'Because he who is mighty*
Lk 1:49 *has done great things for me: holy is his Name'*. Blessed be that Mighty One who conferred on you these great deeds!

'Great things', you say. We desire to learn from you what these may be. Perhaps among them is your royal lineage as an offspring of David; perhaps it is your beauty and virtue, which no blemish beclouds. Or is it that the Scriptures speak of you, before whom fountains of water appear and spread out over the
Cf. Ps 17:16, Sir 24:42, Gen 1:11 meadows for you to gather living herbs? These things are surely great, but we await to hear from you still greater. We know that the Mighty One is rich and generous with his gifts, and that he has granted you many gifts in the abundance of his grandeur. But which of these do you account as great?

Again she speaks: If you would know what greatness was bestowed on me, I will gladly tell you, since it is your love for me that bids you ask. That greatness is not like these other mighty deeds; its singular privilege stands high above all the rest. Indeed it has no peer. But I think you know of what I speak: you have read in Isaiah of the Virgin who was to bear Emanuel, and you do not doubt that this refers to me. But as it delights you to hear of these great deeds from me, I shall make them plain for you. The Mighty One, whose Name is holy, is the God and Lord of all, who created heaven and earth and sea and everything therein. He slays and he gives life, strikes down and heals: none can escape his grasp, nor can anyone resist him. He performs his will not merely by deed, but by word. He spoke, and the world and everything upon it was created. He commanded, and it came into being; established, and it perdures; set forth his law, and it shall not pass away. This Mighty One leaned down from heaven and descended into my womb, so that he who was my God and my Creator should become my Son. I, a virgin, conceived God of God. God became a creature, the Word became flesh, the Son of God became a man; for so it was prophesied: *A woman shall encompass a man* in her womb.[105] And also: *Behold, a virgin shall conceive and bear a son, whose name she shall call Emanuel,* God with us. Do you not think it great that a virgin has conceived and borne not only a man of great esteem but the author of salvation, not man merely, but her God and Creator? Who

Cf. 2 Cor 3:6, Hos 6:2, Deut 32:39, 2 Ch 13:8

Jer 31:22

Is 7:14

[105] With *Mulier* for *femina*. The passage is correctly cited and otherwise developed by Bernard (*In laud.* II.8, 9); Ogier's argument suggests Augustine (Sermon 14) as an additional source.

has ever heard of anything so great as this, that a woman should conceive, not of man, but of the Holy Spirit; that she should become a mother without violating the privilege of her chasteness; the mother of him who created all things and is before all things, the beginning of all things, from whom and through whom all things exist? *Great* indeed are these *things* that *the Mighty One—holy is his Name—has done for me*.'

Ever blessed be that Mighty One, God the Father and Christ his Son, who has done such great deeds for you, that he who made you should be made in you; for through these great deeds we receive great things each day! God came down into your womb to take on flesh from you, and through you was given the Holy Spirit who dwells in our hearts. In your womb he clothed himself in our humanity, and so he made us sharers in his divinity, for, clothed in your flesh, he clothed us in his godhead. From heaven he descended into you, so that through you he might draw us unto himself in heaven. God came to earth and there became man, so that as man he might ascend to heaven, there to be God. Life himself came down to our death, so that our death might be reconciled and united inseparably with life. For the sake of our death eternal life died, so that our death might live and never perish. That life was buried in the tomb, so that our death might live and reign in heaven.[106]

[106] Here follows, as if anticipating the later, expansive treatment of Mary's participation in Christ's Passion and Death, an artless digression: "We know a certain Virgin whose name, I think, was Mary—and, unless I am mistaken, you know her well also—who, shedding many tears, beheld that life dying on the tree.

You said that he who is mighty—whose Name is holy—has done great things for you, and we believe that much good has come of this to us. Because of these great deeds, his mercy has flooded the world for all the generations of those who fear him. Through you the Most High has spread his mercy far and wide, even as it is written: *You shall save men and beasts, Lord God, to the extent that you have multiplied your mercy.* The wondrous mercy of Ps 35:7
God was established in heaven, and there his truth was prepared. Now the universal Church sings: *The earth is full of the mercy of God.* Ps 32:5
Through you the Lord of all has become *merciful, long-suffering and compassionate.* Henceforth Ps 102:8
he shall have no wrath towards us. *He shall not deal with us according to our sins, nor shall he pay us back according to our iniquities. For on earth, even as in the heights of heaven, he has vouchsafed his mercy to those who fear him. As great the distance from sunrise to sunset, so he has distanced us from our iniquities. Even as a father has compassion for his children, so the Lord has had mercy on us* Ps 102:10-13
through you who pleased him without peer.

Fear the Lord then, you, his consecrated brides, and all his holy people, for *to those who fear him there is abundant glory. The proud and the haughty shall hunger and be in want, but those who fear* Christ *shall rejoice in the abundance of all goodness.* Those who fear the Lord shall be Ps 33:10-11
blessed on their last day, and at their parting

I believe she loved that life more than words can tell and mourned bitterly to see him die. You are, I know, not ignorant of how that woman grieved, when, in the throes of death, he who was *comeliest among the sons of men* said to her, with respect to John, '*Behold your son.*' But let us set this grief aside just now and return to your joy and ours."

they shall have abundance of bread.[107] Those who fear the Lord shall take on wings as of the eagle; they shall fly to the heights of the sun, and with Christ, their sun, they shall shine throughout eternity. *Peace* and mercy, joy *and safety,*[108] shall attend their rich reward of rest. The fear of the Lord is *the two-edged sword** that shall overcome the foe in perfect safety. The fear of the Lord is *the sharp javelin* of Christ's irrevocable authority. It is our confidence of strength. All who steadfastly persevere in the fear of the Lord shall gleam bright against the foe of humankind. They shall never be brought low by adversity; they shall cast forth every adversary, ever fearless, ever secure. They shall be feared by every adverse spirit and shall know no fear of the foe. Before the judgment seat of Christ they shall stand secure who have ever preserved in their fear of him; nor shall they cringe in terror of him whose fear possesses them in love. To all who fear him shall be given that mercy and abundance of everlasting sweetness that now is hidden in their earthly pilgrimage.

Cf. Is 40:31, Prov 23:5, Mt 13:43

** Rev 1:16*

Rev 2:12

Let us then fear the Lord, so that we may at last attain his mercy. Jesus will hasten in mercy to meet those who fear him, consoling and caressing them.[109] He banishes fear and promises safety. If thus you long for Jesus' consolation, keep the fear of him ever before your eyes. Chaste fear is the certain guide that leads to God and lasts for ever. It is the fear that

[107] Cf. Sir 1:13, on which this appears to be in part a gloss.
[108] *Pax et securitas,* as the fruits of justice: Is 32:17.
[109] *Demulcens,* suggesting indebtedness to Ambrose (*De virg.* 93).

drives out every fear that proceeds from the punishment of sin: it converts all fear to love, and brings forgiveness. O blessed fear, that appeases the wrath of God and transforms the strict judge into a loving redeemer! Blessed is that fear that blesses the God-fearing; when that dreadful judge comes, they shall not fear the dreaded words, *'Go, accursed ones, into the everlasting fire.'* They shall hear instead these *Mt 25:41*
words of benediction: *'Come, you whom my Father has blessed, receive the kingdom prepared for you before the beginning of the world.'* For: *His* *Mt 25:34*
mercy is from generation to generation of those who fear him. *Lk 1:50*

We have heard how, with supreme loving-kindness, the bestower of all good, our compassionate Lord Jesus, stretches forth his mercy in the abundance of his goodness to all who fear him; but he smashes the proud with the might of his terrible arm, even as our Lady declares in the next verse of her hymn: *He has used the power of his arm to rout the proud-minded.* *Lk 1:51*
We understand 'the arm of the Lord' to mean Jesus, his Son and yours. The Father's Son, without a mother; yours, without a father. His Son, born of his own nature; yours, conceived of the Holy Spirit. But how God the Father *has used the power* of his Son and yours *to rout the proud-minded,* do now make known to us. We know of that arrogant creature who lost his head in wishing to ascend above God: that wretch lost his head when he abandoned himself to such evil. Seeking the lofty, he was dashed from on high; thrusting at heaven, he fell into the depths; coveting a throne above the stars of heaven, he crouches below the

earth condemned for ever. It is of this arrogant one and his band of followers that you speak, O Mother of such might. *The Lord's arm scattered the proud-hearted* when he condemned for ever Satan and all the airy powers who opposed him and drove themselves far from his mercy.

Nothing is more displeasing to God than a neck stretched out in sin. The proud and the haughty have no part in the kingdom of God and Christ. The first proud creature was dashed headlong from heaven to the depths from which no proud one ascends. Pride was thus cast out from heaven so that it should never again rise to heaven, but be fittingly held in the abyss. Therefore let every virgin and widow beware, who desires to be joined in love to Christ, the bridegroom of consecrated virgins, lest her heart swell up with pride and thus be turned away from God, the author of all good. Pride separates us from the kingdom of heaven and casts us headlong into fire and brimstone. Pride first infected the fallen angels; let us then not be slain by the same evil poison! Alas, how many in shepherd's garb or holy veil it slays with the sword of depravity! How many are so drunk with that viper's drink that, utterly mindless of their profession, they neither resemble humans nor recognize God! How many, male and female,
Mt 11:7 are no more than *reeds shaken by the wind!* How many are dashed to the ground as if by blast of gale; there is scarcely remedy to heal the wounds of such a fall! Oh the number of miserable wretches who, by some sign or gesture, or vulgar little word, are dashed to the ground, as if they had been struck on both

cheeks! Let them blush, humbled and ashamed: *God withstands the proud but grants favor to the humble.*

Virgins, servants of God: *what can separate* you *from the love of Christ?* Did he not suffer death himself to free you from death everlasting? Did he not wash away in his blood the filth of your bodies and souls? He has chosen you out of the world so that henceforth you are no longer slaves to sin; then keep your flesh whole, lest together with your soul you prostitute yourselves to the Corrupter. The Lord is *comely of form before all other sons of men;* it is fitting that he choose for a bride one who is wholly beautiful, in whom there is no blemish of impurity. Christ the humble seeks to choose himself a humble bride. Are you humble? Then you are beautiful, lovely, utterly pleasing to the God of all. If you have no humility you will no longer be his friend or his bride, but rather the devil's harlot. Oh what a wicked bridegroom, what a hateful spouse! His brides know no mercy from him; he reeks and stinks worse than heaps of dung. Oh how badly wed is the bride of such a marriage! How foul and doleful the conjugal act! Servant of God, make your marriage with Christ; let him be your lover, your spouse, for he is the Lord your God.

Rom 8:55

He, as his Virgin Mother bears witness, *cast down the mighty*—the archangel-turned-devil and his pact—*from their thrones*. For his pride that angel was cast forth from God's glory; but other spirits who stood steadfast in humility have been greatly and irrevocably elevated in the glory of their Maker. I want you to know

Lk 1:52a

what happened to the fallen angels, because it happens to us mortals every day. He condemns the proud and thrusts them into the fierce pit; but he saves the lowly and draws them to himself in heavenly glory. His anger flares out at the haughty and brings them to scorn; the humble he loves most of all, he blesses the blessed for ever. Every proud spirit is seized in hell's everlasting prison; the humble are nourished with eternal glory in the royal hall of the saints. Cruel and severe the punishment of the proud; the lowly are joyously welcomed to endless repose. The proud are consumed in the fires of hell; the humble are made sublime in glory. The struggles of the proud are never over; the glory of the humble never ends. It is good, then, not to be proud, since such are their pains and torments; but to be humble, so joyful their rich reward.

Pride is doing that which counters God's will. What greater pride could there be than to demean the precepts of the Most High? The commandments of Israel's God are these: *You shall not kill, you shall not commit adultery, you shall not steal,* and so on. Thus every murderer, every adulterer, whore, fornicator, and effeminate, every brigand and thief is proud and puffed-up; as such they can never possess the kingdom of heaven. Whoever is such as these will be cast down by the Mighty Humble One from arrogance and pride into the cauldron seething over a fire blown white-hot by
Jer 1:13 the north wind, there to be punished for ever. For thus sang Mary, Queen of the world and Mother of Humility: *He cast down the mighty from their thrones and raised up the lowly.* The

God of humility lifted up the humble angels, since, when he gazed upon them standing there in their humility, he raised them to greater excellence. It was of course fitting that they who had chosen to submit themselves to the subjection of their Creator should ascend to unaccustomed heights,[110] and to retain by their humility what the apostate angels had lost through their pride. All who are humble share the lot of the angels, which is none other than God himself, even as the Prophet sang: *My lot, O Lord, is to keep your Law.* *Ps 118:57*

O happy lot, O blessed possession! O treasure beyond compare, O overflowing happiness and sweetness! Who could be richer than those who possess God as their lawful inheritance? Who could be happier than one whose lot it is to have the Lord of happiness? If you are humble, God will be your treasure. Therefore be meek of heart, you who wear the habit of humility: let what your habit professes outwardly preserve you inwardly in virtue. Thus you will be pleasing to God, who emptied himself and, accepting the form of a servant, gave himself up to suffer, dying on the rood, lest humankind die and for ever live in the abyss of savage cruelty, where every grief and torture dwells, eternal struggle and continual mourning, where no order obtains, but everlasting horror. Happy indeed are those who so live in this mortal life that they may rejoice in that life to come; when death comes, they

[110] *Culmen antenomasie:* a problematic reading, even correcting to *antonomasiæ* ('naming by epithet'), with perhaps the sense that the submissive angels have taken the place of their erstwhile angelic superiors.

will not mourn what they must leave behind, but will exult in God whom they have loved with all their hearts. God will be the eternal joy of all who have made themselves unpleasant to themselves, so as to be wholly pleasing to their Maker.

Therefore, bride of Christ, whatever your past, take no pleasure in what is displeasing to your Creator, but in him alone, whom you have vowed yourself to please in all your actions. If you have lived chastely, if you have not strafed the citadel of humility with bolts of pride, then you will be comely and beautiful in the sight of the Most High. He himself—who *filled the hungry with good things and sent away*
Lk 1:53 *the wealthy empty-handed*—will find it good to be your spouse. How blessed the hungry whom the Lord fills with his lasting goodness! All who hunger and thirst shall be filled by the Lord. Blessed the soul of our Prophet, who so hungered that he wept and cried aloud: *As the hart yearns for springs of water, so my soul yearns for you, O God. My soul thirsts for God, my living fountain; when shall I come to stand before the face of God? My tears have become my bread day and*
Ps 41:2-4 *night; every day they ask me, 'Where is your God?'* Who indeed among us has not wept and groaned, exiled from our homeland, wayfaring pilgrims far from the glory of heaven? Who indeed do not drench their cheeks with tears? Who does not writhe in grief, unable to see the true Sun, or the Moon, our glorious mother gleaming in her comeliness? Who does not grieve who cannot see the shining stars that are the angelic orders, or the bright troops of the patriarchs and prophets, the

choirs of apostles and martyrs and confessors, the throng of virgins following the Lamb with sistra and lyres, wherever he may lead?[111] Anyone who does not groan and weep, who does not yearn with heartfelt eagerness for the coming of Christ the Lord, is not among the hungry to be filled by Christ, the Desired of all the nations.

All who hunger and thirst for justice will be fed by the Bread of Angels that came down from heaven to give life to the world. These hungry ones Jesus does not *turn away empty-handed;* he satisfies their desires with his goodness, by enriching them with the good of everlasting life. They are indeed rich when they share in the wealth of joy in the glory of heaven. There true wealth lies, where no one is wretched or poor; for there dwell glory and life, utter joy, and total bliss. With such *good things* the author of goodness will fill those who in this life have rid themselves of sin, who suffer torment in order to possess Him, and who find no pleasure except in the true joy of God, and the supreme bliss of Christ. He enriches holy paupers with his ineffable goodness, but he impoverishes the wicked wealthy, and sends them away empty. Death separates the rich from their passing wealth, but when the poor of Christ pass on, they gain eternity. The rich pass from wealth to destitution; the poor in spirit rise to eternal riches. The true pauper has nothing of mortal sin. Even if he has earthly riches, he reckons them as worthless, because he does not yet

[111] The musical instruments are borrowed from 2 Sam 6:5.

possess the true wealth of the Lord Jesus. To see him, to hold him: this is the desire towards which he labors with all his heart.

The *rich* of our text are those whose lives
are doubly mortal:[112] they covet passing gains,
and neglect to live for God. O what an evil
wealth is the enormity of sin and vice, which
plunders the soul of divine riches! The greater
the accumulation of such wealth, the more its
possessors will be cast down and despised by
Christ, who will dismiss them empty-handed,
saying: *Depart from me, workers of iniquity; in*
Mt 25:41 *truth I tell you, I do not know you!* Such wealth
reduces all who horde it to the wretchedness
of eternal poverty, where every miser will live
in misery who in this life had nothing of true
riches. They shall enter the punishment of
eternal fires, for ever to burn there with that
Lk 16:19-31 rich man who took no pity on poor Lazarus.
Let us instead love him with all our hearts and
might in whom the storehouse of wisdom
and knowledge is hidden, namely, the Lord
Jesus Christ, that chosen *pearl,* that *treasure*
buried in the field of heaven, desiring and loving
whom that *certain rich* but wise *man sold all he*
Mt 13:46, 44 *owned to buy*. Let us rid ourselves of worldly
wealth and sin. Let the rich whose true wealth
is Christ bestow their goods on the poor and
needy, so that they—and we—may join the
company of the angels in the Kingdom of his
Father, and he says those wondrous words of
welcome: *Come, blessed of my Father, receive the*
kingdom prepared for you before the beginning of
Mt 25:34 *the world*.

[112] *Qui in hac vita mortali mortaliter vivunt,* i.e. who lead a life of mortal sin.

All this he had promised through his servants, the prophets. But even before it had come to pass, *he came to the aid of Israel his servant, mindful of his mercy.* Adam, the first of all whom God had formed of clay, who from the moment of his creation merited to enjoy the sight and conversation of God, could well be called Israel, since that name means 'seeing God'.[113] To that Israel God had revealed himself face to face; but this wondrous privilege was lost through disobedience to the Most High. He who had witnessed the sublime forgot himself, becoming undiscerning as a beast of burden. Thus the Lord clothed Adam and Eve in hides and cast them out of the Garden of Delights into this vale of calamity and death; those who had lost the company of angels through their immodest appetites were thereafter to share the lot of brute animals, as slaves to their bellies. But the Lord of mercy, who could not forget his compassion nor persist in his wrath, *remembered his mercy* and came to seek *the lost sheep,* and finding it carried it back to the heavenly flock, *coming to the aid of Israel his servant*—humankind—*as he promised to Abraham* in these words: *All nations of the earth shall be blessed by your seed.* God came to the aid of not just any Israel, but such as was his servant—such a son and servant, Lady, as your Son.

Lk 1:54 *Gen 3:21, 24* *Mt 18:12* *Lk 1:54* *Gen 22:18*

There is a wicked Israel, a false Israel, a true Israel, and an adopted Israel. The wicked Israel is that apostate people of whom the

[113] Jerome *Heb. Nom.*; on the discrepancy of this etymology with that given in Gen 32:29, cf. Jerome *Heb. Quæst. in Gen.*

Lord says, in Isaiah: *I nourished and raised up
sons, but they have spurned me. A cow knows its*
Is 1:2b-3 *owner, but Israel does not recognize me;* and in
Jeremiah: *My people have twice acted wickedly:
by abandoning me, the spring of living water, and
by digging themselves wanton cisterns that cannot*
Jer 2:3 *hold water.* Truly it was that Israel which killed
the Lord of life on the wood of the cross. The
false or disguised Israel is the one whose reli-
gious habit portends signs of holiness, but
who inwardly is empty of the good outwardly
displayed. Of such it is said: *They profess to*
Ti 1:46 *know God, but the facts deny it.* True Israels are
those born of the Holy Spirit, who from the
first moment of their being have burned with
love for their Creator and, ever clinging to
him, contemplate his face with radiant gazing.
Such is the Israel of God, of whom it is said:
You who rule Israel, hear us, you who guide Joseph
Ps 79:2 *as a sheep;* and elsewhere: *How good is the God*
Ps 72:1 *of Israel to those who are upright of heart;* and this:
*You are the King of Israel and David's excellent
offspring!*[114] The adopted Israel is that people
of whom the Lord of Israel says: *A people I have
not known have done me service, they have hearkened*
Ps 17:45 *and obeyed me;* and this: *The people that shall be*
Ps 101:19 *created shall praise the Lord.* All who have been
reconciled to God the Father through the
blood of Jesus Christ are rightly called Israel,
for they shall ever see God, from whom those
who live evilly shall ever be cut off. All who
from the fullness of their hearts abandon the
paths of error and justly and piously tread the

[114] Theodulf of Orleans, *Gloria laus et honor* (hymn for Palm Sunday).

ways of truth will, with the true and holy Israel, see the Lord of everlasting bliss.

There is, similarly, both a good servant and a wicked one. The Latin word *puer,* 'a child, a servant', is said to derive from *purus,* 'pure'.[115] Some are pure by goodness, others purified of evil and iniquity. But alas, how few the servants whom wickedness, uncleanness, petulance, anger, hatred, and worldly distractions have not made impure! How rare are they who are like that child the Lord Jesus Christ stood in the midst of his disciples and said, *'Unless you humble yourself like this little child you shall not enter the Kingdom of Heaven'*. Every truly humble person is that little child, pure of every wickedness. Such is the servant of God, whom the Lord upholds and loves. We read of certain children (who were surely not innocent of wickedness) who mocked Elisha's baldness. *'Come down, baldy!'* they laughed and taunted. Elisha cursed them, and suddenly they were devoured by lions.[116] No servants of the Lord's these! Elsewhere we read of quite different children who cried out to Jesus, *'Hosanna! Blessed is he who comes in the name of the Lord'* as he entered Jerusalem on a donkey, on his way to the Place of the Skull to be crucified for our salvation. All such children are blessed of the Lord who with all their hearts bless their Maker. Those who curse Christ the Lord will be cursed, and those who bless him will be filled with blessings.

Mt 18:4a, 3b

Mk 11:9b-10a

[115] This appears to be the author's invention; *puer* and *purus* are unrelated.

[116] 2 Kg 2:23, apparently recalled from memory: *descende* is given for *ascende*, and 'lions' for 'bears'.

But let us return to our text: *He came to the aid of Israel.* After recalling in general God's loving-kindness and justice, the singular dispensation to our Lady—the flower of virgins, the pleasure-garden of pomegranates, filled with the beauty of all fruit, our wholly beautiful Virgin Mary—gives another meaning to the words: *He came to the aid of Israel, his servant.* He came to our aid like a physician to the sick, made visible among men so that he make an Israel, that is, one who sees God, of his humble and obedient servant, for no one will be saved by him who is not obedient and humble. *As he promised to our forebears, to Abraham*
Lk 1:55 *and his seed for ever.* Abraham is mentioned by name, since it was to him that salvation was revealed, and to whom the incarnation was made know, to him and to his seed, not those begotten in the flesh, but those who followed in his footsteps, to those whom the coming of Christ was promised. This promise of eternal inheritance knows no end, for believers will want for nothing at the end of time, but will enjoy beatific glory for ever and beyond. May the Mother of glory deign through her merits to bring us to that bliss, together with her consecrated virgins.

To her be glory and honor
through Jesus her Son,
who with the Father and the Holy Spirit
lives and reigns,
blessed God for ever and ever.
Amen.

X. Tenth Homily

Mary's sojourn with Elizabeth and Zechariah
Joseph's response to her pregnancy

WE HAVE HEARD the honey-sweet voice of the turtledove; we have heard her song with joy. What that fair and blessed Maiden, full of sweetness, bore in her heart and put forth in words of sweetness and the sound of rejoicing and praise, all *youths and maidens, elders and children,* should receive in gladness and rejoicing with all devotion. Sweet is that song, *sweeter than honey and the honey-comb;* dear is the sing, dearer *than gold and topaz!* Sweet are the words; sweeter their effects! Indeed, mere honey is but wormwood in comparison. Her sweetness is that of one who has given herself in love of Him, and in his outpouring of sweetness she pours out her very being, cinctured in his love. She is worthy of all our laud and love. Blessed are they who love; more blessed are they who love and praise. Blessed are they who love the mother of our love in fact; more blessed are they who love and praise the mother of our rejoicing and praise, in perfect harmony of voice and heart. She is well praised if perfectly loved. Love of her is very praise itself, unless it is darkened by the gloom of perversity. Let us therefore love her in our hearts and praise her with our voices. Let us learn the canticle

Ps 148:12

Ps 18:11

Ps 118:127

she sang, the canticle of her own example, of her humility and sublimity, the canticle of justice and loving duty, of the promise of her God, whom she bore in her womb, the author of our salvation, the life of our life, our glory's glory. Let Mary's Magnificat be sung with great reverence, since she who composed it was not a prophet or Sybil, but Mary the Mother of God!

The ever blessed Virgin Mary—the beauty of virgins, the comeliness of holy women, the decorous grace of the saints—*stayed on three*
Lk 1:56 *months with Elizabeth before returning to her home.* She remained long enough to see the birth of the Forerunner, the primary reason for her coming. She had not stayed so long merely to be with her kin, but in order to be of ever increasing assistance to Elizabeth and John. For if at her very coming they were filled by the Holy Spirit, how much more was added by so long a stay?[117] Oh how blessed the house in which such a Lady remained for three months! Elizabeth and Zechariah could well have said: *How good and pleasant it is for* Mary
Cf. Ps 132:1 *to dwell* among us! *Good and pleasant it is,* Zechariah, for you to have dwelled with Mary! Not merely fortunate, but utterly blissful is anyone who has enjoyed a single day of her companionship. True and consummate happiness it is to enjoy a vision of her, and of him she bore in the increasing modesty of her virginity. To gaze upon the face of the Queen,
Ps 44:12 and of the King who desired her: this alone would be enough! How few and rare are

[117] The entire passage is a transparent paraphrase of Ambrose (see n. 92).

those who yearn to be dissolved of this mortal coil and be with them, with whom to dwell is ultimate happiness! How blessed they are! How happy the cloistered who seek nothing else, who neither long for nor love nor desire anyone other than their Redeemer Lord and his glorious mother, to live with whom is all they live for! If only for us to live were Christ and Mary his mother; if nothing else turned in our hearts, resounded in our mouths, was pleasing in our actions, than the Lord Jesus and that blessed Virgin who conceived him by the Holy Spirit!

The Virgin was now manifesting visible signs of pregnancy: pallor and heaviness beset her; in time her womb began to swell, the veins palpable in her neck. So Matthew reports in his Gospel: *When Mary the mother of Jesus had been betrothed to Joseph, but before they came together*—that is, lived together—*she was found to be with child by the Holy Spirit.* She had been *Mt 1:18* betrothed in the Lord's generosity to that saintly and just man Joseph, so that he might take care of her and the child. As well, the betrothal sheltered her from being stoned as an adulteress; it would, moreover, hide her child-bearing from the devil.[118] The Lord had rather that the manner of his conception be unknown than that his mother should be defamed. He had rather be called a carpenter's son[119] than that his mother be thought an adulteress. The blessed Virgin had not wished

[118] See n. 33.

[119] *Maluit dici filius fabri quam matrem suam fornicariam putari*—cf. Bernard (*In laud.* II.12.) *tolerabilius vero atque honestius fuit putari ad tempus Christum de coniugio fuisse natum quam de fornicatione* 'it was rather more endurable and honorable that

to tell Joseph what the angel had told her, but left it to be known by the Holy Spirit how she came to be pregnant. Seeing his bride's swelling belly, her gaunt face, Joseph recognized the signs of pregnancy, though he had not touched her in the role of husband. As he was saintly and just, he did not wish to betray her or see her disgraced, and *intended to divorce her privately. Privately,* because he was kindly and merciful—or because he recognized the power of the mystery, that magnificent sacrament she bore, and felt unworthy to be near her. Abasing himself before so great and ineffable a reality, he sought to distance himself, just as Peter, abasing himself, told the Lord:
Lk 5:8 *Away from me, Lord! I am a sinner.*[120] Or perhaps he acted like the centurion who sent the Lord the message: *I am not worthy that you should enter under my roof; I did not deem myself*
Lk 7:6b-7a *worthy even to come to you.* Or perhaps like Saint Elizabeth, when she said to blessed Mary, *'How is it that the mother of my Lord should come*
Lk 1:43 *to me?'*

So Joseph, cautious and fearful of joining himself to such holiness, abased himself. 'I shall send her far from me and my kinfolk', he thought, 'so as to separate her from my unworthiness. Then her dignity will be all the greater, all the more excellent her sanctity.' *But as he was thinking these thoughts, an angel of the Lord appeared to him in a vision, saying,* "Why do you hesitate, Joseph? Why such imprudent

---

Christ be thought to have been born of wedlock than in consequence of fornication'.

[120] Substituting *recede* for *exi*. The argument is Bernard's (*In laud.* II.14).

thoughts? Why are you so irrational? He who is to be born is God, and she who is to bear him is a virgin. You will safeguard this birth, not as a proud father, but as a humble servant. The child will not be yours; you will belong to him. *Joseph, son of David, fear not to take Mary as your spouse.* Do not dread it, do not be confounded; but sure and fearless take her to yourself. Take her as wife, according to the precept of the Law, but hold yourself from her, according to the custom of marriage and cohabitation. Take her therefore as an entrusted heavenly treasure, as the wealth of the Deity, as the fullness of sanctity, as the perfection of justice. Receive her as the dwelling-place of the Only-begotten, as the honored temple and house of God, as the childbearer of the Creator of all, as the immaculate home of the King and Bridegroom of heaven.

'*Fear not to take Mary as your wife.* Your wife, I say, but do not hear this with dread or confusion, neither you nor anyone to come until the consummation of the world. You shall take her as your wife so as to keep her virginity private from the devil; so that she might be spared the ostracism of the Jews. She is to be your wife, in accordance with the Law of marriage, but not according to its custom. Nor is the Son that is born to be believed to be yours. *For what is to be born of her is of the Holy Spirit:* her partner in this birth is none but God. *She will bear a Son whom you will call Jesus;* so was he named before all time. It is not you who give him this name, nor you who chose the word. With rejoicing, call him Jesus, Saviour: not a savior who begins to save from this time forth, but the Savior of old. *He shall save his people from their sins* [Mt 1:20-21], ransoming all in his blood, freeing from the power of death by his own death. He will be the Savior of all faithful believers.'

All this came to pass: the descent of the Only-begotten, the incarnation of the Lord, the commissioning of the angel, the Virgin's chaste betrothal. All this came to pass for the salvation of all the world. All this came to pass, so that one thing might be accomplished. What may that be? you ask: that a Virgin should give birth? that she should remain a Virgin? that she should become a mother and retain intact her maidenhood? *Behold the Virgin shall be with child*—not by earthly fatherhood, nor deceived by the serpent's persuasion, nor infected by his poisonous venom. *The Virgin*—welcoming the angel's proclamation, fulfulling the witness of the Prophets—*will be with child,* so that she might worthily bear God incarnate to the world. *'Behold',* the angel says; and what he proclaims is a mystery of such amazing greatness as to awaken all as if from sleep: *'She will bear a Son* to undo the curse of Adam and, by her obedience, reverse the disobedience of Eve, so as to raise again that race whose first mother's rash credulity had cast down. *And his name shall be called Emanuel, God with us.'* *Mt 1:23*

His name was first called by the angels, singing praises at his birth and rejoicing to see the King of Peace and God of all come down to humankind. Then the apostles called his name, preaching the power and dominion of the Only-begotten of God to all the nations. Then at their deaths, defying fire and sword, the martyrs called out his name. And so all believers everywhere shall call and recall that name until the consummation of the world. "God with us!" shall be the cry of all who on earth have been called by a new name, when at last they see him, no longer in figure and mystery, but face to face: when Emanuel appears before us in the abundance of his grace and joy and beauty, to fill us with himself. For he is the comeliness of all grace, the nectar of all sweetness, the fragrance of choicest scents, the singular goodness of every good:

Christ the Lord,
who with the Father and the Holy Spirit
lives and reigns, God, blessed for ever.
Amen.

XI. Eleventh Homily

The Birth of Jesus. The Presentation.

LET ALL WHO DESIRE to come to our Emanuel, the Word of the Most High
Jn 1:14 Father who *became flesh and dwelled among us,* bind themselves to the Virgin who bore him with bonds of utter love. She is the gate of heaven, the doorway to Paradise. She is the way to life, the straight path to eternal glory. All who yearn for the supreme happiness that is Christ will obtain it, if so long as they live they burn with love for his most holy mother with all their being. Happy alone are they, and worthy of perpetual happiness, who have not been estranged from the love of this Ever-virgin's Son; for Son and Mother shall ever be the blessed possession of all who in this desert exile are joined to them in love. O incredibly blessed possession, more blessed than words can tell! O glory of glories, to see Christ in the fullness of his glory, and the Virgin who bore him, adorned in her beauty! Great glory indeed it is to be clothed in the robe of blessed immortality and stand in the company of the angels, to be like an angel of God and drink one's fill of the sweetness of Paradise; yet greater than this and every glory of heaven shall be the glorious sight and enjoyment of Christ and his mother. Far exceeding every

glory, far surpassing the sublime, far excelling every sweetness of eternal bliss:[121] to see Christ the Lord in the glory of his Father's majesty, and to see seated beside him his Virgin Mother. There, as virgin choirs sweetly serenade them with their supple song, the radiance of the sun is beclouded by their sweet and matchless beauty. Therefore, consecrated virgins, for whom to live is Christ and Mary his glorious mother, pour forth your prayers to them for me, that I might be found worthy to praise them, whom all that has breath should ever praise.

You have heard, Daughters of Jerusalem, what Gabriel told Joseph, the spouse of the Queen of the world, when he appeared to him in a dream. Let us now turn our hearts' attention to the birth of Divine Majesty. For when nine months had run their course, our divine Virgin, who conceived of the Holy Spirit, gave birth to our Redeemer. Virgin she gave birth, for Virgin she conceived, conceiving without lust, and giving birth without pain. Intact she conceived; unopened she gave birth.[122] No man had entered her: the Lord impregnated her, the same begetting and begotten. The author of birth himself was born; he, the Creator, became the created, the Former himself the formed. O marvel, O wonder! It is God

[121] Ogier's rhapsodic language echoes Leo the Great (*Serm.* 29): *supereminet humani eloquii facultatem divini operis magnitudo* 'the grandeur of God's workings far outstrips the power of human speech'.

[122] *Peperit clausa*, cf. Ambrose (*De institutione virginis*, VIII.53): *Bona porta Maria, quæ clausa erat et non aperiebatur; transivit per eam Christus sed non aperuit* 'Mary is that good gate which, closed, was not opened: Christ passed through it but did not open it'.

who gives life, and God to whom human life is given! Mary gives birth to him who from nothing made all that is. The Virgin, without the aid of a man, gives birth to God and man. God, the Creator of all, becomes a new crea-
Dan 7:9 ture: the Ancient of Days for us becomes a tiny child; the incomprehensible becomes comprehensible, the immeasurable takes on human measure. Let heaven be struck dumb with awe, and let the world quake in dread.

What came to pass? *The Word became flesh*
Jn 1:14 *and dwelled among us.* The Only-begotten of God the Father became the first-born of the Virgin Mary. He is born in Bethlehem—that is, 'the house of bread'[123]—for he is that true bread that came down from heaven, so that humans might eat the Bread of Angels. The God of angels saw fit to become man. The Word became hay so as to become the feed of loving beasts of burden. The Word by which the angels in heaven are fed was placed in a manger by the Virgin, as if the feed of beasts. Oh what amazing honor—but oh, what a loving and unheard-of emptying! He who is before all time takes his place in time; he who created everything is born of a woman. Immensity becomes brief, the lofty is made lowly, the Maker something made, the Creator a creature. In being born of a mother, he became a creature who is the eternal Creator, one with the Father and the Holy Spirit.[124] *Mary*—the comely Virgin, the beauteous, beautiful Virgin, flower of flowers, beauty of virgins,

[123] Not in Jerome, but a transparent and well-known etymology.

[124] *Flamine*, as in the doxology of Hom. XII of the *Expositio* On the Lord's Words (see n. 143 there).

the jewel of all who are consecrated to God, the confidence of brides, the glory of widows, Queen of the world and heaven's Mistress—*gave birth to her firstborn child and laid him in a manger, for there was no room for* him *in the inn.* *Lk 2:7*

O worthy of the Worthy One, immaculate Mother of the Holy One, O fragrant nard, what scent did you give forth? O Mary, splendor of earth and glory of heaven, what Son was this that you bore? His excellence is inestimable, his grandeur utterly sublime. He who gave all things beginning had no beginning: he is God of all, Lord of all, the Life that never dies. His glory shall know no end. Yet such grandeur, such excellence, the author of glory, the giver of life, Creator and maker of all, Lord of the universe, the Most High God, who worked his weal in you—you would confine to a manger? What have you done? What can you have been thinking? Is this not he who stretches out the vault of the heavens and adorns it with twinkling stars? Is this not he who made the sun and the moon and gave them such brilliance as to illumine day and night and dispel the darkness? But what am I saying? Whatever I might say of his sublime majesty—and whatever the angels might add—is nothing in the face of his surpassing greatness.

Yet he was born in a stable—of you, blessed glory of maidens, Mary—because there was no *house of cedar,** no *bed of ivory,*† where you might give birth to our Creator and Redeemer. Thus like an exiled pilgrim, you gave birth to the Lord of the world in a stranger's home, and like a pauper's wife wrapped, not in silks but in coarse swaddling, and laid him in a

** 2 Sam 7:7*
† Am 6:7

manger: the child from the moment of whose birth you worshipped as your Lord and God. O fortunate stable, O blessed manger, in which Christ is born and the God of all is laid! There the angels served as midwife; there millions upon millions of angels rejoiced. In the stable the child began to whimper;[125] in heaven *a multitude of the heavenly hosts sang out: Glory to God in the highest, and on earth, peace to all of*
Lk 2:13-14 *good will! To all of good will,* since the Goodness of heaven has been born on earth. True *Peace* has descended from heaven; thus the angels sing God's glory on high. The angels rejoice, but Mary quakes to have become the Mother of God. The angels rejoice in solemn dance[126] before Christ, before whom his mother stands in dread and awe. The mother bears Christ, the Virgin nurses her son, rejoicing in holy fear. She bears the Bearer, she nurses the Nurse and feeds the Feeder, not only of herself, but of all in whom there breathes the breath of life.

O most blessed of all women, whose womb was God's canopy,[127] the temple of the Holy Spirit, Christ's ivory bed, the bridal-chamber of divine majesty, the banquet seat of the King of everlasting bliss! What sanctity was yours we can only imagine, when, created and fashioned in the image of God, your flesh so pleased your Creator that from it he should fashion himself a mantle of praise and a breastplate of victory, and that through it he should triumph over

[125] The rare verb *vagiebat* suggests Venantius Fortunatus *(Pange lingua)* as the source of the image (see n. 74).

[126] *Tripudiando,* see n. 97.

[127] *Reclinatorium:* Sg 3:10.

the author of death and ransom humankind. Blessed is your womb, from which our Valiant One fashioned himself a sword to slay the foe of our salvation, and free his people from perpetual bondage! You are wholly beautiful, glorious, and desirous, undarkened by any blemish, clothed in comeliness and enriched with all holiness. More beautiful of flesh than all other virgins, you are in mind more holy than the angels. You are full of God, full of the Holy Spirit! Virgin most blessed, you bore him in heart and in womb. You bore him in your arms, you nursed him at your sacred breasts, held him in the embrace of your love. You bent to kiss him as often as you wished. Oh bliss beyond reckoning: Jesus himself you held in your power to do with however you thought best! He was completely yours: he was your Son! I truly believe you could not have your fill of kissing and hugging him, so immense was your love.

What can I say, my Lady and, through your own Son, my hope, my salvation and life, my sweetness—I who have not yet seen him, whom you possessed in such delight? Will you ever show me your servant mercy, and hold him forth to me in all his comeliness? Shall I see Christ and the Virgin that bore him? To see Christ and his mother is the whole of my happiness; I seek nothing else. So long as I am wanting in this good, no other good is good to me. But ah, what goodness will be mine when this goodness is bestowed on me! Since this has not yet occurred, let tears and groaning be my lot until he comes in utter gentleness to comfort every mourning soul. O happy mourning, O blessed grieving that might merit so great a consolation! O blessed eyes, whose tears the Savior of the world shall wipe away!

Who will grant my eyes a torrent of tears with which I might weep day and night until the Lord Jesus appear to comfort my soul?[128] Daughters of Jerusalem, beloved brides of God, let your tears flow with mine, until our Bridegroom reveals himself to us in all his comeliness! Call to mind again and again with singular attention, you who bound yourself to him with holy vows, how bitter to be bereft of him you wed. You made your vows: repay them now! You vowed yourselves to Christ: give yourselves utterly to him! Run, daughters! Run, consecrated virgins! Run, all you who have known motherhood, all you who have promised Christ your chastity—run to the Virgin who bore him! She continues to bear the King of Glory, and she will give him to all who seek him wholeheartedly.

She gave birth to him and suckled him; on the eighth day she had him circumcised, and on the fortieth she presented him in the Temple with a burnt offering of a pair of doves.[129] Fleeing Herod, she brought him into Egypt, nourishing him at her breast. She continued to minister to him wherever he traveled.

[128] The *Planctus Mariæ* begins with this sentence, known by its incipit *(Quis dabit)*; see Introduction.

[129] *Duos turtures vel columbas:* cf. the responsory for Candlemas, *Obtulerunt pro eo Domino par turturum aut duos pullos columbarum,* an awkward narrativizing of the alternative offering ('a pair of turtledoves or two dove pullets') prescribed in Lev 12:6 and cited in Lk 2:24; the antiphonist—and Ogier—might well have chosen one.

She was, I believe, among the women who followed Christ and cared for his needs. We need hardly wonder that she accompanied him: he was her heart's sole sweetness and desire. She stood as well among those women who grieved and mourned the Lord with keen lamenting. She could have been among the women on the way to Golgatha to whom Jesus turned, not radiant with authority but disgraced by scandal, and said: *'Daughters of Jerusalem, weep not for me but for yourselves and for your children!'* *Lk 23:28*

Was it not so, Mistress of the world, beloved Mother of Christ? O heaven's jewel and joy, I beseech you now to tell your worthless servant the truth of the matter—but forget, I beg you, the pain that rent you then! If only that pain might daily wrench my heart, even as it cleaved yours! Tell me instead what you felt on the day of your Assumption into heaven, there to rejoice for ever in the presence of your Beloved! Tell me what tears you shed, that I might know the depths of your bitter grief when you beheld Jesus your Beloved (and—alas!—once mine), nailed to the cross; when you saw him bow his head and breathe his last most sacred breath! But, I pray, do not be overwhelmed by these words of mine, though they might well rend rocks. Ah, but who, whether reigning in heaven or yet a pilgrim here below, could stem the flood of tears to hear with fully rapt attention how the King of Angels himself became the reproach of men? How the Son of God the Father became the outcast of the people? Well can you rejoice now, Lady, whom he has glorified in heaven, he whose most dutiful death transfixed you then with bitterest agony. Let me share the tears you shed for him at his passion. Then, so that his suffering might even more abundantly afflict me, recall for me the words you exchanged with our Lord and God. Assure me of your tenderness; grant me what you have promised! I remember that you spoke, at the very beginning of this work,[130] of the grief you bore at the death of your only-begotten son. It made me shudder with woe to hear those words. Their bitter sorrow lingered in my soul, even as you bid me wait until such time that we would return to those dark tidings. Tell me now, I implore you, I insist! Reveal to me the truth of what occurred, O Virgin Mother of Truth himself!

[130] Introductory Homily I.

XII. THE LAMENTATION OF OUR LADY

'WHAT YOU ASK pierces me through with great grief; but as I am now glorified and can no longer weep, write, then, with tears what grievous pain I felt.' To weep, my Lady, is what I dearly wish—and nothing else! Let it be as you command, only grant me my desire. Your servant listens; speak, my Lady! Most blessed Virgin Mother of God, tell me if indeed you were in Jerusalem when your son was arrested and led, bound, before Annas. *Jn 18:13*

'I was, and when I learned of it I hastened as close to my Lord as I could come. There, beholding him beaten with fists, his cheeks roughly slapped, his face spat upon, his head crowned with thorns—made *the scorn of humankind*—my whole being was stirred, and *Ps 21:7* my spirit fainted away. I could hardly speak or feel. Bewailing him with me, as if their only child, were my sisters and many other women, among whom was Mary Magdalene. She indeed grieved more than all the rest except the one who now is speaking to you. When at cockcrow Pilate ordered him to bear his cross to the execution site, the crowds swelled along the way. Some were weeping; others laughed him to scorn.'

To the extent she could, his most doleful mother followed after him along with the women who had accompanied him from

Galilee to minister to him.[131] These now held here, as if a corpse, and bore her along until he had reached the place where they crucified him. Before her eyes he was raised up on the cross and fastened to the wood with most horrible nails. He himself, *like a lamb before the*
Is 53:7 *shearers, made no sound nor opened his mouth.* His handmaid gazed upon her Lord; his mother beheld her Son hanging on the cross, dying the basest of deaths. Grief beyond all telling seized her mind. And little wonder! Blood oozed and flowed from his hands and feet, nailed to the rood.

'All the beauty of his face was drained, and he who was comelier than all the sons of men now seemed the unsightliest of all. In him, I now perceived, the prophecy had been fulfilled: *We saw him, and there was no charm or*
Is 53:2 *beauty in him,* for his countenance had been bruised by savage fists and truncheons. As if abandoned by my own offspring, my one and only Son, I could not contain my grief. My voice scarcely sounded, yet I groaned and sighed. I wanted to speak the words that welled up in my mind, but my heart's anguish broke in on them as I tried to form them with my mouth, and what issued instead was the sound of my grief-wounded spirit. Love then spoke hoarse words, for my tongue, the mistress of my voice, had lost all use of speech. Watching my soul's Beloved as he died, I melted utterly under the press of grief . . .'

[131] The dialogue is temporarily abandoned by the introduction of an omniscient narrator. Perhaps we are to infer that the account thus imparted has resulted from information revealed to the author by Mary, but the voice is, with the exception of a few affective intrusions, quite unlike the persona of the author.

while he, with countenance divine, gazed upon his weeping mother to console her with his words. But she was beyond consoling. 'Too aggrieved to speak, I wept and said: "My Son, my son, would that I might die in your stead!"[132] My Son was dying—why not then his wretched mother with him? O my sole love, sweetest Son, do not leave me here alone! Take me with you! Let me die with you! You die ill alone; let death destroy your mother as well. I would not have death spare me in my wretchedness; death alone I seek. Come, death, wield your power, slay this mother! Destroy alike both mother and son! Son, sole sweetness, singular joy, sustaining bliss and desire of my soul: let her also die with you who bore you into mortality. Do not die without your mother! Behold my wretchedness and hear my prayer, for indeed a son should hearken to his mother. Hearken then, I implore you: take me up with you upon the rood, so that two who lived as one in flesh might perish, one in death. O impious Judeans, spare not the one who bore him whom you have crucified. Crucify his mother as well, or slay her by some other savage means, to put an end to son and mother together. He dies all alone, while I, bereft of light, am deprived of son, of joy, of sweetness. Why would a mother live in grief after the death of her son? Take up the mother; hang her as a pledge of love! Unsparing of my son, do not be lenient with me, death: to me alone be cruel! If I might die with Christ—oh, greatest joy! How sweet to

[132] David's lament for Absalom, 2 Sam 18:33.

die wretchedly! But death, desired, denies me. Alas, I cast myself headlong, unhappily before you. How much better to die than lead a life of death! But longed-for death leaves wretched me unhappily behind. O gentle Son, receive your mother's wretched prayer! Do not now be cruel to her to whom you were ever kind. Receive in death with you your mother, so that I might live with you for ever after death. Nothing would be sweeter for me than to die with you; nothing more bitter than life after your death. You were father and spouse to and son to me. Now I am orphaned, widowed, bereaved. My Son, what more am I to do? Where could I go? Where could I turn for succor, where find support? Dearest Son, to you all things are possible; but if it is not your will that I should die, grant me some measure of gentle counsel!'

Then, beckoning to her with his eyes and head, the Lord says, with regard to John,
Jn 19:26 '*Woman, behold your son.*' His gaze was vivid, as if to say, 'O my tender one, so wracked with tears and grief, you know that it was for this I came, to be flesh of your flesh, so that I might save humankind on the gibbet of the cross. How else should the scriptures be fulfilled? Suffer I must, for the salvation of all, but on the third day I shall rise again and appear openly to you and to my disciples. Desist from tears and grieving, for I am going to the Father, ascending to take up once again the glory of my Father's grandeur. Rejoice with me rather, for at last I have found the errant sheep that for so long was lost. I die so that the whole world may live again. Through the

fault of one the rest perished; now, through the merit of one, all are saved. How can you be displeased at what is pleasing to God the Father? The chalice my Father gave me, did I not will to drink it? Do not weep, Mother—oh, do not weep, sweetest Mother! I am not forsaking you. I am with you, and I shall be with you till the end of time. To death's command I now submit, according to the flesh. According to my divinity I am and was and will be immortal and unsuffering. You know where I came from. Why be sad if I now ascend to the place from which I descended? The time has come for me to return to him who sent me. Where I am going you cannot come now, but you will come afterwards. Meanwhile your nephew John is to be as your son. He will take care of you and be your ever-faithful comfort." Then, nodding his head towards John, he says, *"Behold your mother.* Watch over her and keep her; I commend her *Jn 19:27*
to you. Receive her as your mother; yours, yes, but mine indeed as well.'

Both virgins, John[133] and Mary, now stood silent; neither martyr could speak for grief. They heard Christ speak, and soon after they saw him die. But neither could answer him as they watched him dying. They themselves were as if dead, without the breath to speak. They listened and were silent, for grief had robbed them of the power of speech. Their spirits failed within them; mournful grief alone befriended them. Weeping they loved,

[133] John is called *virgo electus a Domino* ('the Lord's chosen virgin') in the antiphon *Ioannes apostolus et evangelista* (Vigils, December 27).

and bitterly they wept.[134] Bitterly they wept, for bitter was their grief. The sword of Christ's Passion and death pierced their souls—pierced them, and destroyed them. But she who loved the greater grieved more piteously. As only a mother can feel, she felt Christ's anguish. The Virgin who bore him suffered the sword of his pain. The torments of his death wounded her, tortured her, lashed her motherly soul. Her martyred consciousness was lanced by the spear with which the wicked servants pierced the limbs of Christ. Grief impaled her: measureless grief seized her mind, raged within her, and found no outlet. Christ paid the debt of death in his flesh; his mother paid it with her soul. Then, having commended his mother to John, Christ said, *'I thirst'*. Those who crucified him *gave him vinegar mixed with gall to drink, but when he tasted it, he would not drink it,* but said: *'It is finished!'* Then *he cried aloud,* saying: *'Father, into your hands I commend my spirit', and thus expired.* At this the earth quaked, the sun hid its light, and all the stars began to mourn. The moon, grieving, lost its luster, and bolts of lightning fled the upper air. Hard rocks were cleft, the Temple's veil was rent. From opened tombs many rose up from their graves in public proclamation of Christ as God.

Jn 19:28; Mt 27:34; Jn 19:30; Lk 23:46; Mt 27:51-53

Well may we desire to know what sorrows assailed Mary as she grieved beyond the point of comprehension—but our minds fail us, nor can our tongues form words. Near the cross of Christ stood, as if lifeless, the Virgin: she

[134] Wordplay on *amare* (as the infinitive 'to love' and the adverb 'bitterly').

who as a virgin conceived him by the Holy Spirit. Bespattered, motionless, struck mute by grief that drained her of all strength, she lingered there, pale and wan as a living corpse. Alive though dying inwardly, alive there next to death, she could not die, though living she was dead. Fierce was the grief that raged in her soul, for though she longed to die, rather than live on after Christ's death, wretchedly she lived, though dead within. There she stood, transfixed by grief, as she waited for Christ's body to be taken down from the cross. At length she spoke:

'Return to me his lifeless body! You have worked your will, now take him down and bring him to his mother—or, if you would rather so, join me to him in death, so that my pains and his might now be ended. Take him down, I beg you, so that I may have his lifeless body. Even in death he will be my solace.'

Near the cross she stood, contemplating Christ as he hung on the savage trunk, supported by his feet, his hands raised high to embrace the crossbeam. How gentle his countenance! Ah, to kiss the wounds that gushed with blood! To hold him in her arms, or, as that was impossible, to rest at least his hand in hers! But love urges hope for that which is rarely to be had, for love will not suffer limitation. To hug him there, aloft upon the cross! But no: she withdraws her hands and strikes them against her breast. Rising from the ground, she stretches up towards Christ. Then, unable to touch him, she collapses roughly to the ground. Cast down, she lies there under the immense weight of grief; yet love still more intense compels her to get up. Borne up by love she stands, her hands outstretched to touch him. Once again the crush of grief hurls her to the ground. O grievous lot, more dreadful life like this than death by cruel blade at the hands of the wicked! A deathly pallor blanches her face. Her cheeks and lips are stained by the blood of his wounds, which drip upon the ground, where she bends to kiss them as they moisten the earth.

Meanwhile a certain nobleman named Joseph, one of Jesus' disciples (though secretly), went with confidence to Pilate to request the body of his Lord. This being granted him, he sought out Nicodemus, a legal expert known for his wisdom (and likewise a secret follower of Christ). Together they came to the site of the Lord's crucifixion with instruments to pry up the nails and take down the body. When she saw their purpose she rose up, as if reviving a little from death, and offered them what aid she could render. One of them pried the nails from Jesus' hands, the other supported the spent body lest it fall—while Mary lifted high her arms to draw Christ's drooping head and arms to her sorrowful breast. There she showered insatiable kisses upon her Beloved, though he was dead. Then, when they had taken him down, she clung to him like a dead woman standing, overwhelmed by uncontainable grief and immeasurable love. Mary's tears began to wash the head of her dead son as she writhed sobbing. Again and again she kissed his brows and cheeks, his eyes, his nose and mouth. So wrenching the flood of her tears, you would have thought she was dissolving

Cf. Jn 19:38-39

body and soul. So drenched with tears was her dead son's body, the stone was moistened where they laid him.

Recall to mind just who it was this Virgin had conceived without lust and borne without pain: how he was all she lived for, her God and her Lord, her only Son. Could any loss be more dreadful? Reckon, you who would, the measure of her grief! None can tell what grief that was—yet it was equaled by her love. She did not lose hope, but mourned his loss as a mother should—as only a mother could. She grieved for the death of her innocent Son, yet hoped for his rising again on the third day. Certain holy women, few in number, wept with her; fewer still the men who mourned with Mary the Virgin. Yet there were angels grieving, too—to the extent that angels can grieve—with pious and justified grief. They suffered together, mourning the death of Christ, even as they rejoiced at his redemption of humankind. I imagine it was the sight of Christ's mother in the grip of such grief that made them weep with bitter agitation. Which of the angels and archangels there would not have wept: for if grieving was contrary to angelic nature, how much more so then was human death contrary to the nature of immortal God? They saw Christ's body so wretchedly abused, his flesh so cruelly lashed and torn, there where he lay lifeless on the ground. And there was Mary, his most loving, most holy, wholly good and beautiful, utterly sweet and delightful mother most blessed: wracked by sobbing, swooning with bitterest grief, so bitterly weeping. How could they hold back their tears? Oh, there was mourning and wailing among the angels present there, such mourning as befits nurturing spirits. I should marvel if they did not weep, even in their state of bliss where weeping is impossible. I believe, and thus declare, that if they were capable of grieving, they grieved; for even as it was possible for God to die in his human form, so it was possible for the blessed angels to bewail the death of their Lord.

Then, as the Gospels bear witness, Joseph of Aramathea, that just and saintly man,[135] joined Nicodemus in taking Christ's body down from the cross, wrapped him in a clean shroud perfumed with costly spices, and laid him in the new tomb Joseph had had hewn for himself. At this a million angels, flocking to his tomb, sang their Lord's exequies. It was lauds they sang, though Mary joined to it her sighs and moans. They raised praises heavenwards, while she wept bitterly before the grave. When Joseph and Nicodemus laid the Lord in the tomb, his mournful mother wanted to be buried with him, to rest there with her Beloved, to embrace him, to kiss him again and again in the full sweetness of her love. 'Have pity on me, have pity, you at least, my friends! Let me be with him awhile, so that I might draw back thc shroud and gaze upon his face. Do not consign him so swiftly to the grave! Give him to his wretched mother to hold him yet a little, though he is dead. Or if you would bury him, bury me with him,

[135] The epithet *iustus et sanctus* has been transferred from Joachim and Joseph, Mary's husband, to this namesake of the latter.

too wretched to live on after him.' As they laid him in the tomb, Mary drew him to herself. She wanted to hold on to him, but they wished to consign him to the tomb. Thus there arose a gentle quarrel among them, a compassionate contention, even though those present were so moved to tears they could scarcely form the words. Seeing Christ's mother so destitute of comfort, they mourned even more for her than for their dead Lord. Greater was their sorrow at her sorrow than their grief at his death. All wept, beset with passionate grief, as to the tomb of death they consigned the Lord of life. They buried him; then Mary embraced the tomb, and with what voice she had she blessed her son. At the tomb she sat with drooping head, her arms outstretched, pressing her lips to the stone, and with tremendous sobbing she bewailed her Lord.

Then John drew near—he to whom Christ had commended his mother—and, mourning, lifted her as she mourned. Wracked and spent with groaning and weeping, her legs would not support her; but even as she was, she returned to Jerusalem, all tears, in the company of the holy women who helped her. Many of the women who saw her were moved to tears by her grief and broke into bitter mourning. Some of them followed after her lamenting. Many wept because their hearts went out to Mary: her grief made many grieve. None who saw her could restrain their tears. So piteously she wept, so bitterly she grieved, many were moved, even against their will, to mourn at the sight of her weeping. She wept; they wept as well who walked with her. Many wept who came upon her on the way. And so she was led weeping by those who wept, until they had reached John's house. Here she settled and remained. John kept her with him in his house and loved her as his very own mother. O blessed John, to whom the Lord confided such a treasure! May the Lord reward you with his love for the love in which you always held the mother he entrusted to you! You were blessed by Christ; you were blessed as well by his mother.

Above all may her Son
Jesus Christ our Lord be blessed,
who with the Father and the Holy Spirit
lives and reigns,
blessed God for ever and ever.
Amen.[136]

[136] Here ends the *Planctus Mariæ*.

XIII. Final Homily

The Resurrection
Mary's Assumption into Heaven
Conclusion

MAY JESUS CHRIST, our Lord and our God, grant us all that we know and are meant to learn concerning the Mother of everlasting salvation and glory, the delight of the angels and the sole bliss of all the elect. Then may our thoughts and words ever serve his honor and glory, and that of the ever-Virgin from whom he chose to take on flesh, so as to save us and free us from everlasting death. For when we recall his death, we ought as well to die with him. So long as we enjoy the breath *Cf. Rom 6:8* of life, let us bear in our bodies the marks of his Passion, not merely recalling his suffering *Gal 6:17* in pious homilies, but living it in our actions. Let us, to the depths of our being, be dead to the world, and live in love for Christ who for our salvation died upon the gibbet of the cross and was buried in the tomb. It is my hope that all who here on earth were partakers of his most blessed Passion may gain the resurrection of eternal salvation.

Now when the Lord had been buried, the Jews sealed the tomb and kept it under watch. Meanwhile Mary sat in John's house. Sat? Should I not rather say she lay there? I would say both: she sat and lay in the house of the beloved apostle; for so beset with grief was she, she could not walk without great difficulty. In John's house she wept day and night, nor could she be comforted by any who were dear to her, not by her sisters, not even by John. She poured forth the bitter grief of her grieving heart in bitter tears. In her mind she revisited the sites of his suffering; in her heart she relived all he had suffered. She bewailed him, nailed to the cross, with moans and sighs. She cried out with grief, recalling now the vinegar and gall they gave him to drink, now the cruel spear that bore through his dead body.

'Jesus, sweet Creator of all! Jesus, my Lord and my God made man! Oh what a savage death was yours! You whom earth and sea and air and heaven could not contain, now lie—alas—with the confines of a tomb! You through whom the human race returns to life now lie lifeless in the wretched tomb of death! True God, Life eternal, came to earth: came to take on the body of human frailty; but was *Jn 1:11* not received by his own, who ever plotted against him. Against him raged Herod the King of the Jews, and with Herod all Jerusalem, even as he was but a babe at his mother's breast. When grown to manhood he spoke the words of salvation, bursting the bonds of illness and infirmity, healing the sick from every ailment, raising the dead from cruel death—only to suffer himself the insults of many a son of Juda, the Scribes, the High-priests, the Elders, the Pharisees. They plotted together his destruction, now openly manifest on this very day. All this the Son of God suffered in the human flesh he received from his handmaid, so that in the flesh he might deliver the flesh from the death of the spirits which he had created. He gave his flesh in death as food for the author of death, that cruel death should itself die. And overcoming death he is to conquer death for ever and bring life. Oh may my future joy come quickly! God the Father shall raise him from death, and he shall die no more; no longer shall death have power over him. As man he died, as God he lives for ever!'

Meanwhile Jesus, whose tomb was sealed with a stone and guarded by soldiers, *now triumphed in splendor and rose from death in victory.* To the women who came weeping to the tomb to anoint the Lord, *a radiant angel spoke, banishing all grief and the pains of death: 'The Lord has risen!*[137] *Do not be afraid,'* said he, *'I know that you seek Jesus, who was crucified. He is not here: he has risen. Go, tell Peter and the disciples that he goes before you into Galilee. There you will see him; lo, I tell you in advance'*[138] Hastening to tell the apostles, they see the Lord—alive!—and kiss his feet. At this news the disciples proceed to Galilee to see the longed-for face of their Lord. Then,

[137] Lines from the Paschaltide hymn at Lauds, *Aurora lucis rutilant* (vv. 3-4), partly rendered in prose paraphrase *(qui clausus fuerat lapide et custodiebatur sub milite = ille quem clausum lapide | miles custodit acriter),* inaccurately recalled *(solutis iam gemitibus | et inferni doloribus* for *inferni iam gemitibus | solutis et doloribus),* and interlarded (cf. n.139).

[138] Mt 28:5-6; Mk 16:7; Mt 28:7b: the accounts overlap, and Ogier may well be citing a presumed single source from memory; the Matthean clausula *(ecce prædixi vobis)* is rendered here in the present tense.

The sun beamed bright with Easter joy,
to flood the world with light,
When the Apostles recognized
the countenance of Christ.

With their own eyes they saw the wounds
resplendent in his flesh.
'The Lord is risen again!' they cried
to one and all alike.[139]

He appeared (as some[140] maintain) first to his mother, in the beauty of his comeliness far beyond all the sons of men, and said: 'Hail, Mother, blessed above all women! Cease your tears now, for I have risen from the dead.' Then he rushed to embrace her; but she fell to his feet, touching and kissing them, thanking him for all that he had suffered for the salvation of the world, and blessing God for having raised him from the dead. Whereupon he bade her farewell and vanished from her eyes, appearing next to Mary Magdalene, and then to all the apostles. Others say that he did not first appear to her, since she was utterly certain of his resurrection and did not doubt it for a moment; but that he appeared first to Magdalene, then to certain apostles, and at length to them all.

[139] Hymn at Lauds, *Claro paschali gaudio* (vv. 1-2); *videntes ipsi vulnera* (2.1) is an otherwise unrecorded variant of *ostensa sibi vulnera* 'the wounds having been shown to them'. In the twelfth-century Molesme Breviary (cf. CLS IIA), these verses constitute the ninth and tenth verses of *Aurora lucis rutilant* (n. 290 there); the hymn was sung at Lauds on Easter Sunday.

[140] Ambrose (*De virg.* III.14), for one: *Vidit ergo Maria resurrectionem Domini: et prima vidit et credidit. Vidit et Maria Magdalena, quamvis adhuc ista nutaret* 'Mary saw the Lord's resurrection; she saw it first and she believed. Mary Magdalene also saw it, though she still wavered'. In the Byzantine liturgy (e.g. Ninth Ode at Easter Matins) the resurrection is announced to Mary by an angel.

What great joy there was in heaven, on earth and sea—yes, even in hell! The angels rejoiced, the archangels were glad, so too the cherubim and seraphim, as all the orders of heaven cried out: *All hail to our God who sits upon the throne, and to the Lamb. Salvation, honor and power to God* Almighty! Then the sun re- *Rev 7:10*
gained the brightness it had lost, shining with seven times the brightness it had shone. The *Cf. Is 30:26*
earth spun joyously in orbit, announcing to all the world the joys of the living Christ. The clouds were driven away by radiant light, and rays of bliss illumined all the earth: Christ was risen from the dead! The stars shone with three times their erstwhile brilliance, and greater light flashed over all the seven planets. The moon with gleaming horns proclaimed Christ's praise, radiant with joy throughout its phases. Heaven sang for joy to Christ, and earth and sea and the abyss echoed the glory of God.

> *Hell restored to life the just*
> *whom Adam's failing there had doomed*
> *through guilt not of their own.*[141]

Christ rising, so too they arose, as witnesses to the truth. The earth rejoiced, adorned with flowers, to serve the living Lamb whom God the Father had given over to death, that by the Lamb's death we might be given over to life in God, and with the Lamb, our God, we might partake of life in heaven. The sea, becalming its storms, became gentle and restored

[141] Three lines (source unknown) of dactyllic hexameter: *Reddidit ad vitam infernus mortuos iustos | quos Ade culpas iuste possederat ipsa | vita protoplasti, non actibus propriis reos.*

blue skies to seafarers. Joy flooded the heavens, and true joy shone upon earth, when Christ arose for ever victorious over death.

Then gladness was restored to the mother who had so bitterly mourned his death. She
Jn 20:20 *rejoiced* with great joy *when* she *saw the Lord*.
And little wonder! He who had lost his life
Cf. Lk 15:24 had found it again. The son who had died was restored to her alive. The flesh of the Messiah living again, the spirit of Mary revived. Through the life-giving Spirit Christ's flesh was restored to life; through the life restored to Christ's flesh the lifeless spirit of his mother was restored again to joyous life. All her mourning turned to joy; from the depths of her woe she was raised to bliss. Oh, how she rejoiced, how she leapt for joy, inwardly and outwardly. Happier still was she as often as her blessed eyes beheld the Lord Jesus. How sweet it is to imagine her, gazing upon the Lord, enflamed by the fire of his all-consuming love! How she must have held him in her arms, how she must have showered him with kisses, until the time that he must ascend to heaven and take his seat at the right hand of the Father. And when Christ ascended to heaven, her spirit ascended there as well, so that wherever he might be her spirit might be with him. Thus in spirit she lived with him in heaven, even as life on earth became for her the unbearable burden of the body. How she wished to be rid of the body and be with Christ! Daily she poured forth her tears and sighs to him, that she might be loosed from the prison of the flesh and join her spirit with his in heaven. Day and night she frequented

his tomb, the site of his crucifixion, and the place from which he had risen to heaven to receive again from his Father his heavenly realm. She hoped to find some measure of joy in the joy of her Son. But there from the measureless welling of love her tears gushed forth, recalling the grief of his death, desiring the embrace from which she had again been separated. Thus weeping and wailing she cried: '*As the hart longs for fountains of water, so my soul longs for you, my God,* my Son, my life, my love, my only joy, my singular comfort. *When shall I come and see your face?* Why are you so far *Ps 41:2, 3b*
from me, my God, my comforter, the consolation of my soul? *Look on me with pity and have mercy on me!* O most beloved Son and Lord, *Ps 24:16*
do not let me be so long apart from you! Take up my soul, for life is full of bitterness. My soul *seeks you and finds you not, calls and is not answered. Lord, I have loved the loveliness of your* *Sg 5:6*
house and the dwelling-place of your glory! Take *Ps 25:8*
me to you, for life is death without you.' This and like words were her daily prayer.

At length it pleased her Son to call her in his grace, two years after his ascension,[142] so that where he was his mother too might be. *Jn 14:3*
The disciples, who had scattered abroad throughout the world to preach the Gospel, gathered together to celebrate her passing, to bear her most sacred body to the grave. The Lord himself arrived, crowned with his Father's diadem, to take his mother's soul to the glory of eternal bliss. And with him were a million angels, singing sweet songs, now

[142] So the Latin apocryphal account of Pseudo-Melito.

hymns of joy, now shouts of exultation, at the leave-taking of the sacred soul of the blessed and spotless Virgin. Thus Mary was called forth from her body, more beautiful than myriads of angels, more radiant in her virtue than the moon, more brilliant than the sun. Leaning upon her Beloved, she was taken up by her Son, and so rejoicing, accompanied by choirs of hymn-singing angels,[143] the whole court of heaven exulting to gaze upon her beautiful countenance and lovely form, she entered into the joy of her Lord, her sovereign boon.[144] What a rare and wondrous fragrance wafted between them!

Meanwhile, as the funeral rite proceeded, virgins undressed her most holy body to wash it. Magdalene was there, along with the spotless Virgin's two sisters and certain of the other women who had followed the Lord Jesus, ministering to his needs. Since his ascension into heaven, their love for him had kept them close to his mother, whom they cherished in his honor. How the sight of her was pleasant to them! How her company refreshed them! More and more her devotion and sweetness daily nourished them by word and example, so as to love Christ in heaven as God, whom they had loved as man and prophet on earth (for they had not believed him to be more than that at first). Thus through her their hearts and souls grew ever more ardent for him. Among them, I believe, were the conse-

[143] *Hymnidicis angelorum choris,* cf. Gregory the Great (*Ep.* XIII.39): *reddatur ergo Creatori omnium ab hymnidicis angelorum choris gloria in cælo* 'let therefore glory in heaven be rendered the Creator by hymn-singing choirs of angels'.

[144] *[Se habet] optime in optimo,* Augustine *Contra Acad.*

crated virgins who through her example strove to please Christ her Son in their virginity with all their hearts and minds. The washing of the spotless Virgin's body was thus entrusted to these consecrated virgins, so that, untarnished by any carnal stain, they might undress and wash and perfume the body of the Mother of him who had so undeservedly borne the stains of the world. Yet even in death the brightness and beauty of that most blessed body surpassed the power of tongue to tell or words to describe. It was brighter far than snow, more brilliant than the sun, more redolent than balsam of the glory of the resurrection to come—even before reunited with her soul. It could be touched but not looked upon, so like lightning did its brilliance wound the eye. Many holy angels stayed behind to guard the body of the Queen of the world, the Mother of the Most High God, looking after her and caring for her with all due honor and reverence, until the day of her resurrection, which (so we would believe) was on the third day, when the blessed Virgin, rising from the dead, now immortal, went to reign with Christ her Son in everlasting bliss. The Virgin's sacred body, the treasury of eternal happiness, the Temple of the Son of God, the dwelling-place of the Holy Spirit, was buried by the apostles, weeping together with the many holy women who had gathered there. They wept, yet they rejoiced as one. They wept to see her taken so far from them; they rejoiced that she was ascending to be received with utter happiness into her Son's bridal-chamber of bliss. It had not been so long before that the Lord of angels, her only-begotten Son, was removed from them in his human form; now she who had been since then their sole comfort and joy, the Mother of the Savior of all, was removed from them as well.

In heaven, however, Mary's departure from the world was a cause of great joy. When at last the blessed Queen of the World came to be raised above the choirs of angels, there had not been such joy since Christ's ascent into heaven. All the cherubim and seraphim applauded her coming; every rank in paradise sang out in jubilee: 'How lovely, how beautiful is the Mother of Jerusalem's King, *more awe-*
Sg 6:9 *some than an armed camp!* The fragrance of your ointments surpasses all aromas; how comely and sweet are your delights, Holy Mother of God! *Blessed are you, and blessed is the fruit of your*
Lk 1:42 *womb!* Rejoice now, blessed one, blessed for ever: worthy are you to be elevated above the choirs of angels, and to be enthroned next to the God of Ages!' O brilliance of the heavens, sweetness of Paradise, delight of God, glory of the angels, happiness of the saints, blessed jewel of virgins: O gladsome joy, O blessed benediction of all whom you love and cherish, of all whom you embrace in your love!

Who will grant that you might love me? Who will grant that I might come to you: that I might come to you, see you, possess you, my weal, my love, my life, my glory, my crown? O Lady of glory, O Queen of happiness, fountain of motherly love, vein of mercy, richness of sanctity, pleasant delight: shall my desire ever be fulfilled? Shall I see you whom I love, whom I long for with all my being? Shall my hunger be stilled when, with all the elect, you appear in the fullness of your loveliness? O wholly beautiful, matchless Queen, sweet with the delights of God, Mother of the Most High: what shall I say? What shall I do? Where shall I go? Where shall I seek you? Where shall I find you? Alas, how far from me you are, the hope of my salvation, the solace of my sorrowful soul! Alas, O Christ, I have seen neither weeping Mother nor dying Son. At the birth of the King the angels sang *'Glory to God in the highest'*—but I did not hear them. The shepherds saw you; I did not. You dwelled among people; I did not know you. You died and were buried; I was not there to mourn you. You arose and ascended to heaven; I was not there to witness your glory, nor have I seen you yet. What is a wretch like me to do? If I travel to the East I will not find you. If I journey to the South I shall not look upon you. In the North you will not appear to me. I seek and do not find, call and remain unanswered. What further grief might I endure, my Lord and my God, you who create and refashion, who form and inform, who kill and revive, strike down and heal? You have struck me down and wounded me with the javelin of your cherished love; and you have healed me through your death from every mortal ailment, ransoming me to God in your blood. Surely my grief is enough as it is. Yet, woe is me, another grief to this is added, stripped as I am of the power to see and come into the presence of my Lady, your beloved Mother. You ascended into heaven and drew her to you there; yet I am unworthy to ascend to you or to look upon her. You exalted her; you elevated her above the choirs of angels, above all the order of the holy spirits. I thank you for that; yet be merciful to me and pity me, that I might see both you and her. This alone will satisfy me; nothing else would I seek. May my Lady, your Virgin Mother, obtain this for me. To her I commit myself entirely in body and soul; to her I commit my life, my death, and my rising again. May she be blessed for ever and beyond,

with Jesus her Son,
who with God the Father and the
Holy Spirit lives and reigns,
God, blessed for ever and ever.
Amen.

HERE ENDS THE LITTLE BOOK
OF THE PRAISE OF PARADISE,
THE MOTHER OF THE ETERNAL KING,
THE SACRED VIRGIN.
GLORY TO YOU, LORD, VIRGIN-BORN;
WITH THE FATHER AND THE HOLY SPIRIT,
THROUGH AGES EVERLASTING.
AMEN.[145]

[145] *Explicit libellus de laudibus paradisi, scilicet matris regis eterni, virginis sacre. Gloria tibi domine qui natus es de virgine, cum patre et sancto spiritu in sempiterna secula. Amen.* '*Libellus*' suggests that the clausula is Ogier's, not that of the scribe of Staffarda; the doxology is of course that for the Common of the Blessed Virgin during the Nativity season.

On the Lord's Words to His Disciples at the Last Supper

PROLOGUE

YOU WHO HUNGER to be filled at the paschal feast of the Lord, come! Our little table is laid; no one who would eat will be turned away. Whoever you are then, come and be refreshed with crumbs from the very table of the Lord, that most sweet Bread who said of himself, *I am the living bread that has come down from heaven.* He gave *Jn 6:51*
his children their fill while he was still in the world, and when he was about to ascend to his Father, he told them, *Little children, I shall be with you only a little longer.* Then, ascending *Jn 13:33*
into heaven, he *entrusted his little ones with these remnants,*[1] which John set forth, just as his *Ps 16:14*
Master wished. These priceless words I now take up, ever seeking with groans and weeping that most blessed Bread of Angels. In exchange for that indescribable food I gladly offer whatever the world deems precious.

Approach then the little table this unworthy servant of Christ has set, but come with tears, and do not go away without groaning. The food you will find here is not for the belly, but for the mind: not *burnt offerings of fatlings* nor *bullocks and goats,* but the Lamb the *Ps 65:15*

[1] *Reliquias* also echoes the account of the multiplication of the loaves in Mt 14 (cf. v. 20).

Virgin bore, who *like a sheep before its shearers*
Is 53:7 *never opened his mouth.* May my soul confess
him, and may he save me, who have sinned in
his sight! May he be my *Way* in this little work
and in all my actions; let me follow him in
everything I undertake, pursuing wherever he
leads. Let me *proclaim the Lord's name in Zion*
and his praise in Jerusalem, so that, *when peoples*
Ps 101:22, 23 *and kings are gathered together to serve the Lord*,
I might be found worthy to see him *in the*
goodness of his elect, and to rejoice *in the gladness*
Ps 105:5 *of his people.*

Blessed is the Lord for evermore!

I

FIRST HOMILY

Now before the feast of the passover, Jesus, knowing that the hour had come for him to pass from the world to the Father, having loved those who were his in the world, he loved them to the end. They were at supper; the devil had already put it into the heart of Judas, son of Simon Iscariot, to betray him.

John 13:1-2

GOD'S SON, the Father's *Word,* for our salvation *became flesh and dwelled among us.* Desiring to teach and form his disciples— *Jn 1:14*
and, through them, all who believe in him—he set an example of humility. As that most sacred hour approached when the flesh taken from the inviolate Virgin Mary was about to endure doleful punishment, he *got up* from that noble banquet which closed his time on earth, *put off his outer garment, poured water into a basin, and began to wash the disciples' feet.*[2] *Jn 13:4, 5*

It was, as John the Evangelist tells us, *before the festival of the Passover.* The Jews, by long custom, kept solemn the day on which the Lord divided the Red Sea, led them through

[2] Paraphrased; cited in context in Homily II.

its midst, and struck down Pharaoh and all his mighty hordes. But now there approached that most sacred Passover when the true Moses would pass through the Red Sea, not after forty years, but after forty days. The festival of the Jews, on which their forebears passed over out of Egypt, was but a shadow: Christ, who passed over from this world, is its fulfilling truth. And we, through him, have passed over from vice to virtue, from death to life, and from the world below to heaven above. Becoming for us the victim and the sacrifice, he offered himself to God the Father as a burnt offering on the altar of the cross.[3]

But why do you call it a *festival,* Saint John? Is not a festival a day of joy and gladness? Can it be a day of gladness and delight when *the Lamb is lifted up to be slain on the gibbet of the cross,*[4]
Ps 21:6 the *reproach of men and the outcast of the people?* when the sun grows dark for grief, the rocks are rent, and the whole world shudders in its
Cf. Mt 27:51 orbit? when the mother weeps with the beloved John? For the saints and the elect, this was a day not of laughter and happiness, but of grief. Some there may well have cheered that day as you and your companions wept, but their gladness turned into mourning soon enough when the Apostles' grief was turned to joy.

Jesus, knowing that the hour had come for him to pass from the world to the Father. The Hebrew

[3] The sacrificial *holocaustum* recalls the language of Abraham and Isaac (Gen 22:1–19). The ram supplied there by God is now 'the Lamb born of the Virgin' (Prologue).

[4] Venantius Fortunatus, *Pange lingua* (Hymn to the Holy Cross; *GR* 182–184).

meaning of *Jesus* is 'saviour'. Jesus is indeed that mighty Saviour who can no longer be overcome and who saves all who hope in him. Once he was vanquished for you, Christian,[5] yes, he was put to death. But do not weep; he rose from the dead: *death no longer has dominion over him. For it behooved him* to die for the salvation of the world, *and on the third day to rise from the dead, that in his name repentance for the forgiveness of sins should be preached to every nation.* He ordained it so.

Rom 6:9

Lk 24:46-47; cf. Jn 20:9

His hour had come. An hour before, fearing death according to the flesh, he had groaned and said, *Now my soul is troubled. What, shall I say: Father save me from this hour?* Christ feared dying so that you, relying on Him who raised Jesus from the dead on the third day, might have no fear of death. He who raised Jesus, in Him alone let us put our trust. Christian, do not lose hope in the face of weakness! He has taught us what to say in mortal peril, to whom to fly, in whom to hope. Our hope is in God the Father, who cannot disdain any whose hope in Him is confirmed by their good works. Good works, I say, since, without merit, to hope at all would be presumption. Do good works, then, so that in the hour of death you may be able to say to Him in truth, *In you, Lord, I have hoped. Let me never be put to shame.*

Jn 12:27

Ps 30:2

Jesus foreknew this hour: he chose it, so that in his humanity he might pass over through death to his Father, whom in his divinity he

[5] Ogier addresses a singular *christiane* three times in this homily, coupled once with *monache* ('monk'); 'Christian' recurs once in Homily III and twice in Homily IV (here as well coupled once with 'monk'); see also his address to a *lector* (n. 28).

had never left.[6] This hour is that *end* of which John writes, *having loved those who were his in the world, he loved them to the end*. He had loved them enough to have become human for their sake, and so great was his love that it led him to die for them. You, too, he loved in death, so that by that love you might also pass over from this world to the Father. He loved you to the end, so that by that love you might remain steadfast to the end. If you do so, you will as certainly pass over to the Father, as one who does not will be truly lost for ever. In that love let your love be without measure, for so he loved you, and so should you love him. In dying for you he surpassed love's measure; to love him as much as you ought exceeds your ability. *Love* him *with all your heart, with all your*
Deut 6:5; Lk 10:27 *mind and soul, with all your might;* he asks no
Lk 10:28 more than this. *Do this and you shall live.*

They were at supper; the devil had already put it into the heart of Judas, son of Simon Iscariot, to betray him. This suggests that the supper was prepared but not yet eaten,[7] for later Jesus reclined at table and gave Judas a morsel of bread. O wretched Judas, wicked merchant, worst of disciples! For you was this supper laid, by you its host betrayed! O false confessor, despairer of repentance! You said, *I have sinned,*
Mt 27:4 *I have betrayed innocent blood,* and in the grasp of despair, O wretch, you snuffed out your life!

[6] Cf. Thomas Aquinas, some sixty years later: *Verbum supernum prodiens nec Patris linquens dexteram.*

[7] *Nondum transacta* appears to depend on a reading of *cena facta* as 'supper having been laid'.

Judas, we are told, was Simon Scariot's son. The name Simon means 'obedience',[8] but what sort of man this Simon might have been God knows, not I. Scariot refers to his place of origin, which is also known as Marmoth, or 'evil death'. Was there ever anyone worthier of such a death than Judas? Not believing that Jesus was God, Judas was prompted by the devil to betray him.

Christian—and you, monk of Benedict—do you not shudder when you consider what became of this disciple of Christ? The devil *put it in his heart* to betray life, and betraying that life he lost his own in the grasp of despair. If the wolf did not fear to enter the Lord's flock and destroy one of the Twelve—so small a number!—what is to become of the flock consigned to the shepherd? Let each of you, my dear brothers, see that you do not become a Judas. See that you walk cautiously, not as the foolish walk, but as the wise, wary of the wily foe's ambushes. He *put it into Judas's heart to betray* the Lord. What is it to betray the Lord? It is to sell him out, to estrange oneself from him. You estrange yourself from him when you drive him away. O monk of God, O disciple of Christ, hear me, heed my counsel! The devil seeks to snatch you away from the Lord's flock. Do not consent! Do not believe him! *He is a liar, the father of lies.* He means to *Jn 8:44*
slay you and destroy you. He wants you to be lost with him in hell.

[8] 'Hearkening' *(audiens):* according to Jerome. The association of Scariot with *marmoth* ('violent death') is from some other source.

Jn 12:6

It is said of Judas that *he was a thief who kept the common purse.* Thirsting for gain, he hies to the snare; losing his life, he gains his death. Beware of purses, beware of pouches and pockets![9] They are the devil's pitfalls—how many, alas, come to grief by them! Alas, how many pouches and pockets there are in our monasteries! How many of us who wear the cowl and bear the tonsure have pockets of the mind, pouches of self-will, of murmuring, backbiting, and wavering. How many have pockets of pride and malice, pouches of envy and ill-will! Those who do, dear brothers, follow Judas the betrayer. Unless they change their ways, they will never possess the kingdom of God. Beloved, be disciples of Christ in truth, I beg you, not in falseness. Be his not in your garb but in your hearts, not merely by the shaving of your heads but in the pureness of your minds. Forsake Judas who despaired, and follow Peter who truly repented. Forsake Judas despairing in the depths of hell, and follow Peter into heaven's glory. Make Peter's tears your own, and so through Jesus Christ our Lord attain his glory. May my soul confess the Lord, and may he save me who have sinned against him

he who with the Father and the Holy Spirit
is blessed for ever.
Amen.

[9] *Loculis, marsupiis.* The plural form *loculos* ('purse', 'money-bag') occurs only in Jn 12:6; the singular is used in the Vulgate as a euphemism for 'burial place', 'bier' (e.g. Gen 50:25, Lk 7:14), and by Ogier in the sense of a 'secret cache' *loculum propriæ voluntatis*. For most of the argument Ogier uses *marsupium* ('pouch', 'bag', 'purse'); this is the 'common purse' (among thieves and plunderers) in Prov 1:14.

II

SECOND HOMILY

Jesus knew that the Father had put everything into his hands and that he had come from God and he was returning to God. He got up from table and removed his outer garments, he took a towel and wrapped it round himself. He then poured water into a basin and began to wash the disciples' feet and to wipe them with the towel he wears. He came first to Simon Peter; Peter groaned and cried out, 'Lord! You—wash my feet?' Jesus replied, 'You do not know now what I am doing, but later you will understand.' Peter said, 'Never shall you wash my feet!' Jesus replied, 'Unless I wash you, you can have no share with me.' Simon Peter said to him, 'Lord, wash my feet—and not only my feet: wash my hands, my head!' Jesus said to him, 'No one who has had a bath needs washing, except the feet, but is clean all over. And you are clean, though not all of you. Then, when he had washed their feet and put on once more his outer garments, he went back to the table.

John 13:3-19

JUST AS *THE EAR cannot be sated by hearing, nor the eye by seeing,* so we must never cease to proclaim the loving works of Christ. *Ecc 1:8, reordered*

These indeed are *sweeter to me than honey and* Ps 18:11b *the honey-comb,* dearer *than heaps of gold and* Ps 118:72 *silver.*[10] May the Lord increase my desire and gladden me with the delight of his face, in the company of all who love him, as I tell what the Lord did then!

Jesus knew that the Father had put everything into his hands. Elsewhere we read that God the Father *put all things under his feet, sheep and* Ps 7:7-8 *cattle, all of them, and even the wild beasts. Everything:* both good and ill, for from evil good resulted. Through the evil of Judas's betrayal Jesus made good our redemption. He knew *that he had come from God* without having left him, and that *he was returning to God* without deserting us. He came *from God* by coming from the bosom of his Father into the womb of the Blessed Virgin, for, *being in the form of God, he did not count equality with God something to be grasped, but emptied himself, taking the form of a slave, becoming as human beings are, and* Phil 2:6-7 *being in every way like a human being.*

And so he came *from God* to be present among us, to be seen and touched, to be—oh, how my heart groans as I set this down, how my eyes are aflood with tears!—to be bound and struck and scourged and spat on and, finally, to be put to death. This is what *he had come from God* means. But do not weep, dear brother, for *he was returning to God*, for *Christ has been raised from the dead and will never die* Rom 6:9 *again; death no longer has any power over him.* He

[10] The entire citation may be the product of misremembering Ps 18:11—*[iudicia Domini] desiderabilia* super aurum *et lapidem pretiosum multum, et dulciora* super mel et favum (the order being reversed, as in the initial citation from Ecclesiastes)—or else an intentional conflation of Pss 18 and 118.

ascended into heaven and is seated at the right
hand of God, having been made by God the
judge of the living and the dead. Thus, *he got
up from table* when, from his Father's bosom,
where he supped with angels; he came to man-
kind, putting on the garment of our mortality.
He removed his outer garments when he emptied
himself. Uniting himself to human nature, *he
took a towel* and *wrapped himself round with power,* *Ps 92:1b*
the king of glory, the Lord of power who triumphed *Ps 23:10*
gloriously over the proud foe.

*He then poured water into a basin and began
to wash the disciples' feet.* The water he poured
is that blessed water that washes from our
minds all that is vile. It is the water that cleanses
the leper, gives light to the blind, heals the
sick and sets the sinner aright; it is the water
that raises the dead. To this water our Lord
Jesus invites us all when he says: *Let anyone
who is thirsty come to me and drink.* This water *Jn 2:13*
is the Holy Spirit. Of this water Jeremiah says,
*They have abandoned . . . the fountain of living
water and dug themselves water-tanks that are
cracked and hold no water.* *Jer 2:13*

From that fountain let me drink, Lord, *so
that I may never be thirsty again.* How my soul *Jn 4:15*
thirsts for this living fountain—oh that I *Cf. Ps 41:3*
might attain it! Oh that I might slake my thirst
at that fountain most sweet! When shall the
time come for me to draw from it fully? If at
some time, why not now? What shall I say,
what shall I do?—for my Lord delays in com-
ing to me. Most sweet Jesus, may my tears of
restoration persist until my soul is told to
rejoice and be glad: 'Behold whom you seek,
behold whom you desire, and for whom you

weep! Behold your Lord, your God: Father, Son, and longed-for fountain of the Holy Spirit! Drink deeply of the delights of paradise!' Oh, my brothers, let him so inebriate our minds with himself that we can love none else but him!

The *basin* into which the Lord pours the Holy Spirit is the Church of the faithful, wherein the Holy Spirit washes away believers' filth in the bath of regeneration. That he washed the feet of the apostles tells us that he washed away the uncleanness of those who followed in his footsteps. Or we can say that the basin—the receptacle of the Holy Spirit—is the hearts of the apostles into which the Lord poured the Holy Spirit. He washed their feet, ridding them thoroughly of the blight that clung to them. And so by the Holy Spirit he confirmed them in that Catholic faith that conveys the faithful to heaven, and which until then the dust of faithlessness had darkened.

There is more to be said, so long as the love of Christ delights you to hear it. But do not, I beg you, receive without tears what should not be written without weeping. *He poured water into a basin* who, for love of you considering death a delight, poured out blood and water on the gibbet of the cross. He washed the feet of the apostles, that is, he cleansed believers' sin-soiled soles. He wiped them *with the towel he had tied about himself,* that is, with the human flesh in which he was clothed; for his Passion is truly the cleansing of our sins. We do not stray from the path of truth in assigning to the Lord's supper the sense of his

Passion, for just as no further meal followed that supper, so too Christ, having once suffered, suffers no longer. And after the supper of his Passion, he *rises up from table.* He *removes his outer garments,* his former infirmity, *and wraps himself in a towel*—the same flesh, but immortal now. He *puts water into a basin,* washing away believers' sins in the waters of baptism. He *wipes them with the towel he wears,* for, exhibiting himself in his humanity, he urges the Father with indescribable sighs and groans.

O wondrous and unsought-for loving-kindness! O incalculable goodness! O rare and unheard-of humility![11] Christ, God's Son, born of the pure and inviolate Virgin, King of kings and Lord of lords, gets up from supper, removes his outer garments, wraps himself round in a towel, and pours water into a basin. Before his disciples he stoops low, kneels upon his venerable knees, and washes their feet! Who has ever heard the like of it? What astonishing love, God's wondrous kindness! He who from nothing created all things *washed the disciples' feet.*

You there, so afire with ready anger, so prompt to be devoured by pride—what do *you* make of it? What do you think of your Creator, your God, as he stoops to wash the disciples' feet—while *you* refuse to humble yourself before your offended brothers? O wicked servant, seed of Canaan and not

[11] *O mira et inexquisita pietas! O inæstimabilis bonitas! O nova et inaudita humilitas!* cf. the Exultet: *O mira circa nos tuæ pietatis dignatio! O inæstimabilis dilectio caritatis, ut servum redimeres Filium tradidisti!*

Cf. Mt 15:22-27 of Judah, deceived by the author of pride! Consider what an evil one it is you follow in your pride—and how good the one whose humility you disdain to imitate. The one is the devil; the other is God. Choose whom it is better to follow! Do you persist in your pride? Blush with shame, vessel of dung! Do you not know that *God resists the proud but*
Jas 4:6 *showers his grace on the humble? Put off the old*
Col 1:9-10 *man and put on the new,* the Lord Jesus, and he *will refashion the body of your lowliness into the*
Phil 3:21 *likeness of the body of his brightness*. Learn
Cf. Mt 11:29 humility from its author in the words that follow.

When the Lord Jesus began to wash the disciples' feet, *he came* first *to Simon Peter,* the first among his disciples. That God should wash a man's feet filled Peter with terror and dread; he could not bear to see the Lord so humbled. He had watched him pour the water into the basin and wrap himself in the towel; perhaps he wondered what Jesus meant to do. But then he saw him come before him with the vessel, watched him kneel in preparation, and his apprehension was more than words can tell. Terrified, *Peter* groaned and *cried out, 'Lord! You—wash my feet?'* Was the Lord about to serve his servant, the Master his disciple? Would God so humble himself before a man, the Creator before his creature, He who from nothing made all things—before one who was made of clay? 'Get up, Lord,[12] my God! What are you doing? It is too much, I cannot bear

[12] *Surge Domine*—the verb is that of the angel of the Resurrection: *Surrexit* 'he has risen'.

it! My eyes must not behold you so abased, so stooped before my feet! Get up, O Creator! Up, my God, light of the world, my life, my glory! Do not do what I see you mean to do! *Never shall you wash my feet,* Lord!'

At this, *Jesus replied, 'You do not know now what I am doing, but later you will understand.* Do not be terrified, Peter. This is to be sure a great gesture of humility, but you will soon see greater and limitless evidence. It is a mystery beyond your ken now—so it must be—but later you will understand. It is an object-lesson I mean to leave you with as I go to the Father; do not prevent me from doing as I will. *Unless I wash you, you can have no share with me.'* (When he says *you* rather than *your feet*, what pertains to a part is attributed to the whole; this is known as synecdoche.) 'I am the water that washes, I am the water that sanctifies: *if I do not wash you, you can have no share with me.'* Hearing these latter words, Peter shudders profoundly. 'What does it mean when you say, *"You can have no share with me"?* No share with you? What bitter words! You are my life, my sweetness, all my hope, my well-being, my every desire!' Then, no longer contradicting the Master, he offers to be washed not only his feet but himself entirely: 'Here I am, Lord. Do with me what you will! Wash my feet—and *not only my feet: wash my hands, my head!'*

If it is true, Lord Jesus, that no one you have not first washed can have a share with you, then have mercy on me, have mercy! I am that total sinner, wholly unclean and filthy; yet I desire a share with you. *Do not despise me, O God my saviour! God, be merciful to me, a sinner!* *Ps 26:9*

Lk 18:13 Wash what is filthy,[13] wash what is befouled! *Wash my feet, my hands, my head,* my whole body! Wash my mind, wash my soul; wash me within and without. *Wash me thoroughly from my guilt, purify me from my sin; wash me till I am whiter than snow.* *Ps 50:4, 9* Who but you, Lord Jesus, will grant it to me to come into my heart and inebriate me with your water, so that I can forget all my former evil and—oh blissful thought!—embrace you, that Life that shall never die? My sinful soul awaits the inspiration of your grace, that I might sufficiently repent and worthily live.

Your telling Peter, *No one who has had a bath needs washing, except the feet,* suggests that the apostles were baptized, though we do not read where. Whoever has been washed in baptism is wholly clean, but as we have once again been sullied by the dust of this earthly dwelling, we need to wash our feet. These our Lord washes in our stead as we pray to him with contrite heart and stinging tears. Whoever in leisure applies himself to the truth, while at other times hastens to open to the bride's knocking, befouls his feet; for the truth is heard humbly but is not proclaimed[14] without peril. For when the bridegroom encourages her to vaunt herself, the bride of the Song of Songs indicates that she wishes to be shunned. *I have taken off my tunic,* she says; *am I to put it on again? I have washed my feet; am I* *Sg 5:3* *to dirty them again?*

[13] Cf. the Pentecost sequence, *Veni Sancte Spiritus* by Stephen Langton (d. 1228): *lava quod est sordidum.*

[14] The operative verb here is *prædicare,* in the double sense of open declaration and self-vaunting.

The bridegroom had said to her, '*Open to me, my sister, my love, my spotless one, for my head is covered with dew, and my locks with the drops of night.* Oh my sister, my co-heir, my love, privy to my secrets, my dove illumined by the Holy Spirit, my perfect one divested of all earthly cares, *open to me,* make accessible to me by open declaration the hearts of those who have strayed. *My head is covered with dew*, my godhead is surrounded with the fervor of charity; *and my locks with the drops of night.*' (The latter alludes to the threat to the faithful posed by the arguments of heretics.) To these words the bride responds, '*I have taken off my tunic; am I to put it on again?* I have secluded myself from public notice; shall I vaunt myself anew? I have cleansed my thoughts and affections; shall I be sullied again by the world's pollution? *I have washed my feet; am I to dirty them again?*'

Sg 5:2

Sg 5:3

The Lord washes his disciples' feet as a pledge of the prayer he himself taught them: *Forgive us our debts as we forgive those who are in debt to us.* O fortunate feet, to have merited one so great to wash them![15] (I speak not here of Judas's feet but those of the elect.) O blessed Peter, O fortunate apostles, before whose feet knelt in all humility the creator of the angels! O blessed cleansing! O blessed washing that makes the leper clean, the ailing cured, the wounded healed, the scarred mended, granting light to the blind, steps to the lame, beauty to the repulsive, abundance to the needy, to

Mt 6:12

[15] *O pedes felices qui tantum ac talem meruerunt habere lavatorem,* a parody, with much of what follows, of the *Exsultet* (n. 11): *O felix culpa quæ talem ac tantum meruit habere redemptorem.*

the grieving gladness, to the penitent pardon, to the dead—life! O great joy, O boundless gladness!

You are clean, he tells them, *though not all of you.* The Evangelist explains: *He knew who was going to betray him; that is why he said, 'though not all of you'.* Then, *when he had washed their feet and put on once more his outer garments, he went back to the table.*

What follows let us ever keep fresh in our memory; let us ever be guided by these words. *Do you understand,* he said, *what I have done to you, I your Lord and Master? I have set you an example so that you may do what I have done to you.*[16] After he washed the disciples' feet—cleansed us in his blood—he went back to the table, seating himself once again at his Father's right, and spoke through the Holy Spirit, who came in tongues of fire. Having washed his disciples' feet, Christ *put on his garment:* having died in the flesh, he won resurrection's glory; having poured out his blood, he *put on immortality.* Then *he reclined once again at table:* he rested, then he ascended to heaven, where he sits ever blessed at the right hand of God the Father. From that lofty repose he instructs and guides the disciples in the Holy Spirit; through them he thunders forth to all nations.

1 Cor 15:53

Cf. Ps 28:3

What does he say? It is what he promised Peter when he said, '*Later you will understand.* Now he invites them to understand what they did not know before: *You call me Lord and Master, and rightly; so I am,* he says—not in

[16] This compressed form of vv. 12b-16 derives most likely from the Mandatum antiphon, *Dominus Iesus postquam cenavit* (*GR* 165).

arrogance but in truth. He whom necessity compels to tell in truth good things about himself is all the more truly bound to humility the closer he keeps to the truth. 'I am *Master,* I am *Lord.*

> I am the *Master* who knows neither error nor falsehood.
> I am the *Master* of goodness, the *Master* of holiness; whoever follows me walks aright and cannot go astray.
> I am the *Lord* of life and death, the *Lord* of heaven and earth, creator of all, *Lord and Master* of all.

If I, then, the Lord and Master, have washed your feet, it is for you to wash each other's feet.'

Just as before by example, so now by word the Master of truth instructs us. Here the argument for loving-kindness has its heart: 'If I who am Lord and Master have washed your feet, then you who are neither lords nor masters ought to wash each other's feet. *I have set you an example:* you cannot be good servants unless you follow me; you cannot be true disciples if you turn aside from my teaching.'

You prelates in sees of authority, hear me! Do you follow the Lord's example? Let each of us search his conscience. Whoever holds true to the Lord's teaching may well rejoice; who does not is no longer the Lord's disciple. Better for him to be drowned in the depths of the sea with a great millstone round his neck than to bear the title of abbot. Better a *Mt 18: 6*
swineherd he, than the shepherd of monks. O *basin* of the Lord, O humility of Christ,

how long have you been absent! How rare, how few are those who pour water into a basin and beg on bended knee to wash the feet of their disciples! A brother sins, a monk commits an offense, falls into some transgression. There is no basin, no water, no one ready to cleanse him—only to expel him. This is not the lesson of the Lord, prelates; this is not the rule of Christ.[17] Christ washed his disciples' feet on his knees—and *you* will not wash away the filth of those in your charge, prostrate before you? *No servant is greater than his master.* (*Cf. Mt 10:24, Lk 6:40*) A monk errs, a brother sins, his foot tracks in dirt, he is wasting away altogether perhaps. Learn from the Master's basin: take water, run to that brother—not like Pharaoh in his chariot, (*Cf. Ex 14:4*) but like the Redeemer in his humility—with serene countenance and tranquil mind. But be quick as you can! Rush to wash him, lest the dust provoke itching sores that then become leprous,[18] when nothing is left to the leper but to be cast out from the Lord's flock. If he is headstrong, unwilling to mend his ways, if he tells you, *You will never wash my feet,* say to

[17] The correction of wayward monks occupies six consecutive chapters of the RB (23-28) in degrees of severity—other chapters take up the corporal discipline of (boy) oblates (30) and the formal penance to be satisfied by an excommunicate monk (44). Central to Ogier's theme is Chapter 27, on the solicitude an abbot should have for his errant brothers, even as a physician for the sick. Senior members of the community are to offer counsel—discretely, like a 'mustard-plaster' concealed under one's habit. The abbot is moreover required to undertake the cure of infirm souls, not act the tyrant over healthy ones. The medical imagery of the Rule may well have triggered Ogier's more tactile figure (see n. 28).

[18] *Scabies* and *lepra* are afflictions associated with stubborn disobedience in the Pentateuch (e.g. Deut 28:27, Num 12:10). Variations of this dermatological image recur throughout the Homilies (*sciabious sive leprosus*—III, n. 32; *scabiem ulcerosam*—VIII, n. 102; *scabiem cutis*—X; see also *impetigo*—XIV, n. 132); it first appears in Tractate V as *scabiosum in pelle, leprosum in carne* (see n. 61 there).

him, *Unless I wash you, you will have no share* in Christ the Lord. Then if with Peter he assents, wash him in all humility, gentleness, and mercy, so that you, too, may receive mercy from God. Brother in Christ, fellow abbot, keep Christ's example—or else you are no disciple of his. Do you disdain to do what Christ did? Does the servant shrink from doing what the Master has done? *'No servant is greater than his master,'* Christ tells us; *'no messenger is greater than the one who sent him.* Just as I suffer, so also you; even as I humble myself, humble yourselves as well.'

Now that you know this, blessed are you if you behave accordingly. I am not speaking about all of you: I know the ones I have chosen. He was not speaking of all of them, for Judas had turned from him. He had chosen twelve, but one was the devil, Judas Iscariot, who *lifted up his heel* against the Lord. Jesus himself had said of him, *What scripture says must be fulfilled: he who shares my table has lifted up his heel against me.*

O unhappy Judas! You eat the Lord's bread and lift up your heel against him. How many there are just like you! How many live from the altar who do not serve the altar—nay rather, lead the Lord to the altar for naught! Alas, even more to be lamented: how many false priests eat the Lord's bread—his body!—and trample Christ under foot! How they stink of the rot of luxury! How the poison of unfaithfulness infects them! Judases all, let them transform themselves for the better, or else, lest they wish they had never been born! *Cf. Mt 26:24*

'I tell you this now, before it happens, so that when it does happen you may believe that I am he.

Until now I have endured it in silence, but now I draw attention to the traitor before what is soon to happen takes place, so that when it happens you may believe that I am the one of whom the Scriptures foretold it.'

You therefore, my brothers, disciples of Christ, reflect on Judas's deed and see that you do nothing similar. Judas lifted up his heel against Christ; you must prostrate yourselves, body and soul, before him. Judas turned away and left him; you must follow him. Judas sold him out to the authorities; you must sell all you possess—yourselves as well—for love of that pearl of such beauty. Exert yourselves to the limit in pleasing him, and him alone. Then you and I may be able to attain those joys that last forever, which are Christ Jesus himself: through the same Saviour of the world,

who with the Father and the Holy Spirit
lives and reigns blessed for ever and ever.
Amen.

III

THIRD HOMILY

In truth I tell you, whoever welcomes the one I send, welcomes me, and whoever welcomes me, welcomes the one who sent me. Having said this, Jesus was troubled in spirit and said, 'In truth I tell you, one of you is going to betray me.' The disciples looked at each other, wondering whom he meant. The disciple Jesus loved was reclining next to Jesus, leaning on his breast. Peter made a sign to ask whom he meant. So, leaning against Jesus' breast, he asks 'Lord, who is it?' And the Lord tells him, 'It is the one to whom I give the piece of bread that I dip in the dish.' And when he had dipped the piece of bread he gave it to Judas, son of Simon Iscariot. At that instant, after Judas had taken the bread, Satan entered him. Jesus then said, 'What you are about to do, do quickly!' None of the others at table understood why he said this. Since Judas had charge of the common fund, some of them thought Jesus was telling him, 'Buy what we need for the festival', or telling him to give something to the poor. As soon as Judas had taken the piece of bread he went out. It was night.

John 13:20-30

OUR HUMAN NATURE binds each of us, so long as we live in this body, to go out to our work and to toil until evening. Scripture is not to be contradicted on this point: each of us is to work without ceasing at what is for our eternal good. The hour is coming quickly enough when all toil and every concern of our labors will cease, and then each according to his work will receive his reward. As for me, since nothing is sweeter or more just than pondering the Lord's commandments, I have chosen to meditate on the law of Christ—for *the law* of my Redeemer *is greater to me than countless sums of gold and silver.* I give the fruits of my labors to anyone who asks. Hearken diligently, dear reader,[19] and observe whatever Christ says in my place. No one is greater, or greater in goodness, than Jesus; no one more comely, none sweeter, none dearer. He is the glory of the saints, the splendor of the angels, the author and creator of all. Hear what he tells his disciples!

Ps 118:72

In truth I tell you, whoever welcomes the one I send, welcomes me, and whoever welcomes me, welcomes the one who sent me. Having taught us humility by example, by suffering for us in the flesh, Our Lord and Saviour set aside his honor to comfort us. In all whom we welcome for love of him, it is he himself and his Father who are welcomed. In the one who is sent is confided the authority of the sender, not that of the messenger. Welcoming Christ's

[19] The device of addressing a *lector* characterizes this homily, in which it occurs four times (and once again at the beginning of the next); thereafter the reader is so addressed only once more, in Homily XII (see the *Introduction,* B.), although Homily VIII (end) refers to 'one whom reading our words delights' and Homily IX (at the beginning) to 'anyone reading this chapter'.

messenger we welcome Christ, and, if Christ, then Christ's Father also.

Who is the messenger Christ sends us as himself? It is the pauper, the beggar, the stranger, the homeless one who has nothing to wear, nothing to eat, nowhere to lay his head. He comes to your door, to your home, not as brother to brother or fellow colleague; he comes as a mendicant to a master, seeking bread and clothing, begging lodging for the love of Christ. Do you recognize him as one Christ has sent? He does not come alone: Christ comes with him. Welcome him with rejoicing, refresh him gratefully, serve him devotedly with fear and great reverence: it is Christ you welcome, Christ you refresh. Rejoice and be glad to have merited to enjoy such a guest! Blessed is the table where Christ is entertained, where God is refreshed! Luckless and wretched the table where no such feast is laid; how miserable the host, where the pauper is driven away, where the gates of mercy are closed to the poor! It is a wicked servant whose heart fails to fling open the coffers of loving-kindness to the poor. *Cf. Mt 24:48-51*

Are you not then compelled, Christian, to have compassion for your fellow servant? Was it not the Lord of the poor who gave you what you have? Was not the Creator of the poor your Creator? Did he not create you equal in nature? Will you not depart this life in one and the same condition? Be touched then by your common lot. To works of mercy apply yourself to the utmost: welcome the wretch, embrace the beggar and the wayfarer, refresh the famished, and clothe the naked.

Christ himself accepts your alms to that poor brother; do not refuse to open your hand. I beg you, reader: never shun the pauper, but rush to welcome him the moment you lay eyes on him. Hasten to adore him, however mangy or leprous he may be, however filthy his rags, however fetid his breath.[20] Clasp him in the arms of charity, and in all charity grant whatever he asks. In truth it is Christ you give to, Christ who accepts—as he himself assures you. And it is he who will reward you on judgment day, for all eternity.

Having said this, Jesus was troubled in spirit and said, 'In truth I tell you, one of you is going to betray me.' Jesus is troubled by our weakness, not by his power: our weakness, not his power, churns in him. He suffers it, he willingly accepts it, so as to free us from despair. To be *troubled in the spirit* is to suffer that turmoil of the loving heart as when some urgent cause compels a separation of the weeds from the wheat before the day of harvest: excommunication, that is, before the day of judgment.[21] To be *troubled in the spirit* is one thing; to be troubled in the flesh is quite another. The one is fear and anxiety; the latter is carnal passion. It was in the spirit, not in the flesh, that the Lord was troubled as he was about to disclose his betrayal, not because he had just then sud-

[20] The details recall the practice of Saint Francis, the founder (in 1209) of the Friars Minor; Christ in the person of the beggar recalls the Life of Saint Martin of Tours, the *Vita sancti Martini* of Sulpicius Severus, whose language Ogier echoes *(petenti in Christi nomine)*. On *scabiosus sive leprosus* see n. 18.

[21] 'Before the day of judgment' suggests monastic exclusion (*excommunicatio*, cf. RB 23-28); the allusion to the parable of the wheat-tare (Mt 13:24-30) is correspondingly altered from 'at the time of' to 'before' the harvest.

denly apprehended it and was troubled by the unexpected evil, but because it would at last be made known. And it troubled him that the one who was leaving him was about to deliver him up to his enemies. Just as Jesus was troubled by his own imminent suffering, when the hour of his passion was drawing nigh and he said, *Now my soul is troubled; what shall I say?,* *Jn 12:27*
so even now his betrayer's present peril unsettled him. *'One of you'*, he says, *'is going out now to betray me. One of you,* but not one united by the bond of love; *one of you* is bound *to betray me.'*

The disciples looked at each other, wondering whom he meant. Do you suppose that Peter and the holy apostles could enter the secret recesses of the Lord's thoughts and, encountering there something so sinister, not be greatly troubled? The pallor of their faces betrayed the grief that overcame their minds. Yet no grief was betrayed by the one whose frenzied breast concealed the cunning fox: the one about to wreak prodigious grief did not grieve! O goodness of the Creator, O loving-kindness of the Redeemer who wishes none to be lost but all to be saved! He makes a point *Cf. 2 Pet 3:9*
of not naming his betrayer, lest Judas, found out, become even more rash and shameless. Jesus manifests the crime, but leaves room for remorse, so that the traitor, seeing he can no longer hide, might repent. But this son of perdition felt not the slightest twinge of regret; now even worse off than before, Judas is past all return in the affections of his heart. Meanwhile those whose hearts were wracked by an immense storm of grief began to look

about at each other, *wondering whom he meant.* Each knew his own conscience but could not know his neighbor's.

The disciple Jesus loved was reclining next to Jesus, leaning on his breast. How fortunate that disciple, with whom the author of present and future life was so familiar! How greatly honored[22] to have the venerable breast of Jesus, creation's Lord, as a resting place for his head! Oh how well one rests who rests on the breast of Christ! O blessed apostle of God, disciple of Christ, blessed John! Might it be granted to me to kiss and bathe with tears the feet of him on whose breast you merited to sleep! Oh that I might contemplate at least from afar the face of him on whose breast you slumbered!

In recounting the moment, John speaks of himself indirectly rather than appear to vaunt himself. By 'bosom' or 'breast' is meant that secret place from which the Godhead drinks its mystery.[23] With respect to the others, Jesus loved John not more, but more familiarly, so that John might depart this life in peace rather than through suffering. It is to John *Peter made a sign to ask whom he meant,* for Peter knew that Jesus favored John with a certain privilege of love and would not conceal from him the secret of his divinity. *So, leaning against Jesus' breast,* John asks him who it is, and in virtue of the fact that he did not fear to ask

Cf. Jn 21:20-23

[22] Ultimately, Ps 138:17; the immediate source is the introit *Mihi autem nimis honorati* from the Common of Apostles (*GR* 425).

[23] *Illud secretum de quo bibit divinitas sacramentum:* the construction is vaguely reminiscent of Tertullian; Ogier's general argument would lead us to expect instead 'that intimacy through which [John] tastes the mystery of Christ's divinity'.

the Master about his betrayer, being as he was in the bosom of divinity, the Master of truth ordained to reveal heaven's secret to him. *'Lord'*, John asks, *'who is it?* Who is this unhappy and accursed man? Who is your betrayer? Do not conceal him from me, to whom you have deigned to reveal the secrets of your divinity!' And the Lord tells him, *'It is the one to whom I give the piece of bread that I dip in the dish.'*

And when he had dipped the piece of bread he gave it to Judas, son of Simon Iscariot. The dipping of the bread signifies the feigning of Judas, the false friend come to supper. (Dipping does not cleanse, it stains.) Now this *bread,* dipped and given to Judas: what or who might it have been? Stay with me here, reader, I will not long keep you in suspense. But let us first recall that 'bread' has many meanings in holy scripture. It sometimes signifies the Lord, sometimes spiritual grace, sometimes the understanding of godly doctrine, sometimes even the discovery of heretics.[24] Bread may symbolize relief in our present life, the enjoyment of human delights. The Lord says of himself, *I am the living bread that has come down from heaven.* We therefore do not stray from the path of truth in saying that the *bread,* dipped *Jn 6:51*
and given to the betrayer, was the Lord.

Judas received the bread *dipped,* because he reckoned that the Lord Jesus was man merely and not God. He ate the morsel, the hearthbread,[25] soaked, in that although he

[24] On this last cf. 'the bread of falsehood' (Prov 23:3).
[25] *Panem subcinericium,* cf. Gen 18:6.

believed Jesus would die, he did not believe that he would rise again. This most blessed bread was dipped and soaked when Jesus' feet were fastened to the cross for our salvation, when his face was no longer comely or beautiful. The Jews, whom Judas represents, ate this bread dipped when they consented to his death but did not yet admit his resurrection. Like Judas, all who seek to weaken the Catholic faith are unfit to eat solid bread. All who deny Christ as the Virgin's son before all ages, and all who swerve from the firmness of faith, take their bread *dipped*.

Bread signifies spiritual grace, as in this passage from the prophet: *Whoever stops up his ears to matters of bloodshed and shuts his eyes to evil, dwells in the heights. Bulwarks of stone are his on high; he is given bread to eat, and does not want*
Is 33:15-16 *for water.* This means: whoever withholds consent from those who are swayed by carnal sin, or recoils from anything opposed to righteousness, the same, though still bound by the flesh to what is below, has joined his mind to the sublime. Trampling on the cast-off desires of earthly intercourse, he lifts himself up to his heavenly home by the examples of those who went before him. Amply sustained by spiritual graces, through the gift of contemplation *he is given bread.* The gift of spiritual grace has taken possession of him: fixed on heavenly things, he is suspended above all that is weak and base.

This very *bread*—grace—the Lord gave Judas. Judas received it *dipped,* for towards Jesus, the consummate source of virtue, Judas exercised not love but rancor. For him, whose face paled with false piety, the bread had to be dipped. Like Judas are all whose faces feign the religion they lack in their minds. Like him they don a habit of sanctity that does not clothe the heart: outwardly Christ's disciples, apparent lambs—inwardly lurking wolves, the devil's own. *Dipped* bread is what is eaten by those who are monks in name alone. In the monasteries of Saint Benedict, how many monks laugh while others (rightly) mourn, how many rejoice at that which they should grieve! Their stability is physical; their minds are elsewhere. Lazy at *lectio,* tardy to prayer, they sleep in church, but are wide awake in the refectory. They complain of long vigils, but long for merry feasts. They curse the cloister, but love the auditory.[26] 'Too ill' for choir, they frequent the infirmary 'to regain their strength' on meat![27] Forever murmuring and back-biting, dipped bread is what such wretches eat. On they trod in the steps of Judas the betrayer; unless they come to their senses, they too, like him, will be damned.

At that instant, after Judas had taken the bread, Satan entered him. Jesus then said, 'What you are about to do, do quickly!' Some are of the opinion that it was then that Judas received the body of Christ, but it should be recalled that the Lord had already distributed the sacrament of his Body and Blood to everyone, including Judas.[28] It was the *dipped* morsel that exposed the traitor. Many a false monastic

[26] *Auditorium,* the reception room for guests of the monastery.

[27] RB 36.9: 'To regain their strength, the sick who are very weak may eat meat, but when their health improves, they should all abstain from meat as usual.'

[28] Interpolating the synoptics (Mt 26:26-28, Mk 14:22-25, Lk 22:14-20).

receives the Lord's Body along with the sincerely pious of the community. He goes undetected—except for those 'dipped morsels' of backbiting, murmuring, disobedience, loose language, secret property, and still graver sins. Such a one is a Judas, not a monk; let him fear the consequences and repent. Satan *entered* Judas so as to possess him more fully, to ensnare him, to draw him away from the fellowship of the apostles. Satan used Judas, no longer in secret, but openly, fully, so as to slay him, to destroy him in the abyss of perdition.

And what the devil did to the betrayer he will not shrink from doing to those who are like him. He does not relinquish the slave he has long held in his thrall within the monastery, for he has already destroyed without that traitor who is no monk, but monks' companion merely. That the end of the world is at hand the devil does not doubt, and so he hides his cunning from the minds of the corrupted, so that he might smite unawares with sudden death those whom he has long bound in the wickedness of their ways. Many he permits to remain in the monastery until they die, so that through their depravity he may corrupt others and undo them; and because it is thought hardly possible, he is all the more able to destroy wretched souls, either within the monastery or outside it.

But with the Lord's protection let us shun the devil's wiles and pursue the meaning of Jesus' words: *What you are about to do, do quickly*. In saying this, Jesus does not enjoin Judas's evil, he foreshortens it, even as he hastens our good; for he desires the quick ensuing, not of his betrayer's doom, but of the salvation of the faithful. O boundless love, O incalculable loving-kindness, O unfathomable affection! '*What you are about to do* I long for, I desire, I seek! It is for this I came into the world. Would you sell me to the Jews? That is my will. Would you hand me over to be crucified? So be it! Would you have me killed? That is my very purpose and desire. *Do it*, then—and *quickly!*'

Jesus, my life, my every desire, unfailing, delectable, glorious sweetness, splendor of the angels, brightness and glory of the saints! How much you loved those for whom you longed to die! Life you won for us, death for yourself. Oh wretch that I am, he whom all this time I have wickedly offended, from whom—alas—I once shrank back, Jesus, my Lord and my God: would that I might suffer a thousand years of purgatory fire before my Lord Jesus were ever again to suffer offense from me! O reader, pour out your tears for me to the Lord, that he might hear my cry, open to me as I knock, console me as I mourn and grieve—might lovingly accept my repentance! O Lord Jesus, have mercy on me and grant me the delight of your countenance! You who deigned to die for sinners, let this sinner, I beg you, escape the eternal flames!

Pay heed, dearest brothers! Consider most carefully how greatly he is to be loved and cherished who suffered such vile reproach for our sake—he who, willing his own death, urged Judas to hasten its coming! *None of the others at table understood why he said this. Since Judas had charge of the common fund, some of them thought Jesus was telling him, 'Buy what we need for the festival', or telling him to give something to the poor.* Judas held the common purse in which offerings for their needs and those of the poor were kept. The practice has been instituted for the Church as well, not to give thought to the morrow nor strive for earthly gains, but to keep only what is necessary, lest the fear of penury cause her to abandon justice.

As soon as Judas had taken the piece of bread he went out. It was night. So the son of darkness went out to do the work of darkness. We who are Christ's disciples, let us see that we do not eat our bread dipped. Let us serve with our minds the religion with which we clothe our bodies. Let our dispositions maintain the holiness that our habits betoken, lest, reproved, we go out from the Lord in the hour of night
Rev 20:9 into the *lake of fire and sulfur,* there to be consumed together with the devil. Let us cling to the Lord with all our might, for it is good to
Cf. Ps 72:28 do so. May my soul cling to you, Lord! May it so cling to you that you never permit it to slip away from you, and that whenever it sighs for you, you are swift to console it. Grant this, Lord,

to whom be honor and glory
for ever and ever.
Amen.

IV

FOURTH HOMILY

When he had gone out, Jesus said, 'Now has the Son of Man been glorified. And in him God is glorified. God will glorify him in himself. Little children, I am with you but a little while. You will look for me and as I said to the Jews so now I am saying to you, 'Where I am going, you cannot yet follow me'.

John 13:31-33

THE MORE OFTEN we savor the Word of God in our mouths, the sweeter its taste in our hearts. Our minds, once imbued with the savor of the divine Word, rush with longing to open the alabaster of its ointment.[29] Having tasted a little we ever cry for more; we cannot bear further concealment of that treasure. I have long gathered the fruits of divine utterances in the orchard of the Lord, where he himself has lavished them. To anyone who eagerly longs to hold them in his hands, I am only too glad to bestow them. But I beg you, reader, do not cast them away from

[29] Cf. Mt 26:6, Mk 14:3; *alabastrum unguenti* distinguishes the anointing account from that of Jn 12:3.

the loves of your heart; for from them emanates a most delicious fragrance that heals the heart of the contrite and mends the scars of the wounded. This fragrance holds sway over every other sweetness, exceeding the scent of
Cf. Sir 24:20 balsam. Cling to that sweet scent with all your heart, and you will never perish; for this is the resurrection and the life. *All who believe in me,*
Jn 11:25 he promised, *though they die, shall live.* This aroma, this consummate perfume—the fragrance of every good, sweeter than milk and honey, more delicious than nectar, more precious than gemstones and gold—is the Lord Jesus, the Word made flesh, who *lived among*
Jn 1:14 *us*. May my words ever proceed from that Word, and let no other words resound than the Word himself, the Lord Jesus!

Judas, on whose account Jesus had said, *Not all of you are clean,* had left. Only those whom Jesus had cleansed remained behind with him. This foreshadows Christ's glorification,[30] where, separated from evil, he remains for ever with the saints. Well might we dwell on this joyous truth—but the love of Christ enjoins another discourse here, one that can neither be written nor read without tears. At the imminence of the suffering and death he will undertake for the salvation of the world, Jesus rejoices, is glad, and says, *Now has the Son of Man been glorified.*

O Lord Jesus, Son of man, son of Mary the Virgin, most illustrious, sweetest, most beautiful Lord, life of the saints and sweetness of the angels! How are you *glorified,* how made

[30] After the Resurrection; cf. Augustine, *Div. Quæst.* 83, 62.

bright? Are you not about to bear the executioner's fetters and lashes, the reproach of men, the reviling of the people, the spittle, the nails, the cuffing, the crown of thorns, the mock scepter of a reed, the cross, the lance?[31] Are you not about to be bound, your hands tied behind your back, and led before the judge? Are you not to be jeered as if you were a criminal? Is this your glorification? Are you not soon to climb the gibbet of the cross, there to bear its doleful torment? Is this your gladness? Is this your joy, to die for the salvation of humankind? What can be our response to this, dear brothers? Here let the voice be mute and let tears speak! Here let speech be silent and let weeping cry out! Christ our God, for no guilt of his own—but for joy!—draws a death that frees us from death everlasting. About to die, still he declares himself *glorified,* for in suffering and dying he glorifies his members, his faithful ones.

Good monk, good Christian, recall your years of sin with great compunction. Place Christ crucified on one side and your sins on the other. Contemplate the Lamb, contemplate Christ your Lord stretched out on the cross, suffering for your sake. Then consider the baseness of your flesh, the perverse affections of your soul, and pour out your tears to the Crucified, for he who so suffered for your sake is ready to save you. *Now has the Son of Man been glorified.* Son 'of Man', indeed, and not 'of men', for he was born of the pure and inviolate Virgin without man's seed, and he

[31] Cf. Venantius Fortunatus, *Pange lingua* (Homily I, n. 4).

was begotten in heaven of the Father without a mother, his mother a virgin, his father not knowing woman. This *Son of Man* has been greatly glorified, for whatever the Son of God had by nature, the Son of Man has by grace.

In this *Son of Man,* this son of the Virgin Mary, *God has been glorified.* How? His brightness has been manifested in the healing of the sick, the enlightening of the blind, the raising of the dead, his Father's will in all his works. *God glorified him in himself,* for he is one God with the Father, one godhead, one majesty; and this glorification is for all eternity. When death approached, Jesus, insofar as he was man, sought to be given this glorification by God when he said, *Now, Father, glorify me with that*
Jn 17:5 *glory I had with you before ever the world existed.* The glory that he had as God he wished to have as man, so that, united to the Word, his human nature, which could suffer and die, would quickly become immune to suffering and death. That is what is meant by *God will glorify him very soon.*[32]

And so, Christian, as you long to enjoy the inheritance of Christ, remember always to glorify God the Father with pureness of thought, calmness of speech, and orderliness of action in all your behavior, so that all who

[32] Ogier recasts the argument of these verses: in 13:31 *(Nunc clarificatus est Filius hominis, et Deus clarificatus est in eo)* he divides the clauses into two sentences, omitting the consequential conjunction between them and supplying the antecedent for the pronoun in the latter; the introductory conditional clause of 32 *(Si Deus clarificatus est in eo)* may not be Ogier's omission (it is not found in several manuscript transmissions of John), but he has changed the tense of the verb (to *clarificavit*) in the first of the remaining clauses *(et Deus clarificabit eum in semetipso),* but not the second *(et continuo clarificabit eum),* and suppressed the introductory conjunction in both.

see you may glorify God and bless him, saying, 'Blessed be God in heaven and on earth, who performs such deeds through his servants!' Furthermore, if with Christ you glorify the Father, you will with Christ share the same Father's inheritance. This is a great truth. It surpasses the value of the human condition, that of earthly man made of the dust, to rise up to Christ in heaven and reign with him there without end. Who has ever heard the like? Who has ever seen such a thing as this?[33] Truly it is greater by far than anything we can imagine! Truth himself declares, 'It is my will, Father, that *wherever I am, my servant* be *there also*. In truth then, monk of Benedict, be a good servant of Christ, not feigning your religion, not merely cloaking yourselves in holiness.[34] Do not forsake humility, but persevere unto death in your obedience. Then you will reign with Christ.

Jn 12:26

Little children, I am with you but a little while. He calls his disciples *little children* because their understanding was still childlike, not yet matured in the full vigor of faith; accustomed to the nourishment of milk, they were not yet ready to take solid bread.[35] They had known Christ in his humanity, but as their minds

[33] *Quis unquam audivit simile? quis unquam tale vidit aliquid?* Cf. Is 66:8, *Quis audivit unquam tale et quis vidit huic simile?*

[34] . . . *religionem non simulans, sanctitatem non pallians;* cf. Pomerius (fifth century), *De vita contemplativa,* on false monks: *religionis imaginariæ nomine palliati* ('cloaked in the name of a religion in appearance only'—itself perhaps a paraphrase of Augustine *Sermon* 9: *palliatur nomine christiano*). The *pallium* ('cloak') is synonymous with monastic garb in the sixth century. In the *Regula ad monachos* of Aurelian of Arles, *pallium accipere* = 'become a monk'.

[35] On *teneritudo* as 'newness in the faith', see Augustine, *De peccatorum meritis; vivere lacte* recalls 1 Pet 2:2.

were still enveloped in darkness, they wavered in their understanding of his divinity.

We can also say that he called them *little* children because of the magnitude of his love. The littlest stand greatest in our affections. Thus it is natural that parents provide their youngest children with more delicate nourishment than they do their older ones, and to fondle and kiss them more frequently. And when cruel death snatches the youngest from this life, our bereavement is far keener than at the passing of adults. No greater grief than that of parents bereft of little children: oh how they unbosom the depths of their love, how they clasp their little ones in their arms, how they rain kisses upon them!

They also seem *little children* whom a parent's passing deprives of protection, even though they are yet linked by a chain of invincible love. So our Lord, with infinite loving-kindness, called his beloved disciples *little children* as he was about to go to his Father.

'*I am with you but a little while*. This *little while* that I am with you in the flesh, you can see me, you can discern my presence; but I shall soon take up the cross and undo death's dominion. The time and hour are coming quickly when I am reckoned *not a man but the*
Ps 21:7 *scorn of mankind, the contempt of the people*. Then *you will look for me* and long to follow me, but, stricken by the fear of death and not yet imbued with heavenly power, you will not be able to *lay down your lives* for me.[36] That is

[36] Cf. Jn 15:13. The verse, omitted in Homily XIV (which treats only vv. 12 and 14), is alluded to in Homily V ('Some of you may perhaps say, ". . . surely I

what I mean when I say, *where I am going, you cannot yet follow me.*[37] Through the eye of the needle, through the straits of suffering, through the torments of death, *I go to the Father. You cannot follow me now,* since, fearful and afraid, you are like the kid in its mother's milk, unfit for sacrifice. But the time and hour will come when, freed from your fear, you will be ready in my love to undergo punishment, not only of the cross, but of torment even more vile than anything you can imagine.'

Cf. Mt 19:24; 2 Sam 1:9; Ps 17:5

Cf. Ex 23:19; Lev 23:27

But a little while—O Lord Jesus, your love ever yet compels me to utter *a little while* longer, 'Jesus! Jesus, my Lord and my God! Life of my sinful soul, my pilgrim's prize!' How bitter for you that *little while*, when you became the scorn of men and the butt of their mockery, when you were *poured out like water and all your bones were disjointed*. In that *little while, the shepherd was struck and the sheep of the flock were scattered*. In that so bitter *little while* the comeliest of men *had no form or charm to attract us, no beauty to win our hearts*. In that *little while* my David—nay, rather, my Jesus, my Lord—drummed upon the drum of his flesh before the city gates.[38] *Eloi, Eloi,* he cried, *lama sabachthani? My God, my God, why have you*

Ps 21:15

Mt 26:31

Is 53:2

could not die for my brother as Christ willingly died for our salvation."') and cited in Homily XIII (n. 190).

[37] The citation of 13:33b begins in the previous sentence ('you will look for me'), omitting *et sicut dixi Iudæis;* Ogier's *nondum potestis me modo sequi* (for *non potest venire, et vobis dico modo*) appears to be based on Jesus' reply to Peter in 13:36 *(non potes me modo sequi)*.

[38] *Tympano suæ carnis tympanizabat,* cf. 2 Sam 6 (David dancing before the Ark to the accompaniment of *tympanis*, 'when the Ark of the Lord entered David's city'). Ogier's dual persona, David and the Son of David, prepares the cry of the Psalmist (Ps 21:1) on the lips of Jesus on the Cross.

Mk 15:34 *forsaken me?* In that *little while*, my Lady—your mother, the incorrupt, inviolate Virgin, Virgin before and after your birth—suffered the martyrdom not of the executioner's sword, but of her heart's harsh grief. How bitterly she wept, how bitterly she grieved! Could it be otherwise, as she saw her only child, the whole of her desire, stretched out on the cross, near death, his head drooping, breathing his last? May that *little while,* Lord Jesus, so bitter to you and to your most sweet mother, be bitter for me, too, just as if I too had stood near your cross![39] I cannot yet see my Lord dwelling with the Father; let me at least behold him dead upon his cross.

How blissful, how glorious was that *little while* for the thief who heard his Lord say,
Lk 23:43 *Today you will be with me in paradise.* Lord Jesus, what could be sweeter, more delightful, or more pleasing than to be with you in paradise? Nothing—utterly nothing! What then shall I say or do, still bound to the trials of this earthly pilgrimage, exiled from the delights of the paradise of my God? Good Jesus, be mine! Recall, my Saviour, what and why you suffered, and have mercy on me!

By that same loving-kindness, pray
Subdue our wickedness, and may
You spare this sinner by your grace
To gaze upon your radiant face.

In you my every heart's joy lies,
Who are my all, my future prize.

[39] Cf. Homily XII *In Praise of God's Holy Mother.*

Oh may my only glory be
In you, throughout eternity![40]

you who live and reign
with the Father and the Holy Spirit,
one God for ever and ever.
Amen.

[40] Verses 4 and 5 of the hymn *Iesu nostra redemptio* (*LH* 88), substituting the singular for the plural in lines 3/4 (*compotem/me* for *compotes/nos*), 5 *(meum gaudium* for *nostrum gaudium),* and 7 (*mea* for *nostra*).

V

FIFTH HOMILY

> *I give you a new commandment: love one another just as I have loved you. It is by your love for one another that everyone will recognize you as my disciples.*
>
> John 13:34-35

I GIVE YOU a new commandment: love one another just as I have loved you. Those who are not ignorant of the Lord's commandment must not neglect to live by it. *The servant who knows his master's will* and fails to do it *will be*
Lk 12:47 *given a great many strokes of the lash;* but the master whose servant does his will rewards him with many riches and honors, even as the Lord of all says to his disciples, *Blessed are you if you do what I command you.*[41] Sweet is the commandment our sweet Lord proposes here! He who *loved us and washed away our sins in*
Rev 1:5 *his blood* offers us a commandment of incomparable sweetness: a commandment of life, of salvation everlasting! On this commandment
Mt 22:40 *hangs the whole of the Law and the prophets.*

[41] Conflating Jn 13:17b *(beati eritis si feceritis ea)* and Jn 15:14 *(vos amici mei estis si feceritis quæ ego præcipio vobis).*

Whoever observes every commandment but fails in this *one,* the commandment of love, *is guilty of them all.*[42] Thus the Apostle dismisses as worthless, in the absence of loving-kindness, even the noblest gifts and virtues of the Spirit: *If I am without love, it will do me no good whatever.* *Jas 2:10* *1 Cor 13:3*

The commandment of love is that *pearl of great price* which the bride of the Beloved found and gave her all to buy.[43] This is the *ladder* of Jacob's dream that seemed to stretch to heaven;[44] the angels came down by it, and by it we ascend to the angels, for without it none can attain the heavenly realms. Scaling that ladder we come upon the very Lord of angels himself, who commands our mutual love. He instructs us to love one another, even as he desires that his servants love him with all their hearts. It is reasonable that a servant's affection for a master be commensurate to the affection shown by the master. How much more greatly then should a master be loved, when it is not the servant who stands by the lord, but the lord who steadfastly supports his servant! Yet even servants who love the Lord wholeheartedly have all they can do to observe his command with all their might. *Cf. Mt 13:46*

When a command is disregarded, the one who has issued it is slighted; thus those who do not truly love their neighbor disregard Christ's commandment and, thus, its author,

[42] Substituting *omnia mandata* for *totam legem.*

[43] A curious commingling of the pearl-merchant parable with the Song of Songs.

[44] Gen 28:12. Jacob's Ladder prefigures, in the Rule, the Twelve Degrees of Humility (RB 7).

Christ. Dear brothers, let us love Christ and keep his commandment, *for the command of the Lord is clear, and it gives light to the eyes* of the
Ps 18:9 mind; Christ's commands *are sweeter than honey that drips from the comb: observing them brings*
Ps 18:11, 12b *great reward*—namely, the Lord himself. Keep the rule of his precept, then, and await with confidence the author of the commandment as your prize. How excellent the commandment, how great the prize! Let us unswervingly observe it, so as to be worthy of Christ the Lord. It is this commandment he left his disciples as he was about to go to the Father. It is no less than the testament which he, about to die, bequeathed his heirs.

A new commandment, he calls it. In what sense is it new? It is found anew here, but this is not to say that it was not already known; for we find it written in the Old Testament:
Deut 6:5 *You must love the Lord your God*. It is *new,* rather, in that it bring newness to what is old, and youth to the elderly.[45] It is *new,* in that whoever *has been created according to God in the holiness and righteousness of truth* has *put off the*
Eph 4:24 *Old Man and put on the New.*[46] It is *new*, because humankind, once driven from paradise by the sword, is now daily borne across to heaven.

Many love themselves with an affection that does not rejoice in the way of truth; thus our Lord adds, *just as I have loved you.* Love and loving-kindness differ from one another

[45] *Veteres homines transformat in iuvenes,* cf. *Veterem hominem renovans salvator* (antiphon for the Octave of the Epiphany) and see next.

[46] Transposing *in iustitia et sanctitate veritatis.*

as genus and species.[47] Some love is good, some bad, and some is middling. Good love is loving-kindness itself, with which we love God above ourselves and above everything else, and with which we love our neighbor as ourselves. Bad love, shameless, sullied, and adulterous, is the enemy of loving-kindness. The two loves result in contrary and opposite conditions, the one leading to God, the other to the devil. One wins its possessor merit, glory, and life; the other, punishment, torment, and death. Middling love is that such as between children and parents, among kinfolk; it is also the love of things that are had justly and without peril. While it is not in league with lasciviousness, it is neither in union with loving-kindness. Thus middling love falls short as well, since it is not *just as I have loved you.*

Could anyone truly keep this commandment? Has ever anyone loved a neighbor even as Christ loved the apostles? Surely not!—but let us note that *just as* signifies similarity, not extent. We are to love one another the way he loved us. How, you ask? Listen: *For this is how God loved the world: he gave his only Son, so that everyone who believes in him may not perish but may have eternal life.* God the Father so *Jn 3:16*
loved us *that he did not spare his own Son, but gave him up for the sake of all of us.* Christ loved *Rom 8:32*
us so much that he gave himself up to death for us sinners and washed us from our sins in his blood, changing us from sinful to just, from

[47] The distinction is between *amor* and *caritas;* see Homily XIV, where a similar discussion is developed with regard to Jn 15:12 (a reiteration of the 'Rule of Love', as Ogier styles the New Commandment).

dead to alive, from earthbound to heavenbound, from partners of the beasts of burden to consorts of the angels.[48] Blessed be that Lover who in his commandment bids us to love one another just as he has loved us!

Some of you perhaps will say, 'I waver in the face of such love. I scarcely comprehend it. Surely I could not die for my brother, as Christ willingly died for our salvation!' It is precisely you I would remind again that *just as* expresses quality, not quantity. If you cannot walk at Christ's side, at least follow in his footsteps from afar.[49] If you are not strong enough to love your neighbor more than yourself, as Christ did in dying for humankind, love him at least as much as you love yourself. Do for him what you would wish him to do for you. And should you say, 'I cannot do that either', then take my words as a recommendation rather than as an order; for if you cannot observe this, see to it at least that you do not do to another what you would not wish done to yourself. If you love your neighbor even this much, you have fulfilled the commandment. Let the cause of your love for your neighbor be God, not the neighbor: loving your neighbor for himself is no longer loving-kindness but middling love, or even—God forbid!—the worst kind of love. (Anyone so defiled, unless he repent, is deprived eternally of Christ's love.)

[48] Perhaps based on 2 Pet 1:4. The rhyming phrase *(de consortibus iumentorum consortes angelorum)* recalls the style of a short benediction before the Lessons of Vigils; it forms a similar refrain in Homilies IX and X.

[49] Cf. Bernard (*In laud.* I.8.): 'If perhaps you cannot follow him wherever he may go, be worthy to follow him when he graciously approaches'.

So, brothers, we whom Christ calls to be Christians must be founded in brotherly love, for only then shall we truly be Christians, spurning everything earthly, transitory, and changeable, rejecting every blind love and longing to cling solely to Christ. Only then are we worthy to be called—and to be—disciples of him who told his apostles, *It is by your love for one another that everyone will recognize you as my disciples.* It is in this that the children of light are distinguished from the children of darkness, the disciples of Christ from those of the devil: that they extend to each and all the embrace of loving-kindness. Excluding none from the bosom of love, loving-kindness embraces all, contains all, is open to all alike. It is that state of mind in which we clasp Christ to ourselves in love's embrace. Loving-kindness is love that encompasses heaven and earth; invincible love that yields neither to threat nor to punishment. It is the indissoluble bond of love and peace. It is the love of God that disdains the things of this world. The queen of the virtues, loving-kindness, fears no onslaught of vice, for Christ's blood is her dowry.[50] Bearing before her the banner of the cross,[51] she puts all foes to flight. None can withstand the power of loving-kindness; no evil can assail it.

Always and everywhere *love holds fast.* When *1 Cor 13:7*
the embattled David cried out to the Lord, *Take up your arms and your shield, arise and help*

[50] Cf. Acts 20:28. The 'queenship' of the virtues is assigned to humility by Hildegard *(Ordo virtutum)* and (with regard to its extensive treatment in the RB) by Benedict.

[51] Cf. the passion hymn of Venantius Fortunatus, *Vexilla regis prodeunt* (*LH* 58).

Ps 34:2 *me,* love was that armament. And when the same David rejoiced in its protection, he sang,
Ps 5:13 '*You surround us with favor, Lord, as with a shield.* All whom this shield[52] protects shall safely penetrate the assault troops of the foe. This is the steel-hard rock that cannot be broken, that smashes all against itself. It is the *stoutly armed*
Lk 11:21 *warrior* who lays his enemy low by his might, and who slays and destroys *with the two-edged*
Rev 2:16 *sword* his nefarious foe and all his hosts. This is the friend of the eternal King who does not fear to enter confidently into his presence. So
Sg 3:7 love enters Solomon's couch, disdaining rest unless it repose upon the breast of Christ. If this queen of virtues reigns among us, brothers, then all will know, both great and small, that we are truly the Lord's disciples. No one who lacks loving-kindness belongs to the author of love's commandment. It follows then that one who does not love his neighbor does not love God, and not to love is to hate. Anyone who hates his brother hates love's source. So brothers, as we have been gathered together in the love of Christ,[53] let us love Christ the Lord with all our hearts and minds, and love our neighbor as ourselves. For love of him, let us not merely not hate our enemies but love them, even as we love our friends. This is the school of Christ,[54] wherein we

[52] The round metal *clypeus* described here, in contrast to the large, rectangular leather-covered wooden *scutum* mentioned in the two citations from the Psalter. Both defensive weapons are linked in Jer 46:3 *(præparate scutum et clypeum . . . ad bellum).*

[53] *Ubi caritas,* antiphon for Maundy Thursday (*GR* 168).

[54] Cf. the *dominici schola servitii* of RB Prologue 45 and the 'school of love' of the *Charta caritatis* of the early Cistercians.

learn the lessons of the Holy Spirit. Believe me, brothers, anyone who leaves this school and fails to persevere in its teaching is lost for ever. But to Love's lovers, Christ's disciples, what a multitude of sweetness, what riches of everlasting bliss, what joys of never-ending happiness does he himself bestow on us:

he who in perfect trinity reigns and lives,
blessed God for ever and ever!
Amen.

VI

SIXTH HOMILY

Simon Peter said, 'Lord, where are you going?' Jesus answered, 'You cannot follow me now where I am going, but later you shall follow me.' Peter asks Jesus, 'Why can I not follow you now? I will lay down my life for you!' Jesus answered, 'Will you lay down your life for me? Before the cock crows you will disown me three times. Do not let your hearts be troubled. You trust in God, trust also in me. In my Father's house there are many dwelling-places. If it were otherwise I would have told you this, namely, that I am going now to prepare a place for you. I shall return to take you to myself, so that you may be with me where I am.'

John 13:36-38; 14:1-4

Simon Peter said, 'Lord, where are you going?' Peter is responding here to what the Lord had said earlier, *'Where I am going you cannot follow me,* words Peter could not have heard without bitter grief. Jesus has meanwhile given a *new commandment,* but Peter lingers over what was said moments before. Just as the hand instinctively fondles a wound, so the tongue rushes to reveal the heart's bitterness:

what inwardly the mind conceives in grief, the tongue with frankness outwardly gives birth. Thus Peter cannot conceal the pain that grips his heart on hearing of the Lord's impending absence; he can scarcely bear to hear the Master speak further. Overwhelmed with grief, he bursts in on those words of great authority. Saddened to the core he cries aloud, 'Grant it and we will observe intact and undefiled that mutual love you commend to us, and whatever else you command we will do; but when you tell us that we cannot follow you where you are going, we are filled with great and bitter sorrow. *Where is it you are going?* Why do you abandon us? For whom do you desert us? Without you, Lord, what point is there to living? Do not leave me, Lord, do not forsake me!'

The Lord tells Peter, *'You cannot follow me now where I am going, but later you shall follow me.* I am not abandoning you; *I am going* before you, to make a path where none is now, to pave a road where only a by-way now leads. *I am going* in order to give certainty where now there is fear, life where now there is death. *You,* fearful and frightened, not yet strengthened, *cannot follow me now.* I go before you, reviled, to the cross to die, and so, to rise again and ascend into heaven. But you, not yet steeled for suffering, are not yet fit for the prize. *You cannot follow me* in life, since you are not yet ready to die for my sake, *but later you shall.* Upon you I will send the Holy Spirit of my Father to confirm you, *and then you will be my witnesses not only in Jerusalem but throughout Judea and Samaria, and indeed to earth's*

Act 1:8 *remotest end.* You will be ready to follow me then.'

Peter asks Jesus, 'Why can I not follow you now? I am not afraid of punishment or death. *I would be ready to go to prison with you, and to*
Lk 22:33 *death.* What do you mean, *I cannot follow you now? I will lay down my life for you!'* Then the Lord tells him, *'Lay down your life for me?* You deceive yourself, Peter. You are not yet ready, not yet clothed in that great virtue. If you were, you would indeed give your life. Instead, before you know it, you will deny life for fear of my death, and so you will slay your soul. You will deny being my disciple, and so you will slay your spirit. The time draws nigh, the hour is nearly here, when to save your skin you will thrice disown your Lord. *The cock shall not crow until you deny me thrice.* However heroic your words now, Peter, mark mine well: *before the cock crows you will disown me three*
Mt 26:34 *times.* Whether before the first crowing or the second,[55] Peter, your denial will be threefold.'

When the disciples hear this, fear and quaking grip them, and sorrow overwhelms them. Peter, of all the foremost in holiness, devoutest in his love, stoutest in his faith! Was it not Peter who shortly before this had declared Jesus to be God's Son? Had he not confessed, *You are the Christ, the Son of the living*
Mt 16:16 *God?* Peter will disown Jesus three times before cock-crow! They reel to imagine such a

[55] Perhaps an attempt to reconcile this saying, which is essentially the same in Matthew and Luke (22:34), with Mark's twofold denial (*priusquam gallus vocem bis dederit, ter me es negaturus,* Mk 14:25); the verse from Matthew is cited once again in the commentary that follows.

thing. What of themselves, then? Surely the same must befall them when Jesus was no longer among them to guide them. They cannot yet fully believe that Jesus would rise again on the third day; thus the thought that he who was even now speaking to them would soon be dead, made them mourn and wail as if with one voice. Convinced of their dearest Master's impending death and absence, they mourned him as dead even as they beheld him still alive. They see themselves suddenly bereft of the sweet streams of his teaching, his healing of the sick, his raising of the dead to life, bereft of that dearest gentle familiarity he had always shown them. Oh most bitter was their weeping then, my brothers; no one could console them then! *Cf. Mt 26:75*

But the Lord saw them weeping bitterly and wanted to console them about his death. *Do not let your hearts be troubled.* I expect, though, that, without wishing to, he only incited them further to grief with these words. Indeed, I wonder that the Lord Jesus himself did not *groan in the spirit and was* not himself *troubled* when he spoke to them. And when he added *You trust in God, trust also in me,* it was, I believe, as if my Lord Jesus—blessed be he for ever—were saying, 'Do not let my absence and death trouble you. I have the power to lay down my life and to take it up again. Three days dead this body will lie in the tomb, and after three days it will rise again immortal and impervious to suffering. For three days and three nights Jonah lay in the belly of the whale; so the Son of Man will rise again from *Jn 11:33*

the dead on the third day.[56] *Do not let your hearts be troubled.* I who raised up Lazarus can raise up this body of mine. I who raised up the widow's son will not be held up longer than three days by death. *You trust in God, trust also in me.* Do not be afraid about the death of my flesh: I am God, who will raise up the flesh.
Jn 5:36 *My works bear witness to me.* If you trust in God, it follows that you ought to trust in me, since I am God.'

Then, lest they doubted that they were to dwell with God in Christ alive for ever, he told them: *In my Father's house,* where you will reign with me in everlasting life, *there are many dwelling-places,* that is, degrees of worthiness.[57] For *the sun has its own splendor, the moon another*
1 Cor 15:41 *splendor, and the stars yet another splendor.*[58] The house of God the Father is one of his own predestining and foreknowledge.[59] Everyone who has been perfected has a dwelling-place there; each has been paid the same wage, the
Cf. Mt 20:1-16 *denarius* of life eternal. We may also understand *my Father's house* as the temple and Kingdom of God, that is, the just, among whom there are many differences. The various degrees of

[56] Conflating Mt 12:40 *(sicut enim fuit Ionas in ventre ceti tribus diebus et tribus noctibus)* and Lk 24:46 *(sic oportebat Christum . . . resurgere a mortuis tertia die).*

[57] *Dignitates:* cf. Gregory the Great, *Homelia in Ezechielem* (PL 76:977B): *diversæ beatorum dignitates erunt.*

[58] Ogier's use of Paul on the manner of the resurrection is remarkable; the latter chapters of 1 Corinthians have clearly been Ogier's sustained *lectio,* however his pæan to *caritas* echoes chapter 13, and the present argument may reflect Paul's examination of the diversity of spiritual gifts (which include *operatio virtutum*) of chapters 12 and 14.

[59] Cf. Rom 8:29 *(quos præscivit et prædestinavit),* perhaps through a source such as Ps-Augustine, *Hypermnesticon contra Pelagianos: [Deus] quidquid antequam sit præscit, prædestinat.*

worthiness are rooms in the same house; they have already been prepared, through predestination. *He chose us in Christ,* the Apostle says, *before the world was made.* Our dwelling-places are predestined, yet it is through operation,[60] through meritorious action, that we are to hope for them; for Paul also says, *Those so destined he called; those he called he justified.*

Eph 1:4

Rom 8:30

'In my Father's house, merit is variously rewarded. *If it were otherwise*—if these various dwelling-places did not exist—*I would have told you* this, namely, *that I am going now to prepare a place for you.* I do not need to prepare any further dwelling-places there, since they have been appointed in advance.' But since they do not yet exist in operation—since what must be done in order for us to enjoy their effects remains to be accomplished, our Lord adds, *'And if it were otherwise—if these various dwelling-places did not exist—I would have told you this, namely, that I am going now to prepare a place for you so that you may be with me where I am.* Your dwelling-place in my Father's house is foreordained, but you cannot now attain it without great toil.[61] They are yours through God's grace alone, as a gift; I want you to have them now from me.[62] I depart from you according to my divinity, so as to make ready

[60] *Operatione:* so Cassian, *Institutes.* Ogier's reading of Paul in this context is unclear, especially in light of a twofold use of *operatio* as the 'meritorious action' of the Christian, and as the 'divine activity' (redemptive Passion) of Christ; both senses are further entwined in the *operation* of the Spirit.

[61] Perhaps an allusion to 1 Cor 3:8 or 15:58; or, in view of what follows, a reference to the *magnus labor* of Christ's Passion.

[62] In light of Ogier's various distinctions of predestination and operation, *ex gratia Dei et dono,* with regard to the former, may echo his reading of Augustine, *De praedestinatione sanctorum* 1.10.19: *prædestinatio est gratiæ præparatio, gratia vero*

for you according to my humanity that unspeakable bliss which I prepared for you from the beginning of the world. The ineffable joys of everlasting life are not yours to enjoy unless I rid myself of this flesh and clothe myself in it again. I will go up to heaven and will send you the Holy Spirit, so that he may teach you to perform meritorious acts through the working of grace, and that you may possess the kingdom of everlasting bliss that was prepared for you before all time.'

The Lord Jesus daily prepares his faithful a place when he shows his Father the suffering he endured in his flesh for the salvation of humankind. He gives us now, through his humanity, the place he prepared for us through his divinity. *'Cut off from me'*, he says, *'you can*
Jn 15:5 *do nothing'*.[63] Thus, whenever we perform good works, in our fasting and our prayer, in our reading and our meditation, in bewailing our sins and in longing to see Christ, in visiting the sick and feeding the starving, and in all those other salutary actions the telling of which is long,[64] the Lord prepares for us a blessed place in heaven. For when he comes to reward us, each according to his works, he will lead us into those most blessed dwelling-places if we have lived in his faith and love. *'I shall return to take you to myself,* he tells us, *so that you may be with me where I am.* When I appear in judgment, I will lead you into those dwelling-

iam ipsa donatio; on his interpretation here of the latter, cf. Phil 3:20-21, *secundum operationem qua etiam possit subicere sibi omnia.*

[63] Cited out of sequence here, the phrase—and the verse it comes from—is omitted in the commentary on the surrounding verses in Homily XI.

[64] Cf. RB 4: *Quæ sunt instrumenta bonorum operum.*

places where you will be with me for ever.' O joyous, O supreme bliss, to dwell with Christ, to reign with him, to see his glory, his beauty! Who will be able to attain it?

O Jesus, may I be found worthy to see you! My Jesus, I trust in God; I trust in you—and yet my heart is troubled. It would not be so had I heard you tell me, *Do not let your heart be troubled,* but because I cannot see you now—not because I do not trust you—my soul is greatly disturbed. There is nothing else I want, nothing else I seek, nothing I desire and long for, but to see my Lord and God. I seek and do not find you; I call and you do not answer. I desire to see you and I cannot, for you yourself are my desire. O Truth, you are my witness: my heart is sorely troubled, but I trust that in your mercy I may yet see you. Then I shall be satisfied by you and with you and in you and through you, not by dint of my merits but through your manifold great mercy. I shall see you, God my Saviour, when you come to judge the world by fire. But I beg you, directly and through the Mother who bore you, that when you come in judgment you draw me to yourself, where you are now. May I be with you and with your disciples, to whom you said, as you were going to the Father, *You know the way to the place where I am going*. For they knew that you were going to the Father, and that you yourself are the way by which one comes to the Father,

Cf. Sg 3:2

with whom you live and reign
in unity with the Holy Spirit,
God for ever and ever.
Amen.

VII

SEVENTH HOMILY

'You know the way to the place where I am going.' Thomas said to him, 'Lord, we do not know where you are going, so how can we know the way?' Jesus said, 'I am the Way; I am Truth and Life. No one can come to the Father except through me.' Philip said to him, 'Show us the Father and it will be enough.' Jesus said to him, 'Have I been with you all this time, and still you do not know me? Anyone who has seen me, Philip, has seen the Father; so how can you say, "Show us the Father"? Do you not believe that I am in the Father and the Father is in me? If we existed separately we could not work inseparably. Amen, amen I tell you,[65] *whoever believes in me will perform the same works as I do myself, and will perform even greater works, because I am going to the Father. Whatever you ask for in my name I will do.'*

John 14:4-14

WHEN THE LORD TOLD his disciples, *You know the way to the place where I am going,* Thomas doubted. *Lord,* he said, *we do not know where you are going, so how can we know*

[65] Omitting the head of 14:12, *Alioquin propter opera credite* ('for that matter, believe by virtue of the works themselves').

the way? Thomas, who was called Didymus (that is, 'of two minds, doubting'),[66] doubted; and doubtless he believed his fellow disciples did as well. But the Master of truth wins him over. *Jesus said, 'I am the Way; I am Truth and Life.'* Of course they know him, they know he is *the Way;* they therefore know the way. They know he is *Truth and Life;* they must then know the truth and the life to which he must travel. For he is *the Way* by virtue of his being man, and he is *Truth and Life* by virtue of his being God. Thus through himself as *the Way* he was going to *Truth and Life,* for by virtue of his being a glorified human he was returning to himself as God. They thought they did not know this, he plainly proves they do:

'I am the Way by which to go, *the Truth* to which to come, *the Life* in which to dwell.
'I am the Way without misstep, *the Truth* without mistake, *the Life* that knows no death.
'I am the Way by way of example, *the Truth* of my instruction, *the Life* as your reward.
'I am the Way to heaven wending, *the Truth* unbending, *the Life* unending.
'I am the Way, broad and spacious, *the Truth*, mighty and copious, *the Life*, delightful and glorious.
'I am the Way of those commencing, *the Truth* of those advancing, *the Life* of those attaining.

[66] Jn 11:16; Διδυμος, 'the Twin', is the equivalent of *geminus,* but the punning association with *dubius* has become folk etymology.

'*I am the Way* shining and serene, *the Truth* living free from blame, *the Life* contented and fulfilled.
'*I am the Way* of the cross, *the Truth* in the depths of hell, *the Life* of Easter joy.
'*I am the Way* where trial and torture have no sway, *the Truth* where falsehood and error have no say, *the Life* where the dead see anew the light of day.
'*I am the* straight *Way, the* whole *Truth, the Life* everlasting.
'*I am the Way* of reconciliation, *the Truth* of retribution, *the Life* of bliss eternal'.[67]

'*No one can come to the Father except through me*, at once man and God, one with the Father. No one can come to me as *Truth and Life* without coming through me as *the Way:* no one can come to me as God unless through me in my human form. By taking human flesh I set a trap wherein mortals may catch truth and life.[68] I make *the Way* by dying, rising again,

[67] Ogier's remarkable elevenfold trope (perhaps one variation for each of the remaining disciples?) is the single most sustained poetic exercise in the Homilies; each *via-veritas-vita* triolet explores a particular syntactical device, giving rise to a variety of rhymes: (1) *per quam eundum, ad quam veniendum, in qua permanendum;* (2) *sine errore, sine falsitate, sine morte;* (3) *in exemplo, in præmisso, in præmio;* (4) *habilis, irrevocabilis, interminabilis;* (5) *lata et spatiosa, potens et copiosa, delectabilis et gloriosa;* (6) *incipientium, proficientium, pervenientium;* (7) *lucens et serena, vivens absque pœna, felix et amœna;* (8) *in patibulo, in inferno, in resurrectionis gaudio;* (9) *in qua non est spina vel tribulus, in qua non est falsitatis stimulus, in qua reviscit mortuus;* (10) *recta, perfecta, sine fine mensura;* (11) *reconciliationis, retributionis, æternæ beatitudinis*. The whole is densely packed with scriptural and liturgical allusions.

[68] As a figure of the Incarnation, the word *fovea* ('a trap for catching game', 'pitfall') is striking, especially as traps and snares are conventionally emblematic of evil in the Scriptures; *facio foveam,* with its unspecific verb (instead of *fodio*) suggests Ps 7:16 *(incidit in foveam quam fecit),* though the basis of a positive association may lie in Wis 10:13 *(descenditque sapientia cum illo in foveam).*

and ascending to heaven; there I am *Truth and Life,* true and eternal God.'

Wretched man—poor earthling, slumped, bent over, sickly and weak as he is—could never by himself return to the joys of paradise from which he had been expelled. Nor could he, by himself, ascend to God. God came to man; God became man: *the Word became flesh.* *Jn 1:14*
God drew near to man, the Word to the flesh, so as to bear us up not merely to paradise, but to heaven, where, ever blessed, he is *Truth* that is and ever was, *Life* that had no beginning and will have no end. Thus for us earthly mortals God-made-man became *the Way* and led us to himself, true God, having become man by a Word.

'If you knew me, you would know my Father too. From now on you do know him; you have seen him. I and the Father are one: you know him as *Jn 10:30*
he was made known to you through me; you saw him in your hearts when you saw in me his likeness.' Philip cannot comprehend that Jesus is wholly like the Father. Like some of his fellows, he thinks the Father is somehow greater, better than Jesus—thus he knows neither the Father nor the Son. *'Show us the Father'*, he says, *'and it will be enough.* Show us the One who is greater than you; who, unlike you, has sufficient resources in himself.'[69]

At this Jesus chides them for knowing neither the Son nor the Father. *'Have I been*

[69] Ogier strikes a particularly defensive tone at any perceived diminution of Christ's equality with the Father; this response will be provoked again in Homily IX (*Semonem quem audistis non est meus,* where Ogier's objection is cloaked as an issue of syntax) and Homily X *(Pater me maior est)* and may also account for the omission, in Homily IV, of *Si Deus clarificatus est in eo . . .* (see n. 32).

with you all this time, and still you do not know me? You really do not know me, for if you did *you would know my Father as well.'* No one knows the Son who believes the Father to be better than he, not because the Father is of one kind and the Son of another, but that they are wholly alike. That is why Jesus then says, *'Anyone who has seen me, Philip, has seen the Father; so how can you say, "Show us the Father"?* Since I am wholly like the Father, how can you ask this? You seek, not one who is like me, but one you think is better. Why do you wish to know separately what is inseparable? *Do you not believe that I am in the Father and the Father is in me?*[70] You cannot see it, but at least believe it. *What I say to you I do not speak of my own accord,* since I who speak am not of myself alone. What I do I return to Him from whom I am who do it: *it is the Father, abiding in me, who does the works.* Among these are the words I speak; they are good works because they edify, and because in me my Father performs them. *Do you not believe that I am in the Father and the Father is in me?* If we existed separately we could not work inseparably. *Amen, amen I tell you,*[71] *whoever believes in me will perform the same works as I do myself, and will perform even greater works, because I am going to the Father.'*

Amen is doubled here so as to affirm all the more what is said. The hebrew word has several meanings. It is an adverb that affirms

[70] The verb is modified here (14:10), and in its reiteration (14:11), from plural to second person singular.

[71] Omitting the head of 14:12, *Alioquin propter opera credite* ('for that matter, believe by virtue of the works themselves').

and that expresses a wish or desire, as when one says, 'May this good befall you', and you answer *'Amen'*. When at the end of a prayer we hear 'for ever and ever', we respond *'Amen'*, as if to say, 'What you ask of the Lord we also desire'. In the idiom of the Gospels, *Amen* (verily, in all truth) is affirmative, and when it is doubled it affirms all the more what is said. When the Lord says *Amen, amen,* the truth of what follows is to be believed without the slightest doubt. A single word would have sufficed for him to be believed, but his disciples were still weak and wavering in the faith, which was operating through love. They did not yet believe that his power and the Father's were one and the same. Thus he prefaces his declaration with a twofold *Amen*, lest what he promises be met with the least doubt.[72] *'Amen, amen—in all truth—I tell you, whoever believes* that I am one with the Father to be venerated and loved—*will perform the works I myself* now do and shall afterwards do through anyone who believes in me. The works I will perform through the believer *will be greater* still, *because I am going to the Father.*' He goes to Him from whom in his godhead he never departed.[73]

It is of the greater merit to believe in him now, in that we do not see him, than were we in fact to see him. Once ascended to the *Cf. Jn 20:29*

[72] In fact, the doubling of *Amen* is a stylistic peculiarity unique to the Gospel of John, where it occurs twenty-five times; this is its fifth and last occurrence in Ogier's source text (he has omitted it twice, in citing 13:16 and 38, and cited it twice, in 13:20 and 21).

[73] See Homily I., n. 5.

Father, even greater marvels were performed
through him than those he performed in his
person. It is recorded that a woman was cured
of a serious hemorrhage by touching the
Mt 9:20-23 fringe of Jesus' cloak, but after his ascension,
many were cured from every infirmity by
Act 5:15 Peter's shadow. Jesus performed greater works
through Peter than those he did himself. Be-
fore he ascended into heaven, a few were con-
verted to God through his preaching, but after
his ascension, five thousand are recorded to
have been converted to the Lord by Peter's
preaching on one day alone, and three thou-
Act 4:4; 2:41 sand on another. Before he ascended into
heaven he was known only in Judea, whereas
after his ascension he made himself known
through his apostles to all the world, for *the*
Ps 18:5 *message reaches the whole world*. He came into
Jn 1:10 the world *and the world did not recognize him,*
but after he left the world and ascended into
heaven, his fame thundered throughout the
Cf. Ps 17:14 world. Speaking for the Lord, the prophet
Ps 140:10 David says, '*I am one apart until I pass over,*[74] for
I am unknown until I pass over to the Father.
But *when I am lifted up from the earth, I shall draw*
Jn 12:32 *all things to myself.*' Greater are the works he
now performs through his faithful than those
he performed while he rested upon his mother's
lap.

'*Whatever you ask for in my name I will do:* anything for your soul's well-being that you ask for I will give you, immediately or after a while.' Many, we know, are goaded by evil temptations. Their struggle is burdensome and

[74] *Singulariter sum ego donec transeam*; my translation follows Blaise (*DAC* 762).

laborious, and, weeping and grieving, they ask in the Lord's name to be delivered. Fearing failure in the fight, they beg the Lord to help them from succumbing. But when such aid from the Lord is not quickly forthcoming, they feel abandoned by him. When he delays they believe he does not care about them. In this they are mistaken: the Lord loves even more greatly those whom he allows to struggle alone with temptations. The greater the fight, ever greater the victory the Lord provides; the more valiant the combat, the more glorious the crown.

Let Christ's athlete not waver or doubt: who battles the cunning of the ancient serpent wages war for the prize of the joys of paradise. Let him not grow weary nor desert the battle. Let him bravely charge and keenly pursue the fight. Let him be strong and bold of heart,[75] for then the Lord will come quickly and *break the arm of the wicked and the evil* with his mighty *Ps 9:36*
hand. When at last the cunning foe is conquered, the valiant in Christ will reign with him throughout eternity. Let us recall the words of David the prophet: *The Lord is near to the broken-hearted*, and *though hardships without number beset the upright, the Lord rescues them from them all.* *Ps 34:19, 20*

Seek whatever you will from the Lord, so long as it is for the salvation of your soul. Do not be dismayed if it is delayed: what is delayed is not taken away, and when at length it is had it is all the more dearly possessed. In his name let us ask for what he taught his disciples to

[75] Cf. Ps 26:14. On the figure of the athlete, cf. *Tractatus,* n. 71.

ask for when he said, *'You should pray like this: Our Father in heaven, may your name be held holy, your kingdom come, your will be done on earth as in heaven. Give us today our daily bread. And forgive us our debts as we have forgiven those who are in debt to us. And do not put us to the test, but*
Mt 6:9-11 *save us from the Evil One.'* If we ask for anything that is at odds with that prayer, our prayer is in vain; but if we ask in his name for the salvation of our souls, he will grant it to us.

And lest they suppose that what he promised was to be done without the Father, he tells them next, *So that the Father may be glorified in the Son.* Whatever the Son does he does so that the Father might be glorified in him. *'If you ask for anything in my name, I will do it:* whatever you ask me to do as man, I will do it as God, *so that the Father might be glorified in the Son,* God in man united to himself.' In saying this he confirms what he said earlier, for the reiteration of a statement is the confirmation of the act.

Let us therefore ask him, dear brothers, that his grace go before us and come after us, and that it make us securely bent on good works. Let us ask him in his name alone, for he is surely greedy for whom Christ is not enough. Let all who possess the Lord say with
Ps 72:26 David, *My portion, God for ever,* for we can have nothing besides the Lord. All are blessed whose wealth is him alone, for no one can ever again be poor whose inheritance is the giver of all good. If anyone asks for silver or gold, for possessions and sundry furnishings, believe me, he does not ask it in Jesus' name. The Lord will not deign to become the inheritance of

anyone whose possession are so paltry, unless that person considers them less than dung for the Lord's love's sake. We whose portion is the Lord must not hinder ourselves with other obligations, for spending ourselves on any other office diminishes our service to nurturing our vocation and spiritual well-being. Let us then care for nothing beyond what it has been our lot to win as our inheritance, namely Christ himself, for love of whom we have renounced possessions and even our own wills. *RB 33.4*

The heir of this inheritance is truly blessed, for poverty no longer crimps anyone whose fortune is so great. This is our *share in the land of the living* that the prophet David affirms. It *Ps 141:6* was in preparation for this inheritance that the Apostle wrote, *Life to me, of course, is Christ, but then death would be a positive gain.* How *Phil 1:21* joyously he yearned for it when he said, *I want to be gone and to be with Christ!* And now, be- *Phil 1:23* cause he lived solely for Christ in this world, he reigns with him, blessed, in heaven. Now in his heavenly home, he is joined to him whom on the way he longed for with every desire. Dearest brothers, let us therefore ask the Lord for himself, and with our whole hearts seek nothing but him. Fixing our gaze on the great inheritance that is Christ, we shall attain it. May Christ see fit to bestow on us himself,

he who with the Father and the
Holy Spirit lives and reigns,
God for ever and ever.
Amen.

VIII

EIGHTH HOMILY

If you love me you will keep my commandments. I shall ask the Father, and he will give you another Paraclete to be with you for ever, even the Spirit of Truth, whom the world cannot receive, because it neither sees him nor knows him. You know him, for he dwells with you and will be in you.

John 14:15-17

FROM THIS CHAPTER ALONE we can conclude whether we truly love God. We love him in truth if we keep his commandments, for if we do not keep his commandments it is certain that we do not love him. He cannot be loved and disregarded at the same time. He himself says, *Anyone who is not with me is against me; and anyone who does not*
Lk 11:23 *gather in with me throws away.* Only one who strives to the best of his ability to keep the Lord's commandments deserves to dwell with him. It is pointless to say that you dwell with the Lord if you disregard his commands. Dearest brothers, do not be deceived by your religious attire! Believe me, you do not love the Lord if you do not keep his commandments.

What love can our attire profess when our behavior scorns him? The love of God requires a habit of mind, not one of cloth; worthy deeds, not pious notions. Love is proved by action.

What the Lord says is this: '*If* in truth *you love me you will keep my commandments*. Keep my commandments so that I may know that you love me completely, and *I will ask the Father.*' Here he is counseling the disciples to love him and keep his commandments so that they may receive the Holy Spirit, for unless they have the Holy Spirit they can neither love nor keep the commandments.

I shall ask the Father, and he will give you another Paraclete. What Jesus asks for as man he gives as God: he asks for us who himself gives us what is asked for. God himself asks for us according to his humanity when he causes us to pray to him in his divinity: he asks the Father for us when, believing him to be one with God the Father, we ask him. *He will give you another Paraclete to be with you for ever.* It is not that they did not have him, but they had him in a lesser, hidden way, and they were going to receive him more fully and openly. He would be *another,* that is, in person, not in nature or essence. He would be with them to enlighten them, to teach them to proclaim the Kingdom of God, to preach the Gospel—to convince them that he, whom they believed then to be less than his Father, was indeed the Father's equal. '*With you for ever*', he promises, 'to guide you to see the brightness of eternal light; to contemplate me face to face, one God with the Father and the

Paraclete himself, as you will believe me to be.'

The meaning of *Paraclete* is 'advocate', 'consoler', 'comforter'. He is the advocate of the faithful, the defender and protector of all who hope in him; without him nothing is sound, nothing is sacred. He protects his own, defending and doing battle for those whom he glorifies for ever. The comforter of mourners, he is the orphan's father and the widow's husband.[76] The mourners he comforts are those who mourn sinning and its due punishment; those who mourn having become lost in sin and incurring the wrath of Christ the King of glory; those who mourn having spurned by their sins the Lord who died on the cross for them; those who mourn that they cannot see Christ, life's hope, salvation's author. All these the Spirit of Jesus comforts, consoling them with hope in this present life, even as he will console them with the object of their hope in the life of blessed happiness. *The Spirit of Truth,* and of goodness, is one in substance and co-eternal with the Father and the Son. All that he teaches is good, unalloyed by any error or falsehood.

The wicked and deceitful cannot receive this Spirit of truth. No one whose hands are soiled can hold so clean a Spirit. (I speak not of the physical body but of the mind: soiled not with the filth of the dungheap, but with the foul dregs of sin). No one so fouled is

[76] Reversing the imprecation of Ps 108:9 *(fiant filii eius orphani et uxor eius vidua),* Ogier's praise of the Paraclete echoes the Pentecost sequence *(Veni Sancte Spiritus)* of Stephen Langton (Homily I, n. 13).

capable of possessing so radiant and glorious a Spirit. The world—and the worldly one who loves and worships the things of this world—cannot grasp the Spirit of Christ, who hates the world's devotee. The Spirit flies from all who know no other love than that of themselves; he wishes to be loved for himself alone. He wishes to be loved completely, who alone is to be loved above all else. He who has no peer in repaying total love wants no consort in love. He wishes so to be loved that all things may be loved together with him, though nothing may be loved before him. All creation, by virtue of his having created it, comes from him; by virtue of that Creation, every creature is good. Thus creation is to be loved, not for itself, but so that in it the Creator may be loved. The Father's love is not in anyone who loves gold or silver or sundry furnishings and possessions, since these things are themselves the cause of their being loved. It is the Creator who is to be loved in the whole of his creation, and all creatures through him: all things are loved with him, yet he himself alone is loved.

The Creator cannot be grasped by one whose skin is festering,[77] nor seen by anyone whose mind's eye is speckled within. Let the *Lev 21:20*
skin be carefully scraped with a shard until every scab is removed; only then, skillfully *Job 2:8*
treated and polished, can the body become a temple worthy of the Holy Spirit. Let the mind's eye first be cleansed; then it will be

[77] *Qui scabiem ulcerosam habet in pelle:* pustular eruptions of the skin disqualify an animal from sacrifice in Lev 22:22 and are threatened as divine retribution for transgressing the Law in Deut 28:27; *scabies* is a figure of morbid sexual craving in both classical usage and in Augustine (*Confessions* 9.1); see n. 18.

worthy to see the Spirit of truth. If we wish to attain the sight of the Lord's radiant beauty, this is how we must do. Then with the apostles we shall know Jesus, and he will dwell with us in the present life and be with us in the life to come. How happy the bride—how blessed the soul—so cleansed of impurities as to be found a worthy dwelling place of Bliss himself!

These words may delight you, but you must know this as well: the beautiful Spirit of truth cannot dwell in a soul that is subject to sin. Such a soul clings to the depravity that bridles it, neither wanting nor seeking to loose its sinful shackles by imploring the help of the Liberator of souls or expressing the grief of repentance. Like a shameless harlot, such a soul returns time and again to prostitute herself with her corrupters.[78] But a soul that is armed with the sword of abstinence cannot be said to be subject to sin, for such a soul struggles with all its might against the onslaughts of the flesh. Indeed the sword of abstinence is our sole defense in the struggle against the sins born of flesh and blood. Without it the flesh is too weak, the mind all too slovenly, to prevent the crushing of chastity's flower. The withdrawal of food and drink blunts the body's sting of desire, but when the belly is distended by our yielding slavishly to desire, both mind and body become the servants of incontinence, to the loss of chastity. When the gullet is inclined to excess, when

[78] Cf. 1 Cor 6:15; the inclusion of *corruptoribus* suggests as well the language of Rev 19:2.

the hand is friendlier to the mouth than nature requires, then appetite ministers to obesity: the body waxes gross, and extravagance grows addictive. Hew the flesh with the sickle of abstinence, and chastity flourishes in the mind. The body is not to be spared if we wish it to become the temple of the Holy Spirit.[79] May he see fit so to cleanse us of every defilement of body and spirit that we may be found worthy to be, both here and in eternity, the temple of the Spirit

who in unity with Christ and God the Father
lives and reigns blessed for ever and ever.
Amen.

[79] Virtually the entire argument, and its ordering, is inspired by 1 Corinthians 6.

IX

NINTH HOMILY

I will not leave you orphans. I shall come to you. In a little while the world will see me no longer, but you will see me. You will see that I live, and you also will live. On that day you will know that I am in my Father and the Father is in me, and you in me and I in you. Whoever holds to my commandments and keeps them is the one who loves me. Whoever loves me will be loved by my Father, and I shall love him and reveal myself to him. Judas—not Judas Iscariot—said to him, 'Lord, what has happened that you intend to show yourself to us and not to the world?' Jesus answered, 'Anyone who loves me will keep my word, and my Father will love him. We shall come to him and make a home in him. Anyone who does not love me does not keep my words. The word that you hear is not my own, but my Father's. I have said these things to you while still with you. The Paraclete, the Holy Spirit, whom the Father will send in my name, will teach you everything and remind you of all I have said to you.

John 14:18-26

I *WILL NOT LEAVE YOU orphans.* All of us whose lot it is to tread the toilsome paths of this sad pilgrimage, all in whom the love and desire for Christ keep ever mindful of this present exile and that blessed life to come, will surely groan and sigh to read this chapter. So I believe; so I confess. For how indeed could lovers of the Crucified contain their tears, not yet able to see our risen Saviour, the sum of our desire, now seated at the right hand of the Father? O Lord Jesus, without the confidence that your love for me can give, I should indeed believe I am an abandoned orphan, since I cannot see you as you are.

'I will not leave you orphans', you told your apostles, *'I shall come to you';* but I, poor wretch that I am, have not yet deserved to hear my Lord speak thus to me. Let every happiness withdraw from me meanwhile, until I come to see him whom my soul desires![80] Let mourning be my companion, until I gaze upon my Saviour! Happy indeed is that soul which daily mourns and groans to see the world's Redeemer; the day will come at last when that soul will laugh with endless joy with Christ. But let the soul beware which does not grieve at Christ's departure, lest it bewail his coming! She does not love her Bridegroom who does not sigh with desire until he comes. Copious tears are proof of perfect love, and one who daily weeps for love of Christ cannot long be separated from him. He will come quickly to all who grieve for him, and *he will wipe away every tear.* All mourning and wailing will turn into joy everlasting at the sight of Christ. *I shall not leave you* *Rev 22:4; Is 25:8*

[80] Cf. Sg 3:4 *(invenit quem diligit anima mea).*

orphans, he reassures the disciples. 'When the Spirit is given through me, I too will be with you.'

The word 'orphan' is from the Greek, meaning 'a ward, a minor'. Thus by this term the Lord shows himself a father to the disciples. *'I will come to you',* he says, 'after the resurrection of the body, I who am with you in the presence of divine majesty. Yet *in a little while the world will see me no longer, but you will see me.'* (After his resurrection, Christ appeared to good people, not to the wicked and depraved lovers of this world.) We might say that *a little while* means the whole season of our mortal lives, at the end of which the wicked are taken away and do not see God's glory, which is reserved for the just.

You will see that I live, and you also will live. By this we may understand: '*I live* because I am Life, and through that life *you will live.*' He speaks of himself in the present tense, since his future resurrection was imminent; but he speaks of his disciples in the future tense, since their resurrection will come at the end of time. *'On that day you will know that I am in my Father* and the Father is in me, *and you in me and I in you.* On the last day, when your resurrection is accomplished, you will know, even as you have believed, that I am in the Father now, like a ray of the sun, one with him; and
Jn 15:1 you are in me like branches of a vine,[81] and I in you, like the vine among its branches.' But the world—that is, the lovers of this world—neither sees God now nor will see him then,

[81] Jn 15:1, anticipating Homily X.

radiant in his majesty. O accursed world, for ever unable to see the Lord Christ! Do not deceive yourself: no one who loves the world loves God. And how will one see whom one does not love? Who can see God whose heart is not pure, not mild, not gentle, not full of love's sweetness? Eyes deprived of light cannot see the very author of light. Do you truly long to see God? Then cleanse every sin from your heart. Remember what Truth himself said: *Blessed are the pure in heart; they shall see God.*[82] *Mt 5:8*

The Latin word *mundus* has several meanings. As 'universe' it means heaven and all that heaven's span enfolds, that threefold engine[83] of all things *in the heavens, on earth, and in the underworld.* And it is the 'world' of men and *Phil 2:10* their preoccupation with it, their love of the worldly. It is the latter that is meant in *the world will no longer see me.* But *mundus* also means 'clean', washed from every bit of filth and stain, as in the hymn for Prime:[84]

> *Made clean through abstinence, may we*
> *his glory sing eternally.*[85]

Those who are unclean, the lovers of this world, will never see the One who alone is clean: *the world will not see God,* for *if anyone loves the*

[82] *Beati mundo corde* in Latin.

[83] *Trinam machinam,* cf. the hymn, *Quem terra pontus æthera.*

[84] One of the seven services, or offices, of the divine office stipulated in RB, Prime—chanted at the first hour of daylight—resembled the other numbered hours (Terce, Sext, None) known as the Little Hours, though it contained unique features such as a litany and a fixed hymn. To give greater priminence to the morning office of praise (Lauds), Prime was suppressed in the Vatican II Constitution on the Sacred Liturgy.

[85] *Mundi per abstinentiam / ipsi canamus gloriam,* from the hymn, *Iam lucis orto sidere* (LH 233).

1 Jn 2:15 *world, the love of the Father finds no place in him.* To the love of God the love of the world is mightily opposed: where one abides, the other cannot enter. The love of God calls us from the world, but the love of the world calls us away from God. The one casts its possessor down to hell, the other lifts and bears him up to heaven. The love of the world is never sated, its appetite increases by what it feeds on. The love of God seeks God alone; for him alone it ever longs, with him it is content, in him it is fulfilled. Most noble is that love, disdaining the love of everything beautiful besides the flower of inviolate beauty. For Love himself
Sg 2:1 says, *I am the rose of Sharon, the lily of the valley.* Everything that is not Christ, love not only does not seek, it renounces and scorns, as if it were stinking dung. All else love spurns and counts as nothing, for all is worthless compared to that love which Christ alone makes sweet. O happy, blessed love! Blessed are all who possess you! All happy, all blessed are they whose only love is Christ! May we taste that happiness, Brothers, may we know such love for our Creator. You will know Christ's lover: it is one who keeps his commands.

'*Whoever holds to my commandments and keeps them is the one who loves me.* All who love me hold my commandments, hold them fast in mind and keep them throughout their lives, hold to them in action and keep them in persevering, hold to them in word and keep them in behavior: in hearing they have them, by doing they keep them.'[86] Many indeed have

[86] The fivefold trope, a minor variant of the great *via-veritas-vita* invention of Homily VII (see n. 67), is constructed of an interlocking pair of devices: *habet* . . .

the Lord's commandments but do not bother to keep them: they have them in their books, but not in their thoughts; they cite but do not live them. Many remember his commands but do not live by them; they pay lip service to them but set no example by them. No lovers of Christ, these! These *will be given a great many strokes of the lash.* Theirs shall be *weeping and* *Lk 12:47*
the grinding of teeth. For them shall be *fire and* *Mt 8:12*
sulfur, and *a scorching wind will be their lot,* with *Ps 10:7*
the devil and his hosts of fallen angels. But for those who love Christ, how great will be the joy, the great and solemn dance, the exultation, the rhapsody of glory![87]

Whoever loves me will be loved by my Father, and I shall love him and reveal myself to him. O lover of Christ, you who worship God and despise the self, what do you make of this reward of your love? What evil can harm you, what good could you lack, if he who created everything from nothing loves you? O blessed beyond measure, blissful beyond the power of words to describe, you who are loved by God the Father, by his Son, by the Spirit of them both! What richer fortune, what greater bliss than to be loved by the Lord of paradise? His is the power of life and death, his the power to damn and to save—to damn those who hate him and save all who love him. Just as those who hate him cannot be saved, so those who love him cannot be damned.

---

servat (1) *in memoria, in vita;* (2) *faciendo, perseverando;* (3) *in sermonibus, in moribus;* (4) *audiendo, faciendo.*

[87] The 'solemn dance' of the *tripudium,* cf. Est 8:16; on *gloriatio,* cf. Sir 9:22.

But, O Lord Jesus, what will you do for those who love you? Speak, I beg you![88] Tell it so that I may hear it, for although I am a sinner, yet do I love you. What will be the reward of loving you? What will be the fruits of your love? Speak, and let the telling gladden our hearts! All who love you with all their hearts await that reward. They look forward to it, groaning and weeping all the while it is withheld from them. What is that reward? Speak so that my brothers may hear and know, that they may know and seek, that they may seek and find, find and receive, receive and hold, hold firmly—and love as greatly as they can! What will you grant your lovers? What will you reveal to them? *I will reveal myself.* Come, you who moan and mourn the absent Christ, your eternal King: rejoice and be glad, for Jesus will reveal to you himself!

You have heard it, brothers: you have heard it as you were grieving and mourning for desire of Christ, for love of the most blessed Lord, Maker, Redeemer, and Saviour, the Lord of paradise, of sweetness, of glory, splendor, joy, delight! You have heard the reward of your labors, the gift my Jesus will give to all who love him. (Oh, be ever mine, my Jesus!) 'To the one who loves me', he tells us, *I shall reveal myself.*' What could be sweeter, more glorious?[89] What could be greater bliss, than to see him face to face, at whose beauty

[88] Cf. Homilies I and (especially) VII of the Marian tractate, where the rhetorical device is clearly inspired by Bernard.

[89] Cf. *nil canitur suavius,* from the hymn, *Jesu dulcis memoria,* formerly attributed to Saint Bernard.

sun and moon marvel? He whom the holy angels see and ever desire to see, never tiring of the sight of him? The clear beauty of heaven and sweet savor of paradise is Jesus Christ our Lord, the faith of the living, the hope of the dying, the Saviour of all. Nothing is brighter, nothing of greater good than the Lord himself to those who love him. He promises, not gold and silver, not jewels and precious stones, not even heaven and earth: he promises himself, the Creator of all, the God of all!

You who love the Lord Jesus Christ above everything and everyone, this is your love's reward. This is what your love has earned you, who love him not by word of mouth, but in deed, not by your attire, but in your minds, not by habit, but with affection, not shamming, but in truth. He will reveal himself to you. He will give himself to you. Would you ask for more? Would you seek anything else? Without him, all else is paltry. Do you love him? Then seek nothing from him but himself. He disdains the petitioner of whose petition he is not the principal cause. Though he will grant all that is good, he gives himself even more willingly. Do not fear the magnitude and grandeur of the gift. Love him with your whole heart and mind, and you will be able to approach with confidence. You will be able to go in to him and say, 'Yes, Lord, be *all my share in the land of the living.'* O blessed *Ps 141:6*
portion, O blessed inheritance! Lord Jesus, grant that I may truly say, *my birthright, my cup is the Lord!* Be the reward of my toil, my *Ps 15:5*
journey's end, my mourning's consolation! You, Jesus, are the cause of my love; be the

sole cause as well of possessing so great a possession!

Judas—not Judas Iscariot—said to him, 'Lord, what has happened that you intend to show yourself to us and not to the world?' Having been told that the disciples, but not the world, would see Jesus, Jude asks—for all who would ask—the cause of such discrimination. But the cause has already been told: it is love, and love alone, that sets apart a holy people from an unholy people. It is love, moreover, that must be proved: *Anyone who loves me will keep my word.* Thus the proof of our love of God is in our remembrance and observance of Christ's commandments: our actions prove our love. It is pointless to say you love God if

Cf. 1 Jn 4:20 your actions counter his commandments. Not to hold to his commandments is not to love him, but to hate him. Let no one conceal himself in a religious habit, or presume to cloak himself with sanctity as a member of a monastic order. They alone love Christ who set themselves to keeping Christ's commandments to the best of their ability.

That monk, there: regard him carefully. Is he humble in his demeanor? Does he bear reproach patiently? Is he devoted to his superiors, gentle of manner, and reserved in his speech? Does he persevere in silence? In the cloister, does he read attentively? In choir, does he praise Christ with clear devotion? Is he given frequently to tears? Is he sparing in the refectory? Is he ever ready to obey? Is he everywhere subdued, humble in his bearing, and self-effacing? In his prayers, is he ever knocking at the gates of heaven? In his heart, does he ever cry out to the Lord? Is he committed to his neighbor's well-being, and unconcerned with his own? Does he love everyone—and hold himself in contempt? If all this be so, then you can say: this monk keeps his Creator's commandments. How fortunate is such a monk, how blessed! As reward for his toil he shall have the Lord Jesus himself.

But those who have no charity, who do not keep Christ's commandments: they are not of the Lord's own. What will their reward be? The lake of fire and brimstone, death, hell: this is their reward. Is it yours? Would you had not been born! So then, if you desire to have Christ as your reward, keep his commandments, namely: *I give you a new commandment: love one another.* If you love Christ, you must love your brother. If you would not incur Christ's hatred, keep whole the love of your brother.

A great reward ensues. I have already told you what it is, though I delight to tell it again; for the more it is tasted in the mouth, the more like honey to the heart, and all who constantly endeavor to earn it will come to know its sweetness. The reward of brotherly love is nothing less than Christ's love and that of God the Father, for Truth himself says, *Anyone who loves me will keep my word, and my Father will love him.* If God the Father loves you, what possible good can you lack? Whatever you seek you will obtain; indeed you will possess, for ever with his holy angels, the Lord himself, the grantor of all that is good. What greater bliss than to be loved by God the

Father, and by his Son, the Lord Jesus Christ? How blessed the one whom Father, Son, and Holy Spirit love! Oh, if my God, my Creator, my Redeemer, were to love me, I should seek nothing else in this world. In this life Christ's love alone suffices. Christ's sweet, delectable love bestows health to the sick, light to the blind, gladness to mourners, forgiveness to sinners. To the dying it brings life; to the earthbound, heaven. To the companion of the beasts of burden it grants the companionship of the angels. Above all, it lavishes on us the Lord of angels himself, the Master of the universe!

We shall come to him and make a home in him. The Lord comes to us when we come to God. When we come believing, obeying, contemplating—obtaining!—God comes to us to help, to enlighten, to fulfill. Our actions proceed from the love of Christ; his favors flow from God's loving-kindness. Love makes you the dwelling place, makes the Lord your home. *God is love, and whoever remains in love remains*
1 Jn 4:16 *in God and God in him.* O happy builder, love, whose art provides us such a home![90] Not of mortar or brick, that home, not of stone or wood, not of gold or silver, nor of precious stones. It far exceeds all gold, all silver pales before it, and precious stones are cheapened by comparison. To its beauty and comeliness nothing is comparable. Its sweetness makes the taste of honey that of wormwood. All else that is beautiful and lovely is drab beside it. This home is an eternal dwelling, before all

[90] Cf. 1 Cor 8:1: *scientia inflat, caritas vero ædificat* ('learning puffs up, love however edifies').

ages, before time itself; it contains all, embraces all, creates all, gives life to all. In this house the blind find light, the lame a sure footing. Here the crooked is straightened; here the sick are healed, the dead raised up. All who enter here receive. No one there is wretched; all are blessed. To enter that home is to enter the joy of the Lord, which is the Lord himself. There we shall dwell supremely well in that supreme good,[91] which is the Lord for ever blessed!

Dear brothers, does not this priceless home grow sweeter in your hearts than honey in the comb? O christian soul, Christ Jesus' beloved bride, shall you not cry out to your bridesmaids, the souls of the saints and the angelic spirits, and, beseeching with tears and imploring with sighs say to them, *Daughters of Jerusalem, tell my beloved that I am sick with love?* You love him but little if you do not daily *Sg 5:8*
weep and groan for love of him. For in his absence, the bride of the beloved weeps rivers of tears. When she seeks him and does not find him, calls him and is unanswered, her only delight is weeping, and, heaping together all that is doleful, she weeps for him all the more. Of this I am certain: *God will wipe away every tear from* her *eyes* on the day of Christ's *Rev 21:4*
wedding with the Church, when the *virgins shall be led into the King's bridal chamber.* *Ps 44:15*

But why should he wipe tears from your eyes if you do not sigh and lament for love of him? If that is how you are, you are no monk. What, you tell me you cannot weep? I tell you it is because you do not fully love Christ.

[91] *Optime in optimo;* cf. Augustine, *Confessions* 2.10.18.

Tears are love's witnesses. If you do not weep for love of your heavenly home, wail, then, for fear of hell! What, does not the fear of hell provoke your tears? Then truly you neither fear death nor love life. You who have in store the inheritance of eternal life, fear God and keep his commandments! *Anyone who does not love me,* says the Lord Jesus, the Son of God, *does not keep my words*. Oh let us love him with all our might, and let us keep his commands, for our reward will be great!

The word that you hear is not my own, but my Father's.[92] Do not be shaken, I beg you. Do not be disturbed at these words, you who put all your hope in the Lord Jesus Christ and love him with all your heart as true God with the Father and the Holy Spirit. For what he means is: "I am not from myself but from the Father. I am God of God, light of light, Son of the Father, one with him in essence, majesty, divinity, power, might, and in the creation of all things. I come neither after him nor before him. I am neither greater nor lesser, but in all ways equal to the Father. I am another in person but not in nature, *for the Father is one person, the Son another, another the Holy Spirit*.[93] The words I tell you are my Father's, for he sent me: I am from him and my words are from him."

Or we may understand it this way: '*The word you hear is not mine*—that is, not of the

[92] The commentary is introduced by a grammatical aside (*sermonem quem*—for *sermo quem*—*audistis non est meus* is an example of *antiptosis*, where one case is put for another). The remainder of the verse *(sed eius qui misit me Patris)* is similarly 'emended' to *sed Patris*. See n. 69.

[93] The *Quicumque vult* (Athanasian creed).

human flesh I assumed—but of the God who assumed it. It is not that of the Son of Man but of the Son of God. It is not mine as a result of my having been born of the Virgin, but of my having been begotten of God the Father.' Earlier he said, *Anyone who loves me will keep my word.* Here he says, *The word that you hear is not my own.* There is much at variance here: it is, it is not; my word; mine, but not my own. Yet, as Truth is speaking, it must be so. It is his word, as Creator, not as creature, as God, not as man. It is his, since all things are his: *through him all things came into being, not one thing came into being except through him.* The *Jn 1:3*
word is not his, but his Father's, since, *taking the form of a slave, he was humbler yet, even to accepting death, death on a cross.* *Phil 2:7, 8*

Perhaps he said this so that his disciples, who did not yet fully believe in him, might more firmly hold fast to his teachings and more steadfastly keep them, if they knew them to be the teachings of God the Father, the Maker and Creator of all. The Father always seems to be of greater sublimity than the Son, of great excellence and dignity—I say this with regard to the Son's humanity, not his divinity, for in divinity the Son is equal to the Father, not less, nor following after. *In his divinity he is equal to the Father; in his humanity he is less than the Father.*[94] Thus, so that his disciples and their successors might hold his words more dearly, he told them that they were his Father's. It was as if to say, 'You ought to keep intact all that I have taught you, not

[94] The *Quicumque vult.*

violating anything, wholly or in part, for any reason whatever, since the teachings are not mine but my Father's. For I am my Father's Son, and so my words and works are not mine but his. *It is the Father living in me who is doing* his *works,*[95] giving you his teachings through me.'

Cast out from the joys of paradise, earthbound humans, children of the earth and clothed here in this vale of tears in the garment of mortality, did not, in this dismal exile, deserve to hear God speaking, for they had disregarded his commands while yet in paradise. Nor did they deem it worth the misery the way left them by which to return to their heavenly home. But their Lord, in his compassion for them, came to seek the wandering, to console the grieving, to heal the sick, to raise up the downcast, and to restore exiles to their homeland and everlasting life to the dead. So the Word came in the flesh, God to
Jn 1:14 humankind: *the Word became flesh.* God became man, and the Word—that is, God—through that man, spoke face to face with humankind itself and as man gave others the teachings that bring life. This was so that humans might obey that human, and through that God-made-man man might return to God from whom poor humankind had departed. And so God, dwelling as a mortal among mortals, gave them the commandment of life, so that becoming immortal through him they might live for ever blessed with the Immortal One.

[95] Jn 14:10, reprised (from Homily VII) and modified *(Pater in me manens facit opera* sua, for *Pater autem in me manens, ipse facit opera).*

Let us note here the Lord's two dwelling-places: the one along the way, the other in his heavenly home; the one temporal, when he dwelt with us in the flesh, the other eternal, where we shall dwell with him glorified in soul and body. Of the first he says, '*I have said these things to you while still with you*—present in the body. But a time is coming when I will withdraw from you in my bodily presence and will thereafter speak to you through the Spirit. *The Paraclete, the Holy Spirit, whom the Father will send in my name, will teach you everything and remind you of all I have said to you.* He will teach you,' says the Lord Jesus, 'what I have told you.' Not that the Son says one thing and the Spirit teaches another, for whatever Christ says and teaches the Trinity says and teaches. Because God is triune, each person of the godhead must establish himself in our hearts. We should hear each distinctly and understand them inseparably. Thus, when we say, 'the Father, Son, and Holy Spirit', we do not say these words simultaneously, yet those whom we name are simultaneous and could not be otherwise. When the Lord speaks of the Comforter whom the Father will send, we are to understand: 'I am leaving you in my bodily presence but not in the presence of the Spirit. The body I received on earth I now raise up to heaven, but through my Spirit I will remain with you until the end of time. The Father sent me so that I might appear visible in the flesh, but the hour has come for me to pay death's due, and, rising from the dead, ascend to the Father and there be seated at his right hand. Henceforth the world will no longer see me in the mortal guise of the flesh. But *the Paraclete, the Spirit, whom the Father will send in my name,* will comfort you in my bodily absence by the abundance of his sweetness. He will be your teacher, not noising his words abroad but teaching the heart within. *He will prompt you and teach you everything I have told you* through him, all that I will have inspired in you.[96] You will not be able to lament my bodily absence so long as the Spirit remains in your hearts.'

O Lord Jesus, may your Spirit come, my God and Master! May he enter my heart and so flood me with your love that I should seek no other love than yours, that I may love no other beauty than yours, that I may taste no other sweetness! For you are honey and honeycomb: the honey of God the Father, in the honeycomb of the Virgin Mary; honey in the bosom of the Father, honeycomb broken on the cross; honey reigning

with the Father and the Holy Spirit
in heaven and throughout the universe,
blessed through endless ages.
Amen.

[96] The transposition of *suggeret* and *docebit* casts the first verb in another light; *inspiravero* maintains its base sense (as in Jn 20:22) of 'breathing upon or into'.

X

TENTH HOMILY

Peace I bequeath to you, my own peace I give you, a peace which the world cannot give, this is my gift to you. Do not let your hearts be troubled, do not be afraid. You heard me say, I am going, but I shall come again to you. If you loved me, you would be glad that I am going to the Father, for the Father is greater than I. I have told you this now, before it happens, so that when it does happen, you may fully believe. I shall not talk to you much longer, because the prince of this world is on his way, but he has no power over me. The world must recognize that I love the Father and that I obey the command my Father gave me. Get up now, let us go. I am the true vine and my Father is the vinedresser. Every branch in me that bears no fruit he cuts away, and every branch that does bear fruit he prunes to make it bear even more.

Jn 14:27-31, 15:1-2

ALL WHO HAVE LEARNED to love the Lord Jesus with all their hearts taste the sweetness of his words. Nor can they shut out those sweet words who in the secret closet of their hearts fervently embrace Christ the Lord of everlasting life, the delight and joy of beauty's paradise. For the words of the Lord are life's green pastures, the soul's refreshment, *Cf. Ps 22* the cup of sweetness; they gladden the hearts of all who love Christ. To these they are far dearer than gold and precious stones, sweeter far than honey in the comb. But to those who in their wicked lives reject Christ's words, they are as bile, bitter, odious, and in every way distasteful. To them Christ's words speak, not of glory everlasting, but of eternal punishment. Torment they foretell for some, for others the reward of blessed life. Death for some, for others life; hell for some, for others the companionship of the angels. Let sinners everywhere mourn and grieve; let them open their hearts and receive the Word of God. Let them do as he commands, for in Christ are treasures of wisdom and knowledge, of riches and abundant glory. You who delight to hear Christ's words, hear them from this poor sinner of his. But prepare yourselves, I beg you, to hear Christ's words by pouring out your tears. Who indeed could hold back tears at hearing how Christ, about to go to the Father, gave his disciples his peace in the total embrace of his loving-kindness? Listen!

Peace I bequeath to you,
my own peace I give you,
a peace which the world cannot give,
this is my gift to you.

The appointed time had come. Now he would save humankind through his death. Now he would give up his life in ransom for many. Now he would quit the world and ascend to be at the right hand of his Father. And so the Lord Jesus, with the full measure of loving-kindness, embraces in his profound love the disciples he was leaving in the body. Withdrawing from them—deserting them, as it were—he earnestly seeks some means to console them for his absence; but the more he desires to comfort them, the bitterer the grief that fills them. There, clasping them to himself, he bids them as it were a final farewell—perhaps his heart sinks at their kisses. The disciples desired nothing than to be with the Lord, to enjoy the sight of him, to delight in his sweet speech and taste to the full his honey-sweet companionship. All too soon, alas, would all this be taken from them! There wept together love and grief, the twin ministers of tears. Ah, what love—what grief! Who could gauge the torrent of their tears? Whose stony heart would not dissolve in a fountain of tears at so great an outpouring of loving-kindness?

How great was the sweetness of that love, how great the loving-kindness of that sweetness, when their redeemer pressed his lips upon the lips of his disciples! In all truth they could have told him then, '*Honey and milk are under your tongue, your lips distill wild honey.*[97] *Sg 4:11*
Your fragrance exceeds that of the purest balsam, exceeds indeed the headiest of all *Cf. Sir 24:21*
scents'—for so it was. So great the fragrance of that perfume as the abundance of that love:

[97] The order of the phrases in Sg 4:11 has been transposed. Its citation here points as well to the source (Sg 1:1) of the otherwise improbable image of Jesus kissing the disciples *osculo oris* (see n. 99 below).

how great the grief where soon so sweet a fragrance would depart! What violent sobbing plagued their hearts—just imagine it—when they heard the Lord speak of peace! *'Peace'*, the Lord Jesus tells his disciples, *'is my parting gift to you, my own peace, such as the world cannot give.*[98] Returning to the Father, I bequeath you peace. You, about to be guided on your journey to the Father, receive my peace!' *Peace* upon *peace,* as the prophet Isaiah says: *Lord, you will grant us peace; peace, for in you we have*
Is 26:3 *hoped.*

Now there is peace in this world, and so long as we abide in it, loving one another, not judging each other's hidden faults, we overcome the foe. But when, in the world to come, we reign without the foe, there will be peace such that dissension will be impossible, where all is bared and open. Each one there shall be praised of God. God is peace, both here and now and in the world to come. Christ is our peace, for he has made peace for us with God through the shedding of his blood. And he will be our peace in the future, when he
Cf. Rev 1:6 passes on the kingdom to God his Father, *and*
1 Cor 15:28 *God will be all in all.* No further struggle then with flesh and blood: ours shall be the palm and the crown of the contest won, when we shall see him as he is.

Following along in Christ's humble servant's little book, you have heard Christ be-

[98] *The New English Bible* (Cambridge, 1961); like several recent English translations (e.g. *New Jerusalem,* first citation, above), the phrase literally rendered 'not as the world gives [peace]' is imbued with deeper spiritual significance than the contrast with the conventional greeting of a Semitic community (such as used by Jesus himself in Jn 20:19).

queathing his peace to his disciples. Perhaps that surprises you? But I, sinner that I am, may ask why that should amaze you. Why should you be troubled? There is nothing to marvel at here; for what is the more self-abasing, that he should kneel down and wash his disciples' feet, or that he should embrace them in the kiss of peace? Surely he who did not fear to undergo the torture of the cross for them did not shrink from giving them the kiss of peace. But perhaps you object. 'I read', you say, 'in John's Gospel that Christ told his disciples, *Peace I bequeath to you, my own peace I give you,* but I do not read that he pressed his most sacred lips to those of his disciples.' To this I reply: if something is known to have been suggested[99] by the very mouth of Truth, who are we to say that it did not in fact take place? It does no harm to think it; there is no danger in believing it, for it does not run counter to our faith.

Not as the world gives it do I give it to you. What peace the world gives is a false peace, a pretended peace, a deceptive peace, the mere semblance of peace. True peace is the bond of love, of loving-kindness that cannot be dissolved. But what is it the world loves? In a word, nothing: it loves nothing, cherishes nothing, hates everything, destroys everything, ruins everything. From the moment we leave our mother's womb until we enter the bowels of the mother of all, our wretched lot in this

[99] *Prolatum:* no kiss of greeting is recorded in the Gospels except that of Judas; the *osculum sanctum* assumed here derives from the epistles of Paul (e.g. Rom 16:16; 1 Cor 16:20; 2 Cor 13:12) and Peter (1 Pet 5:14), though that is scarcely the *osculum oris* depicted (above, cf. n. 97) by Ogier.

world is nothing but hunger, thirst, nakedness, excruciating cold, scorching heat, itching sores,[100] headaches, gout in the hands and feet, diseases of the spleen and liver, misery within and without! *Outside the sword bereaves; inside it is like death*. In the end, cruel death strikes us down.[101] Such is the world's love. And yet, the wretched lovers of this world do not recognize its trickery. The world they love is hateful, and to its fierce sword they willingly expose their necks. O miserable lot, deprived of counsel! If only they would learn to understand, to make provision for what will befall them on the Last Day! If only they would turn from their love of the world, and hate it!

Lam 1:20

The world is for those who love all that passes away, but the wise see through its paltry peace and superficial harmony. Let us turn our backs on such illusion and return to the peace of our Lord Jesus Christ, that peace which reason attests is none other than his love for us. It is his love that he lavished on us, cleansing us from our sins in his blood. This is the love for which God *gave the world his only Son, so that everyone who believes in him may not perish but may have eternal life*. It was that peace, that loving-kindness, that he left them when he gave up his life for their salvation. It was that most sacred body, received from the inviolate Virgin, that he subjected to an outpouring of contempt on the dreadful hill of the cross. This is the peace he left us, as the blessed apostle Peter assures: *Christ suffered for*

Jn 3:16

[100] See above, n. 18.

[101] *Morte sæva:* cf. Boethius, *De philosophiae consolatione (The Consolation of Philosophy)* I.1.13-16.

us and left an example for us to follow in his steps. 1 Pet 2:21
And elsewhere he encourages us to imitate that love: *As Christ has undergone bodily suffering, you should arm yourselves with the same conviction.* It was this peace he left us when he 1 Pet 4:1
died, but when he rose again it was another.[102] The first peace frees us from sin and bestows forgiveness; the second reconciles us with the Lord and brings us to the joys of paradise. The first he gave us as he was about to die on the cross; the second he will give us as he reigns for ever with the Father. The first occurred amidst grief and sorrow; the second will be in joy and exultation. The first was tearful, in misery; the second will be radiant, in glory. At the giving of the first we weep for Christ, at the second we shall rejoice with him.

With ample cause the disciples wept for their Master, the servants for their lord, as he was about to depart from them in death. And no wonder! They saw well enough why they should grieve—but did not yet know why they should rejoice. They grieved because they knew Christ was going to die, but they did not yet fully believe that he was going to rise again and ascend to heaven. Each of them could truly say (if in their grief they could speak at all), 'How could I not weep? how could I stem my tears? My comforter forsakes me—even as he is comforting my heart!' Doubtless our Lord, as he beheld their bitter weeping, could not in his human nature contain his tears, for he sought at once to console

[102] *Moriendo . . . resurgendo* recalls the Paschal Preface, one of several liturgical and patristic models of Ogier's rhyming tropes (such as the sixfold *prima-secunda [pax]* set piece this sentence inaugurates, slightly compacted here).

them: *'Do not let your hearts be troubled* that I am leaving you; *do not be afraid* that the wolf will attack when the shepherd is away. As a man, I go, but as God I am ever present. Do not be troubled by my death; do not fear it: for after three days I will rise again and come to you, and you will see that I am Life: no longer can anyone who believes in me be subject to death. *I am going,* but *I shall come again to take you to myself, so that you may be with me where I am.*[103] You implore me with your tears who should rejoice to see me depart. I am not forsaking you: *I am going to the Father.* In my divinity I do not leave you when in the flesh I go to my Father: in my human form I am going to the Father, but the Father's Son who took that form stays with you. The body I received from the virginal earth I now raise above the choirs of angels, so that the Son of Man might be seated at the Father's right and enjoy by grace what as God he has by nature. *I go to the Father,* so that humankind, deceived by the devil's cunning and felled by the sting of the ancient serpent, I might now lodge in heaven, and to the angelic flock bring back the long-lost hundredth sheep.[104] *Do not let your hearts be troubled:* so it must be. *It is better that one man should die for the people, than*
Jn 11:50 *that the whole nation should perish.*[105] Three days and three nights I shall lie in the heart of the earth; then, having destroyed the prince of this world, I will rise again on the third day, and

[103] Conflating Jn 14:28a *(Audistis quia ego dixi vobis: Vado et venio ad vos)* with 14:3b *(iterum venio et accipiam vos ad meipsum, ut ubi ego sum et vos sitis).*

[104] Cf. Lk 15:4.

[105] These are, in context, the words of Caiphas.

you will see me, and your hearts will rejoice. On the fortieth day I will ascend into heaven to be seated at the right hand of the Father, and there I will bring you to be with me, to reign with me in bliss. Therefore rejoice!'

O good Jesus, Lord God, my life, all my hope, our every desire! What is this you tell us as we mourn and groan for you? O Life that never dies, you know that you alone are our desire, our only hope of salvation. Our hearts are gravely troubled because we cannot see you as you are. We have not yet been found worthy to see you, Lord, to hear from your lips the words, *Do not let your hearts be troubled.* O fortunate apostles, O blessed disciples of the Lord! You were found worthy to see him present in the flesh. You heard his words of instruction. You walked with him, sat down with him, took supper together. You saw him rise again from the dead, saw him ascend into heaven. And now you behold him, radiant in the bosom of the Father. What could be more fortunate and more blessed than to enjoy completely the sight of God? How lovely the sight of you, Lord God! How my sinful soul longs for it, and, not yet possessing it, languishes and pines away. But I hope in the Lord Jesus Christ that *from my flesh I shall look on God* my Saviour. This faith is firmly fixed in *Job 19:26*
my mind. Meanwhile *I will exult for joy,* and *Is 61:10*
my soul will leap for joy because of Jesus my Saviour,[106] who rising from the dead ascended to heaven and is seated at the right hand of the Father, blessed for ever. For as he was

[106] Paraphrasing the *Magnificat* (cf. Lk 1:47).

about to ascend to his Father, he told his grieving disciples, *If you loved me, you would be glad that I am going to the Father, for the Father is greater than I.*

'I have told you this now, before it happens, that I am going to the Father, *so that when it does happen*—when I have gone up—*you may* fully *believe* that I am God's Son.' *'Believe',* he says, but not 'what you have seen', for there is no praise or merit of faith in that; indeed, what is seen entails no faith at all.[107] *'Believe* that I am God's Son, not with new faith, since you believed it before, but with increased faith, with faith in fullest measure.' Their faith was little when he spoke these words; when he died it would be dashed altogether.

'I shall not talk to you much longer, because the prince of this world is on his way, but *he has no power over me.* The hour is nigh when I must pay death's due, and so I shall not speak with you much longer in this mortal flesh. The devil is coming: the prince, not of creation, but of sinners, not of light, but of darkness, not of life, but of death, not of joy, but of grief. *He has no power over me;* nothing in me is of use to him.' For our Lord committed no sin, nor even willed to; indeed he could not:[108] God did not wish to have what could be lost. He came as a pauper; there was nothing the devil could take from him. To the Prince of humility, patience, and kindliness—the Prince of life and of the resurrection, the Prince of glory and of everlasting bliss—came the prince

[107] Since *faith is the evidence of things not seen* (Heb 11:1).
[108] See Homily XIII, note 150.

of pride, of envy, of jealousy and deceit, the prince of rancor and all ill-will. He came to him, clothed in the trappings of our mortality, close to death, and he thought he might come upon something in him with which he could reproach him as he died. But that wretch was sorely mistaken, for in Jesus the devil found nothing of his own; that ancient right he claimed of others could not be claimed of him. For ever blessed be Jesus, who *during his life on earth offered up prayer and entreaty, with loud cries and with tears, to the one who had the power to save him from death, and, winning a hearing by his reverence, he learned obedience, Son though he was, through his sufferings. When he had been perfected, he became for all who obey him the source of eternal salvation.* *Heb 5:7-9*

Suppose someone might have asked Jesus, 'If you have no sin, why must you die, since it is through sin alone that death comes about?' But such an objection is refuted by a contrary inference,[109] for it is to this tacit question our Lord replied, *The world must recognize that I love the Father and that I obey the command my Father gave me,*[110] as if to say, 'It is true that there would be no death had there been no sin, but I came into the world to die, so that by my death I might blot out sin. It is my Father's will that I suffer the punishment of the cross for the salvation of humankind. I carry out his will so that the world may know that I

[109] Ogier identifies the rhetorical device (as found, e.g., in Mt 21:23-25) as *anthypophora*.

[110] Slightly paraphrased: *hoc mandatum dedit mihi Pater ut facerem* (for *sicut mandatum dedit mihi Pater, sic facio*).

love him who gave me the command.' *Christ*, as the blessed apostle Paul tells us, *was obedient for our sake, even to accepting death, death on a*
Phil 2:8 *cross*.

Get up now, let us go. He is still with his disciples, reclining in the upper room, where they have taken supper together. Now he tells them to rise from table. '*Let us go*—to the place where I am to be betrayed unto death. There is no point in our sitting here any longer: the time for refreshment is past. See, the time of my suffering is hastening. *Rise* and follow me, as I precede you in suffering, for *I am the vine and you are the branches*.[111] I am your head, one in nature with you; when the head swoons, the other members languish sympathetically. As a man, I am the head of the Church; so I am with you, one in nature with you.

'*I am the true vine*—not one gone rank in the wild, producing crude and bitter grapes. I am a fragrant vine of wondrous beauty and fruitful blossoms, bestowing clusters of great sweetness to all the branches that remain in me. I am the vine that produces *wine to cheer*
Ps 103:15 *man's heart*. I am the vine that pours out his own blood to God the Father for the salvation of my people. I am a flowering vine, a leafy vine, a fruit-bearing vine; I need no elm or any other tree to support me.[112] I am the vine

[111] Citing, out of place, Jn 15:5 (omitted in the context of Homily XI), by way of introducing Jn 15:1 *(Ego sum vitis vera)* and 2 *(Omnem palmitem in me non ferentem fructum)*.

[112] Vines were typically trained to elms in medieval viniculture. *Non culta ab homine sed a Deo Patre* paraphrases, without citing, Jn 15:1b *(et Pater meus agricola est)*.

cultivated not by man but by God the Father, not externally by tending, but internally by grace, not merely operating without, but giving increase within.'

Christ is the vine containing all moisture that bears in his body the fullness of the Holy Spirit. His branches are the apostles and all who cling to him in faith. God the Father pruned this vine—Christ's human nature—and made it immune to every sin, investing it with great power. And so he does for the branches, if not in every respect as for Christ. *Every branch in me that bears no fruit he cuts away, and every branch that does bear fruit he prunes to make it bear even more.* All who cling to Christ in faith are branches that remain in Christ, the vine that heals and saves.[113] Some branches bear fruit; others remain barren. Some flower and bud, bringing forth sweet clusters;[114] others open out in dense foliage, but their beauty lies merely in their greenness. And all that persist in their barrenness, or spread out broad foliage without bearing fruit, will be snipped from the vine at pruning time when God the Father finds them fruitless. *They will be cast into the fire* and burn. *Jn 15:6b*

You may wonder how it could happen that some who cling in faith to Christ could be snipped off from him, since someone who clings to Christ is one in spirit with him. In

[113] *Salutifera:* theologically, that which brings salvation; as an attribute of plants, 'medicinal'.

[114] *Botrum;* the rare word immediately evokes the *Cantica,* where it occurs three times (Sg 1:13; 7:7 and 8); the association is reinforced in the next sentence by the phrase *tempore putationis* (Sg 2:12).

order to see matters more clearly, you should know that faith is distinguished by several properties. We speak of faith that is dead, or pretended, or perverse,[115] and we speak of faith that is correct. To the extent that they are Christians, and are thus meant to have faith in Christ, all may be said to cling to him. But the faith of some is dead, or make-believe, or wrong, while the faith of others is catholic. Dead is the faith of the proud and the wanton, of all who hanker after wealth, of thieves and brigands and suchlike. Fictitious is the faith of those who do not obey their spiritual fathers. Ungrateful for the gifts of heaven, they are without brotherly love or the peace of loving-kindness; instead they accuse others, though they themselves are unbridled in their anger. It is pleasure and amusements they love, not God. Theirs is the appearance of piety, but they are utterly without its virtue. Wrong-headed faith is that of heretics, those who rise up against God, proud of their errors, blasphemers—who are worse in all ways than the others. They kick up their heels against the Lord Jesus Christ and defile the blood of that most sweet of vines. But those whose faith is catholic are meek, patient, gentle, humble, celibate, chaste, continent; they are lovers of God and of their neighbors, ready to do any good service. They await the redemption of the children of God. May the Lord find us worthy to be counted in their number!

[115] *Mortua*—cf. Ja 2:17, 26; *ficta*—cf. 1 Tim 1:5; *perversa*—cf. Lk 9:41, and the use of *perversus,* in Tertullian and Augustine, to mean 'heretic', 'schismatic' (cf. Blaise *DAC,* 620).

Dearest brothers, we should very much fear our Lord Jesus' words: *Every branch in me that bears no fruit my Father cuts away*. Let us put no trust in leafy breadth alone; let us put no stock in the spreading of our branches or the greenness of our boughs. For if we bear no fruit we will be lopped off from the vine of the Lord and tossed into the fire. Beloved brothers, recall how the Lord, when he was hungry, came upon a large fig tree along the path. Broad and spacious were its boughs, and its leaves were lush. But finding no fruit on it, Jesus cursed it and it withered up. So it shall *Mt 21:18-19* be with every hypocrite who has the look of saintliness but not its virtue, whose attire is godly, but not his thoughts. It is not the white cowl or the tonsure[116] that make the monk complete, but the purity of his heart and the cleanliness of his mind: his casting off of self in the fire of Christ's love. Let us cling, brothers, to the true vine, Jesus our Saviour, with all our hearts, sprinkled by the fullness of faith and washed of every defilement of flesh and spirit. Let us profess an unswerving hope and faith. Then nothing whatever can any longer come between us and the love of our Lord Jesus. Then we shall be as the vines of En-Gedi, *Cf. Rom 8:39* from which flows a liquor not of wine but of balsam, like that of the Cyprian grapes in the Song of Love. There the bride, rejoicing at Christ's resurrection, breaks forth in song, her

[116] *Corona,* the horseshoe-shaped circlet of hair worn by medieval monks—and cistercian choir religious until 1969; this and the 'white cowl' are obvious emblems of the Order of Cîteaux, but 'the spreading of our branches' (above) may refer more subtly to the Order's rapid growth during Ogier's lifetime.

voice ringing with joy and delight as she sings, *My love is a cluster of Cyprian grapes among the vines of En-Gedi.*[117]

Sg 1:13

The hebrew placename, which means 'the Spring of the Kid',[118] symbolizes penance or baptism, where all who enter as kids acquire the innocence of lambs. We may thus liken En-Gedi to the monastery. Entering as unruly kids, we cast off our kid's skin to be cleansed in every part, and thus with perseverance we are kids no longer, we become lambs. God purges and prunes us to make us bear more fruit. He cleanses our hearts and fills us with the spirit of truth and the dew of loving-kindness.

Every branch that remains attached to the true vine and *bears fruit* God the father purges and prunes, *to make it bear even more.* Tending his vineyard, God practices the vinedresser's art and custom. The vineyard of the Lord is the Church universal, Christ's bride and spouse, of whom God the Father says to his Son, *Your wife* will be *like a fruitful vine in the heart of your house.* When pruning season comes, the vinedresser, cherishing the vine that bears fruit in due season, leaves nothing on it that is dry or withered. Then he digs round it to its lower roots with a sharp hoe, and if it has put out any rootlets, he cuts them away with a pruning knife. The more he removes in this fashion what is less useful to the vine, the more fruit-

Ps 127:3

[117] *botrus cypri* may mean 'grapes of Cyprus', as here, or 'cluster of henna flowers' (κυπρος), which may account for the preceding allusion to the wine's balsamic savor.

[118] *Fons hædi;* on the ensuing argument see Jerome (Ep 36.16.3): *In omnibus scripturis hædi pro peccatoribus accipiuntur* 'throughout the Scriptures, *kids* is taken to mean *sinners*'.

ful it grows. *For the Lord* strikes and scourges *those he loves, and chastises every son he accepts.* Heb 12:6 Those whose fortune it is to receive the lash are granted the joys of eternity; but none who murmur and complain when he strikes them can ever draw near to him who is above them. Indeed they lose their inheritance of heavenly happiness who do not accept God the Father's scourging with patience and love. Those who grumble at the Lord's lashing will surely incur the grumbler's lot.[119]

So dear brothers, if it is your lot to be disciplined by our Lord, do not grumble. Do not become vexed when you are reproved. *Of course, any discipline is at the time a matter for grief, not joy; but later, in those who have undergone it, it bears fruit in peace and uprightness.* Heb 12:11 The Lord's scourging trims away the fleshiness of carnal desire.[120] When the flesh is reined in, the soul soars to heaven on wings of virtue: the flesh loses what it had in excess, while the soul gains virtues it never had. When the Lord chastises us we heap up virtues even as our vices are cut back: spurning the earthbound we savor the heavenly. As we await our eternal prize, let us find strength if some serious illness or powerful temptation or material loss befall us, for as the fight thickens, so bodes a victory all the more glorious! It is when our journey to God is rough and hard—not smooth and calm—that we show how a longing for

[119] 1 Cor 10:10, recollecting Num 17:6-10: 'Never complain *(murmuraveritis);* some of them complained, and they were killed by the Destroyer'. Vigilance against murmuring and complaining pervades the RB.

[120] *Pinguedo carnalis voluptatis,* perhaps an echo of Augustine (*pinguedo carnis: The City of God,* 22.22).

him inflames us. Only through hardships here and now can we regain eternal joys. Thus with the hope of lasting gladness we should reckon every adversity generous good fortune. On no account does divine impartiality allow our sins to go unpunished, but the wrath of his judgment begins with our correction here, so that he is appeased before what is base in us incurs damnation.

Our physician is at work within, cutting away the deep infection of our sins. With the compress of tribulation he draws out the poisonous humors of corruption. For Truth himself says, 'God the Father *prunes every branch that does bear fruit, to make it bear even more.*' Thus when temptation comes we should consider how it drives us from the former firmness of our resolve; let us then dread to lose what has so long been tended in us. Let us seek to resist temptation with all we have and fight it off as valiantly as we can. With the sword of prayer and the tears of compunction we shall break temptation's hold and triumph gloriously over it, not by our own might, but through Christ's grace in us. In this way even we who in good times lie indolent and barren may rise up strong and bear abundant fruit.

Beloved brothers, if we are to be found worthy to have God the Father tend us, we must cling to the true vine, our Lord Jesus Christ, not with faith that is dead or fictitious or erroneous, but with faith that is true, faith that operates through love, without which none can be saved. Let us cling to him, for it is good to do so. Let us place in him our every hope and desire, trusting in God the Father who raised him from the dead, for we will raise up as well our mortal bodies, to seat us together with him at his right hand. May he see fit to be present with us through his Son our Lord,

who lives and reigns with the
Father in union with the Holy Spirit,
God for ages unending.
Amen.

XI

ELEVENTH HOMILY

You are clean already, by means of the word that I have spoken to you. Abide in me, and I shall abide in you. As a branch cannot bear fruit at all by itself, unless it remains part of the vine, neither can you bear fruit unless you remain in me. Anyone who does not remain in me is thrown away like a branch and withers, and it is cast into the fire and burned. . . .

John 15:3-4, 6

LET THERE BE NO DOUBT about what the disciple of Truth meant when he wrote, *Whoever sows sparingly will also reap*
2 Cor 9:6 *sparingly.* We who have been called to be farmers in the Lord's fields should sow mightily, so that when harvest time comes we may gather in fruit *a hundredfold* more than the seed we have sown.[121] Sowing is an act of love: whoever sows in order to gather in must go without for a while so as to rejoice in the bounty of the harvest. Thus, *poor and destitute* as I am,[122] love impels me to give my modest store of

[121] Cf. Mt 19:29.
[122] *Pauper et inops,* cf. Ps 73:21.

seed to anyone who desires it, so that my Lord Jesus Christ may find me worthy to receive a manifold increase of eternal bliss. We do not sow sparingly if we lavish what little we have with the intention of having more. We give generously, even if we have nothing to bestow, so long as we are disposed to generosity. Whatever the funds we have received from the Lord to disburse, let us draw interest on them by disbursing them to all who desire them. Do not fear to draw such returns, for this is not usury that impoverishes the wealthy, but interest that enriches us with goodness and fills the poor and the needy. Come then, thirsting for that wealth, to blessed John's Gospel, and draw joyously from the Saviour's fountains.

Jesus told his disciples, *You are clean already, by means of the word that I have spoken to you. You are clean,* but you must be made clean again so as to bear more fruit. *You are clean*, not on account of your baptism, but *on account of the Word I have spoken to you.* O how good is the Word that washes away the mind's filth and purifies the actions of both the outer and the inner person.[123] That is the Word that heals our wounds and firms up our scars. O excellent Word that *lifts up the lowly from the dust and raises the poor from the dungheap to set him in the company of the princes* of heaven—with *Ps 112:7-8*
those who possess paradise! O how precious the treasure of that Word, which so enriches all who have taken it to themselves so as to transform the partners of the beasts of burden

[123] Cf. Rom 7:22; Eph 3:16.

into companions of the angels! O happy Word, and worthy to be received!

What is this word of bliss? Listen, if indeed you would keep it; but I insist that you be ready to draw interest from it without delay. It is a fine possession that brings increase when given away, but scorns a greedy possessor; for unless it is paid out it quickly diminishes. It rejoices in generosity and slips from the miser's grasp. In no way will it be *hidden under a bushel-*
Mt 5:15 *basket,* it must be *set upon a candlestick,* so that its beauty may be seen by all. *Its flashes are flashes of fire, a most vehement flame that many waters cannot quench. Were one to offer all the wealth of the house* for this possession, *it would*
Sg 8:6-7 *be scorned as worthless.*

This possession is loving-kindness,[124] for all in whom the love of the eternal abounds soon find cheap and paltry the possession of things that slip away. The love of Christ alone is sweet to them, the love of him who said, *I give you a new commandment, that you love one*
Jn 13:34, 15:12 *another even as I have loved you.* This is the word the Lord means when he says, *You have already been made clean by the word I have spoken to you*—by the love I have commanded of you. And as you are now clean, *abide in me, and I shall abide in you.*

O what a sublime promise: that mortals should dwell with the angels, that earth and dust be raised up to heaven, that we partners of the beasts of burden should be lifted up from the dungheap and gathered together with the angelic hosts; that creatures should

[124] *Caritas.*

abide in the Creator, the made with their Maker, the ransomed in their Redeemer, servants in the Master, sinners in the Just One, and those we who were formed of the mud in him who formed everything from nothing; that the passing should abide in the Everlasting, the wretched in the supremely Blessed—indeed, in him who alone makes blessed the blessed and hallows all that is holy: in him who is truth and life and glory everlasting, the world's joy and heaven's happiness, the sweetness of paradise and the bliss of eternity, Christ Jesus the Lord!

O wondrous and inexhaustible goodness! O unheard-of, unfathomable loving care![125] Dearest loving brothers, my fellow servants of Christ (and, for his sake, my masters as well), who could ever find the words to interpret that loving care with which the author of all loving care overflows? Whose pen could put to paper the bountiful goodness in which its very author abounds? Believe me, brothers, even if all were to exert themselves—mortals and angels alike—they could scarcely draw you the least little droplet from that fountain of loving care, so overwhelming is its abundance. It is, I say, with immeasurable loving care and unscalable heights of goodness that God the Creator *emptied himself, taking the form of a servant, become in all respects like man, and clothed in man's flesh,* so that, by abiding in Phil 2:7
man, man might abide in God. He welcomed death, so that death might welcome life. O that the fragrance of this abundance of

[125] *Pietas.*

loving care might daily waft in our nostrils, so that we might truly say with the Bride in the Song of Songs, 'Ever upon my breast I bear my beloved's sachet of myrrh.'[126] O sweet burden, O welcome medicine!

This burden, brothers, is the blessed Cross itself, Christ's Passion. Bearing it does not weigh us down, it uplifts us; it does not bring us low, it bears us aloft. It does not crush, it buoys: it bears all who bear it to where Christ is, in the glory of the Father. This medicine most sweet cures every infirmity and brings strength and courage to the faint of heart. It not only heals the ill, it revives the dead. Hear me, lovers of the Cross: those who avail themselves of that medicine in this life *will not suffer*
Rev 2:11 *harm in the second death.* This is that prophetic
Hab 2:11 *beam that holds in place the rafters of the building.* The Cross of glory binds earth and heaven together,[127] joins human beings to the fellowship of angels, and so reconciles sinners with God that God himself deems it fitting to dwell in them, and they in Him. O supremely solemn dance,[128] O dance of joy, delightful gladness, glad delight: to abide in God and He in us, the redeemed in the Redeemer, the Redeemer in the redeemed!

To this supremely gladsome joy the author of glory invites his apostles. To this everlasting bliss the bestower of bliss rouses his monks. He who is eternal well-being and life

[126] *Fasciculum myrrae dilecti semper supra meum pectus portabo,* paraphrasing Sg 1:12 (*fasciculum myrræ dilectus meus mihi inter ubera mea commorabitur* 'my beloved reposes, a sachet of myrrh, between my breasts') so as to masculinize the image.

[127] *Conglutinat,*: cf. 1 Sam 18:1 *(anima Ionathan conglutinata est animæ David).*

[128] Cf. Homily IX, note 87.

ever-blessed, he who is certain serenity and blissful eternity, he who is all that is sweet and desirable, calls out to the whole of the Christian community, enticing, caressing, consoling, strengthening, encouraging. *Abide in me, and I in you,* he says. 'You who have been washed and made clean, you who have been sanctified through the channel of stone, the sacrament of baptism, and through the banquet of virtues, the proclamation of love: you are in me! But *remain in me,* I pray, during this brief lifetime; for if you do, *I* shall remain *in you* throughout eternity. *In all who* by demonstrating singular love *abide in me, I will abide* as the prize of eternal bliss. I hold dear all who hold me dear. Those who love me during this life will find me after this life, *so that where I am they may be also.* Those who do not love me *Jn 14:3*
will also find me—as an avenger. But you, my disciples, my friends, *abide* in my love. Do not be frightened by my human suffering, the agony of the cross, the entombment of my mortality. Let faith remain invincible in you. Let hope never languish, but let the fire of my love blaze in you. *Abide in me* through faith, hope, and love, *and I* shall abide *in you* through the fruits of faith, hope, and love.[129] For if you do not abide in me, neither shall I abide in you.'

[129] Ogier omits 15:5 *(Ego sum vitis, vos palmites; qui manet in me, et ego in eo, hic fert fructum multum quia sine me nihil potestis facere).* The verse largely recapitulates the opening of Jn 15, which Ogier has taken up in X. Some of the verse is paraphrased here *(qui manet in me per exhibitionem dilectionis, et ego manebo in eo per præmium æternæ felicitatis),* and *per fructum* recalls it as well, though the image is drawn, as if triggered by the verb, from 1 Cor 13:13 *(Nunc autem manent fides, spes, caritas, tria hæc).*

Dearest brothers, you have heard what Truth himself says: *Whoever does not abide in me I will cast out,* and the attendants of torment *will cast him into the fire to be burned*. He who speaks cannot deceive. I therefore implore each of you, beloved brothers, to retire to your cell and scour your conscience, examining the crannies of your hearts and the dark recesses of your minds. If then you find yourselves abiding in Christ, rejoice! But groan and grieve if you find yourself absent from Christ, lest, separated from the fellowship of the saints, you be cast out to burn for ever in the eternal flames.

Abide in me. Alas, dearest brothers, how wretched and unhappy are they who have been struck down by the serpent's lethal venom. Deceived by the devil's guile, led astray by the blindness of their minds, and depraved in their wickedness, they come to Jesus but forswear Christ's companionship, forsaking the friendship of their Redeemer for the sake of worldly attachment. Having spurned their Creator, they who used to bear their heads to God now boldly bend their necks to the devil. Alas, how many, after the glorious Easter triumph, turn their backs on the vanquisher of the prince of this world and, fleeing the victor, bow down of their own accord to the vanquished one!

How many come to the monastery to live the monastic life there, putting on the signs of humility, bearing peacefully every censure, ready like good soldiers of Christ for any good work. But then, having tasted the joys of the contemplative life and the honeyed outpourings of its delights, they forget their profession and, turning aside from their erstwhile intention, revert *like pigs to their slough, to roll once again in the muck,* or, like *dogs returning to their vomit,* they swallow what some time ago they had vomited up![130] Retreating from their holy purpose, they turn away from Christ as well. They might have turned in scorn from the poisons they vomited, had they but held to the covenant they made with Christ; but as it is, they no longer deserve to remain in Christ, because they did not shrink from weakening that covenant. If only they could know and understand what bitterness lies in deserting the fountain of life, the author of honeyed joys, the Lord of the universe, the comeliness of paradise, eternal happiness, the Lord Jesus Christ who saved us from death by the shedding of his crimson blood! If only you might suddenly sense how much you were prepared to offend,

2 Pet 2:22

> *No longer, Myrrh,*
> *would the bark cover your face.*[131]

O what a wretched metamorphosis, what blind lust it is, that turns a virgin into a decay-eaten wench, a woman into a tree, a rule into an apostasy, holy discipline into wanton depravity, the orderliness of the cloister into the lasciviousness of the fields, chastity into pustular lust,[132] a monk into an imbecile, the

[130] The order of images is reversed.

[131] Ovid, *Metamorphoses,* Book X.

[132] *Impetigo;* perhaps the far-fetched image was chosen for its applicability to both human skin and tree bark.

straight into the crooked, the smooth into the rough, a child of God into a child of the devil! This, my brothers, is no *shortcoming of the right hand of the Most High.* O what a bitter falling off, what a harsh departure: to withdraw from Christ and cling to the devil, to spurn the Redeemer and love the Slayer of souls, to stray from the footsteps of Christ and track the wild and winding path to hell! To leave the road that leads to life and follow the course that ends in death!

Ps 76:11

Let all who have suffered such change be attentive to my counsel: *My son, have you sinned? Do not add further sin. Thus speaks the Holy One of Israel: In returning and rest you shall be saved; for the Lord awaits you, to be gracious to you.* Return then to the Lord your God and he will forgive your wickedness. Return to the Lord by the way that leads to him: the way of the heart, the way of the mouth—that is, confession—the way of work, of fear, of sorrow, and of love. Return by the way of the contrite heart, the way of praising lips, the way of the upright act. Return by the way of fear, lest you be dragged before the executioner. Return by the way of sorrow, since you have offended Christ. Return by the way of love, truly at last to love Christ, who for so long has awaited your repentance. Moan, grieve, wail, weep! Do not spare yourself; let God spare you. Do not indulge yourself; let the Lord deem you worthy of forbearance. Gird up your loins, shave your head, don sackcloth, sprinkle yourself with dust, and say to the Lord Christ, your God, 'Good Jesus, have mercy on me! Be my Saviour, Jesus! Have mercy on me, for whom

Sir 21:1

Is 30:15, 18

Cf. Ps 50:19; Ps 62:6; Prov 20:11

you poured out your blood! *Do not enter into judgment with your servant,* for no one will be *Ps 142:2*
justified unless through you alone his sins be remitted. Let not the sentence of your judg- *Cf. Eph 1:7*
ment weigh upon me, whom your manifold loving-kindness buoys up. You who raised up Lazarus even after his body had begun to decompose, raise me up also, a sinner who has *Jn 11*
begun again to trust in you. You spared the harlot Mary Magdalene; spare my soul as well! *Cf. Lk 7:47*
You gladdened the heart of the crucified thief; *Cf. Lk 23:43*
gladden this sinner's soul!' Do this, and you will yet abide in Christ, and he in you, for he is loving-kindness itself. *All who abide in love abide in God, and God abides in them.* *1 Jn 4:16*

Let it be noted that it is one thing to abide in Christ and another to abide with him. And again, it is one thing to abide next to him and another to abide far from him. To abide *in him* is to be partly on the way and partly already there, in our homeland; to abide *with him* is wholly to be home. To abide *next to him* is yet to be in this world; to abide *far from him* is already to be in hell. Let us learn what it is to abide in him, so that we may delight to do so and, not long hence, may be found worthy to abide with him. To abide in him is to cling to him alone in love, to love him whole-heartedly, to prefer nothing whatever to loving him and, *RB 4.21*
for love of him, to reckon everything else as non-existent. In Christ abide all who reckon all else worthless, to whom Christ alone is sweet. What endowment of good fortune, what enrichment of bliss: to find all except Christ worthless, and him alone honey-sweet! May Christ alone be the honeycomb of our

hearts, and may everything transitory be as gall. Let nothing apart from him be to our liking or in any way desirable. O my brothers, let us be worthy of abiding in Christ and with Christ, our true light, our only goodness, life, and joy here below, immeasurable love! May he be our sole desire and our every hope. May we be certain that we still abide in Christ, and that where he is we may be also.

Now anyone who says he abides in Christ
1 Jn 2:6 *ought to walk just as Christ walked. Let no one*
1 Jn 3:7 be deceived or *be led astray*. Let no one trust in his religious garb: it is the purity of his mind, not his habit, and the saving love of Christ, not the shaving of his head, that makes a monk. The Lord Jesus says, *'If anyone wishes*
Mt 16:24 *to follow me, let him deny himself'*, for none who do not forsake themselves can approach the sublimity of Christ the King. For his sake, forswearing ourselves is joyous! Let no one in whom self-denial is not perfected esteem himself as anyone pleasing to Christ. It is vain to seek to please him without casting ourselves aside for his sake. Those who have fully learned how to forswear themselves will know how perfectly to please him.

Therefore if we are to please Christ, self-denial is absolutely necessary. As much as health allows, we should at least deny ourselves as regards our partaking of food. (As much as health allows, I say, not as truly befits our self-abhorrence, lanced through and through by sin, into which hole we might plunge our hand!) We ought to maintain our natural strength without giving way to the enticements of the gullet. We shall never be able to overcome the vices of the flesh that arise from our loins unless we have first learned to rein in our appetite for food with a firm application of abstinence. But once having beaten down the gullet's cravings, let us be careful not to become caught in the mouse-trap[133] of pride. For, should the venom of unwholesome praise seep into the inner chambers of our hearts, the cautering-iron may sizzle but fail to work its weal. Whatever wisp of praise arise about us, whatever fawning favor, let not Humility, the empress of the virtues,[134] abandon the hidden closet of our hearts, where the coiled serpent of human approbation lies hidden in the greenest grass. Remember well the poet's words:

Fly, children, far from here—
there lurks a snake in the grass![135]

Let not that serpent's venomous fangs strike us, lest he capture us and destroy us! Let us maintain great humility in all things, so to abide in the author of humility and be found worthy to reign with him so long as we are with him. Do you abide in him for love? Then do not doubt that he will return that love and abide in you.

We have seen what it is to abide *in* him. Now we shall want to see what it is to abide *with* him. To abide with him is to be where he is, to rejoice with him in bright glory, to

[133] *Muscipula,* a Roman Psalter variant reading of the Vulgate *laqueus* in Ps 123:7.

[134] See n. 50.

[135] Vergil, *Eclogue* 3, 93.

reign upon an everlasting throne, to contemplate him face to face—as the holy angels do and, after the resurrection of the body, all the elect shall do. *When Christ who is our life appears, then you also will appear with him in glory.* (Col 3:4) To abide *next to* Christ but not in him or with him, is not to be on the path of faith, hope, and love, but on the road of error; not to be on the way of his commandments but on the highway of sin. One, therefore, who is neither in Christ or with Christ is next to him. He possesses free will; he could direct his will to loving God. The Lord is knocking at the door; (Cf. Rev 3:20) he has only to open it and the Lord will enter to abide in him and he in the Lord. To abide *far from* Christ is to have retreated from him under sentence of damnation, however you can comprehend that. Let us abide in him so that we may ever be found worthy to bear the fruit of good works; if we do not abide with him we shall surely bear none. Truth himself says, *'As a branch cannot bear fruit at all by itself,* unless it remains part of the vine, *neither can you bear fruit unless you remain in me. Anyone who does not remain in me is thrown away like a branch and withers, and it is cast into the fire and burned.'* That is a fate greatly to be feared. Anyone not remaining in the Lord Jesus Christ will be cast out from the company of the saints with the fear and expectation of everlasting damnation. The henchmen of hell will seize him and cast him into the everlasting fire to be burned for ever. May our Lord Jesus Christ, the author of everlasting glory, deliver us from eternal damnation:

he who lives and reigns with the
Father and the Holy Spirit,
God for ever and ever blessed.
Amen.

XII

TWELFTH HOMILY

If you remain in me and my words remain in you, you may ask for whatever you please and you will get it. By this my Father is glorified, that you bear much fruit, and so prove to be my disciples. Just as my Father loved me, so I have loved you. Abide in my love.

John 15:7-9

IF WE TRULY LONG to lay hold of the way of Truth, we must remain steadfast in our resolve to stretch forth the hand of our hearts towards Christ's teachings, and to live by them faithfully. Only then will that hand be filled with gems,[136] its *belly fashioned of ivory set with sapphires.* Only then can the pyx of the mind contain, through love, the word of the Word, so that the flower of the Word may give off its fragrant scent through an increase of good works. All so resolved to seek from God whatever is good are bound to obtain it: the very Principle of Truth and Essence of Sanc-

Sg 5:14

[136] *Hyacinthis,* a gemstone variously related to beryl, topaz, and sapphire; the stone is listed (among eleven others, including *sapphyris, berillus,* and *topazius*) in Rev 21:20. The allusion to Sg 5:14 *(manus illius tornatiles aureæ plenæ hyacinthis)* is made explicit in the next sentence.

tity has sanctioned it for all time. No word of his can suffer change; nothing he has promised can be deleted from the Book of Life.[137] Listen to the words of Jesus; listen to the promise of God, truth's firm foundation, falsehood's opposite, sins' avenging, the Way of all ways, the Life of life, wholly sweet and good, truthful and wholly true: *If you remain in me and my words remain in you, you may ask for whatever you please and you will get it.*

Great are the gifts promised by Truth himself, who cannot deceive. *'Whatever you please'*, the Lord Jesus says, *'ask and it will be yours*—so long as *you remain in me and my words remain in you.* If you abide in me through love and my words abide in you through the performance of works, whatever you wish (pertaining to the well-being of your soul), ask without hesitation and you will obtain it.'The two conditions are necessarily related; one of them cannot suffer the absence of the other. They form a kind of syllogism: if we abide in Christ, it follows necessarily that Christ's teachings abide in us; it follows then from either premise that whatever we wish we shall obtain. The inference is self-evident. Remaining in Christ, whatever we seek will be granted. And: Christ's words abiding in us, the effect is identical.

Let us pursue this. Suppose some braying logician should object to conjunction of equal members without the conjunction of the

[137] This sentence and the latter half of the preceding are couched in sequence form; it is probably a citation: *Ipsa regula veritatis | omnis forma sanctitatis | sanxit in perpetuum. Nec valebit abrogari | nec de libro iam mutari | veritatis sanctio.*

parts and the whole, contraries and opposites, exceptions and violations, etc. Let us distinguish, then, those who abide in Christ and Christ's words in them, from others who abide in God though God's words do not abide in them. A theologian,[138] for example, who abides in Christ, and in whom Christ's words abide, possesses such doctrinal erudition as to be able to offer his students both the old and the new, the fruit of authority in both Testaments. Let the good he teaches be seen as well in the deeds of his pure and devout life. Another, without this gift of scriptural learning, abides in Christ by virtue of his good life; he may not have Christ's commandment in a book, yet he has it in a *heart laid open* by love.[139] Both are blessed, for indeed *theirs is the kingdom of heaven* [Mt 5:3]. Another has God's word but does not practice it; such is a monk of mere religious show, cloaked in the pretext of holiness, whose life is a perverse contradiction of the rule of Benedict. He does not remain in Christ, nor do Christ's words remain in him, for he neither loves Christ nor keeps his commandments, whatever his pretensions. The true state of such a wretch will be revealed *Cf. 1 Cor 3:13* on the Day of the Lord, when there can be no pretense of religion, no feigned holiness, no sophistry, no well-turned syllogism; for then all things will be plain and open before Jesus the Judge. Judging with truth and discernment, Jesus will expose the crooked deed, the idle word, the foot's misstep, the hand's vain toil, the casting of the eyes.

[138] *Doctor ecclesiasticus.*

[139] Cf. the *dilatatum cor* of Ps 118:32.

Ponder—you whom this describes—what it means to be a monk. You *have washed your feet, should* you *dirty them again?* You *changed your garment;* change your thoughts as well.[140] Are you white on the outside, clad in the white cowl of Cîteaux? Why then are you black within, singed with the branding-iron of your befouled conscience? You are meant to devote yourself to silence; why take such delight in talkativeness? You have vowed to despise the world; and still you try to please it? Love Jesus above all: *prefer nothing to the love of Christ.* Keep before your eyes the fear of the Lord wherever you are,[141] sitting or going, speaking or in silence, in hunger and thirst or when eating and drinking; for in holy fear is the confidence of strength, the hope of eternal bliss, the assurance of forgiveness, the certainty of glory, the remission of sins, the generosity of God, the attainment of gladness, the full enjoyment of the true and most high God. *Happy the man,* says the Psalmist *who fears the Lord, who takes delight in all his commands. His seed will be powerful on earth,* and he shall be blessed of the Lord.

RB 4.21

Ps 111:1, 2

Eternal bliss, the confluence of everlasting sweetness, the joyous vision of God for ever: this is the gift for which all who remain in Christ ask of him. If you abide in Christ—if with pure heart and conscience you have the outpouring of Christ's love—nothing but Christ will be able to satisfy you, nor will you be able to seek anything but him. *Ask what you*

[140] Cf. Sg 5:3 (order reversed here), also cited in Homily II.

[141] This is the first of Benedict's *Humilitatis gradus* (RB 12.25).

will, says the Lord Jesus: that well-being that never ends, that life that never dies, supreme joy, the glory of paradise, sweeter than any honey, more delicious than any nectar, more precious than jewels and gold. *Whatever you wish,* he tells those who love him, *ask and it will be yours.* What a great promise this is!

But note that this 'whatever' does not in itself contain everything; it signifies rather the One who alone contains all things, whose being is ever true: God of God before all time, born man of a Virgin at the end of time. He is the eternal salvation of all believers, the hope and refuge of all who fear him. He is the sole desire of the elect, who can be satisfied by nothing else than God himself, in whom everything exists. They cannot yet gaze upon the author of bliss, and so they groan and mourn. There is no bliss for them: they seek the Lord Jesus and do not find him, they call but are not answered, and so they turn to tears as friends in grief. *Cf. Sg 3:1, 5:6* After him in whose footsteps they cannot follow, they go forth weeping and sighing. Yet how fortunate is the life, how blessed the lot of those whose course is so marked and festooned with the banner of love. It is not to the lazy that such a state is granted, nor is the negligent who attain it. Not the lamed but the one who runs the length of love may claim it.

Let each of us never cease to consider how we ought to run in the stadium of God's commandments, *Cf. 1 Cor 9:24-26* how as Christians we ought to strive to contend with the roaring lion.[142] No

[142] An apparent conflation of *in agone contendit* (1 Cor 9:25) and the *leo rugiens* of 1 Pet 5:8.

one here can hide, no one can be saved, who does not persevere faithfully to the moment of departing this earthly body. One who misses the mark, who fails along the way, cannot reach the finish line of eternal sweetness. Our track is the observance of God's commandments. Love is the goal of our race, or, as the apostle says, *love is the aim of our charge:* *1 Tim 1:5* not the love with which we love God, but that by which we possess him, the love that is God himself.

In the stadium of God's commandments some start the race well but flag at the post. Others get off to a lazy start but speed in the next lap. Still others start swiftly and continue swiftly—while others start slow and crawl along. Only two will successfully finish the race: the one who after a slow start gains speed, and the one who bounds nimbly and keeps up the pace.

Many come to the monastery to glory in the life. They start badly and finish badly, always wandering, never settling down. They grumble and complain when they do not get what they want. They bless their former cellmates,[143] but heap abuse on the brothers they live with. Ill disciplined, uncontrolled in their behavior and actions, puffed up in their bearing, they behave unsuitably and receive favors thanklessly. No prize awaits the likes of these; they have never set foot on the track of the Lord's commandments. No form of holiness, theirs, whose crooked ways and disobedience have poisoned and confounded them. In them

[143] Cistercian monks typically slept in open dormitories of minimal privacy.

the words of Christ do not abide; they scatter to the winds of vanity what few of the Lord's precepts they may have heard. The Lord's commands they despise; their bellies' demands they attend. They *kick the heels* of their wickedness at God the Eternal Almighty, hating their neighbor and denying the Lord Jesus Christ. No longer do they keep what they promised in the sight of all the saints on the day of their profession. All whom this describes must know that damnation awaits them: *God will not be*
Gal 6:7 *mocked.*

Another comes to the monastery there to be punished for the sins he committed in the world; but once there, not only does he not atone for what he committed, he commits further, perhaps even graver, sins. Then, stung through and through by grief, he falls prostrate in great shame. He recalls the severity of the sinner's judge, how great to the damned the punishment of damnation. Further, he considers how merciful the Redeemer is towards the penitent, how kind to those who live righteously. Now he numbers all his wicked ways; now his mind's eye surveys the lot with sorrow. Grief shakes him; the anguish of his punishment alarms him. He dreads the pain of hell, quaking before the torments of fire and brimstone. Nothing delights him; all that befalls him is doleful. With tears and grief he avenges what he perpetrated with such sinful pleasure. He strives with all his might to please Christ the Lord, devoting himself to fasting and prayer, and seeking only what is pleasing to God. Let him seek whatever he wishes of the Lord: without doubt he shall receive it.

My dearest brothers, we whom Christ ransomed with his own blood should love him for lavishing himself on our salvation. We should love him without measure—beyond all measure—with all our hearts and minds and all our strength, from the very core of our being. We should fear him, commit ourselves to him in love, and cling to his discipleship. How sweet and delightful it is, how joyous and cheerful to become Christ's disciple! For *by this,* the Lord Jesus tells his disciples, *my Father is glorified, that you bear much fruit, and so prove to be my disciples.* We therefore who are called—and are—Christians have been established in Christ's Church as if in a field. Some bear fruit; others persist in their barrenness. Some bear paltry fruit: they are lazy and negligent, indolent at prayer, tardy at their *lectio*, half-asleep at Vigils, tender and dainty at work. The Father of our Lord Jesus Christ is not glorified in these, for they neither bear much fruit not prove themselves to be Christ's disciples. Others produce sweet fruit in abundance—sweet to God and man alike. God is glorified in them, and God will glorify them on the day of their reward, when the new crop is harvested, when *they shall come rejoicing, bringing in the sheaves.* Such monks are meek *Ps 125:6*
and lowly, devout, obedient, wakeful at Vigils, fervent at every good work. They are borne aloft in prayer and plunge deep into holy *lectio*. They sigh in their meditation, moan and weep in their contemplation. Indeed they *sow in*

tears, but let them rejoice and be glad, for they shall reap eternal joys!

Others bear no fruit at all, merely bough and leaves. They have the appearance of holiness but not its fruits. The ax is taken to their roots—why should they occupy good soil? A harsh and bitter sentence is meted out to unfruitful trees: *Every tree,* says Jesus, *that does not*
Mt 7:19 *bear good fruit is cut down and thrown into the fire.* So let unfruitful trees beware: hypocrites,
Mt 23:27 *whited sepulchers,* cut and polished caskets that they are. Let that which lies hidden within be rooted out. Let them confess and be healed. Let the cautering iron of conscience sear and strengthen them. Let them direct their steps on the path of God's commandments, and so bear fruit. Then through them might the Father be glorified in the Son, and Christ in his Father, and they in Father, Son, and Holy Spirit. O greatly happy are all whose lives and actions intone the Creator's praises! Happy those whose soul serves their Creator and strives to please their Redeemer. Blessed is the soul to whom Christ is total love, the soul that can be satisfied by none but Christ who was slain for love. Blessed the soul that knows none but Christ who loved us and washed us from our sins in his blood, giving himself as our ransom that through his blood we might become God's adopted children.[144]

Let Christ be blessed by all, he who loved humankind even as his Father loved him—even as he says, *Just as my Father loved me, so I have loved you.*

[144] Cf. Gal 4:5.

O loving love, O everlasting truth!
O sweet eternity, O blessed bliss!
O ornament of angels, O splendor of the
saints!
O good Jesu, O Jesus holy Lord!
O life unsullied, everlasting life,
Unfailing weal, unending glory!
O wholly delectable, wholly lovable,
How you have loved us!
How you cherish us yet!
For us you bore death's embrace.

Your love knew no bounds; your loving-kindness is beyond all measure. *Even as my Father loved me,* you say, *so I have loved you.* Oh, that I could be one whom my Lord might love! One whom he might tell, *Even as my Father loved me!* If my Jesus were to love me, what could I possibly lack? My Jesus, I say, O truly mine! O joyous wealth, O blessed riches: to possess Jesus, to possess Christ the Lord! Possess him in love, dear reader, and so you will possess him for ever in the love he returns. Truth himself says, *I love all who love me; and whoever loves me*[145] *will be loved by my Father, and I will love him and manifest myself to him.* How great the love Christ showed for *Jn 14:21*
us when he died for us, no one now alive could tell. Let tears exclaim what voice cannot explain. *Just as my Father loved me, so I have loved you.* Let us see how much God the Father loved Christ, and how much Christ loved us.

The apostle says, *Christ became obedient for our sake unto death, even death on a cross, and in*

[145] The citation conflates Prov 8:17 *(ego diligentes me diligo)* with the remainder of the Johannine verse, paraphrasing *et qui dilexerit me* for *qui autem diliget me.*

return God lifted him up and gave him a name that is above every name, such that at the name of Jesus every knee must bend in heaven, on earth,
Phil 2:8-10 *and in the underworld.*[146] This includes all the creatures of heaven—such as the angels, archangels, thrones, dominions, principalities and powers, virtues, cherubim and seraphim, every order in heaven—and every creature on earth as well, not only humankind but also the brute animals. So the Psalmist, speaking of him to the Father, says, *You put all things under his feet, all of them, sheep and cattle—even the savage beasts, the birds of the air, the fish that make their*
Ps 8:8-9 *way through the waters.* All must tremble with fear at the sound of Christ's name. And beyond these, every infernal creature trembles and quakes at the invoking of the Holy Name. Behold how much God the Father loved the Son: *The Father judges no one, but has given all*
Jn 5:22 *judgment to the Son.* Great indeed is the Father's love, in thus having raised up the Son and exalted him, putting all things beneath his feet and subjecting everything to his authority.

We have seen how the Father loved Christ. Let us now examine how Christ has loved us. But who could unfold such love? Who could expound in words the overflowing abundance of loving-kindness that Christ has had for us? Christ loved us and washed us from our sins in his blood, and, dying, he destroyed our death.[147] He chose to die for us so as to deliver us from everlasting death and draw us to him-

[146] The latter two verses are repeated later in the passage, following the citation of Jn 5:22, in a loosely ordered argument that I have tightened here.

[147] The phrase is closely modeled on the Paschal Preface *(qui mortem nostram moriendo destruxit).*

self, where he is, in the glory of the Father. For he says, *It is my will, Father, that where I am my minister may be also.* Behold how much he loved us![148] He rose again from the dead to raise us up to the celestial mansions, and he sits at the right hand of the Father to seat and crown and gladden there those whom he redeemed in his blood, those whom he has bonded to himself in love to be with him at his Father's right hand. Therefore let us love and revere Christ without measure, boundlessly, fervently, steadfastly, with all our hearts and minds, with all our might, so that we might be found worthy to come to him and reign with him *Jn 12:26*

who lives with the Father and the
Holy Spirit[149]
blessed for evermore.
Amen.

[148] Perhaps a conscious echo of Jn 11:36, *Ecce quomodo amabat eum [Lazarum].*
[149] *Sancto Flamine,* perhaps recollecting Saint Gregory of Tours.

XIII

THIRTEENTH HOMILY

Just as my Father loved me, so I have loved you. Remain in my love. If you keep my commandments you will remain in my love, for just as I have kept my Father's commandments, so I remain in his love. I have told you these things so that my own joy may be in you and your joy be complete. . . . No one can have greater love than to lay down his life for his friends.

John 15:9-11,13

THE MORE I DRINK of the love of God, the more I thirst; I cannot drink my fill. So it is with all who love Christ fully. Our appetite increases by what it feeds on. Our thirst grows keener the more we quaff. And when that love inebriates our minds—in which it dwells—we can no longer seek or love anything except him *who so loved the world that he gave his only-begotten Son, so that anyone who believes in him* and loves him *should not die,*
Jn 3:16 *but live for ever with him.* It is to this love that the very author of love invites us.

Remain in my love, he bids us, as if to say openly: 'In the same love with which my

Father loves me I love you, and I ask you to love me with that love as well. My love for you led me to my death, but not even that most cruel death could disjoin me from my love for you. Love me, and *remain in my love*.' To show us how we are to remain in his love, he tells us: *If you keep my commandments you will remain in my love, for just as I have kept my Father's commandments, so I remain in his love. Whoever has ears to hear, let him listen;* whoever has a heart to understand, let him comprehend. But surely this exceeds our limits, ranges far beyond our powers of mind and body—beyond our view and ken. What our Lord commands of us is the plan of our salvation, adapted to each of us by the Author of all salvation. But which of us, sprung from the apostate stock of Adam, has been able—indeed, could be able—to keep—spotlessly, without the blemish of the slightest transgression, in perfect love—Christ's commandments undiminished, even as Christ kept his Father's commandments, singly and wholly? He who did not sin, who could not even will to sin![150] No human, whether great or small, was ever endowed with such holiness; nor was any so privileged with spiritual distinction as not to have been born in sin or, thereafter, have lived in sin—excepting the Mother of him who himself did not sin but, blameless as he was, bore the sins of the world![151] With regard to

Mt 11:15

[150] While Ogier's wording reverberates with distant echoes of monotheletism, his assertion that Christ's will was always in union with the will of the Father expresses a rather different, undogmatic sentiment.

[151] On this singular passage—and its eventful reception and transmission—see the Introduction.

sinfulness, brothers, let there be no further questioning about Our Lady! But if the expression, *just as I have kept my Father's commands,* is to be taken quantitatively, then of course in no one else has ever shone such sanctity.

Let us remind ourselves that the expression *just as* denotes a qualitative similarity, not a quantitative one. We have already noted this in the passage where Jesus pronounces the Rule of Love.[152] The meaning here is this: *'If you keep my commands,* to the full extent of your frail powers, until you depart this earthly abode, as I, according to the fulness of divinity that abides in me bodily, obeyed my Father even unto death on the cross; then you will remain in my love, and I in yours, *just as I remain in my Father's love* and he in mine.' In this passage, *just as* does not have its full significance with regard to us; it denotes a similarity to Christ's love and obedience towards God the Father that is meant to remind and admonish us to keep Christ's commands and so to remain in his love. It is as if he said: 'I have ever kept my Father's commands for your salvation's sake, and, thus, *I remain in his love. Keep* then *my commands* for your salvation's sake, and, thus, *remain in my love!'*

Remain in my love! How the love of the Beloved—the loving-kindness of our loving Lord Jesus Christ—compels me again and again to repeat it! O Jesus, the resurrection of the dead, the life of the living, the eternal well-being of believers: how wholly sweet and delightful to all who love and seek you—to

[152] Jn 13:34 (V): *ut diligatis invicem* sicut *dilexi vos.*

all who find you! Make me worthy, servant that I am, to speak with my Master, man to God, creature to Creator, artifact to Artisan, ransomed soul to my Redeemer Lord! Hear me, then; do not be vexed with me! Sinner that I am, still I love you. It is your love that emboldens me to speak to you. It is your loving-kindness that prompts my heart. You told your apostles, through whom we, too, are addressed, *Remain in me, and I remain in you.* O delectable beauty, O honey-flowing sweetness, O sweet fragrance —O fragrant sweetness, highest bliss, everlasting glory! O Life of the saints, O ornament of angels, Saviour of the world, Son of the living God: Jesus most sweet, most comely, most dear! Speak, beloved![153] What is the cause of your love—the bonding force of your loving-kindness—by which you command us to hear and love you? How is it that those who love you grow ever more fervent in your love? Speak, that those who do not love you may hear you and love you, and that those who do love you may grow ever more ardent in your love. *Sweet is the sound of your voice in my ear.* Speak: '*Just as the Father has loved me, so I have loved you,* and because I have loved you, do you repay me with your love. Love me, and *abide in my love!*'

Sg 2:14

Jn 15:9 (cited Homily XII)

It is right and proper that you say this, Lord Jesus, that you command this of us. Reason and fairness dictate that the loved one love the lover: that mutual love bond them. Yet still we seek another cause for that love

[153] This bernardine device is noted above in Homily IX (n. 88). The source of both in the Song of Songs is made explicit here a few lines on.

of yours, by which we should love you even more: tell us who you are! Tell us what you have done for us, and why you have commanded us to love you. Tell us:
Ex 3:14 *'I am who am.*
Rev 22:13 *I am Alpha and Omega, the beginning and the end,* Creator of heaven and earth, *of the sky and the*
Ps 23:1 *sea and all that inhabit them.* I am Maker and Creator of all, King of kings, Lord of lords, ruler of all.' We hear it and we rejoice, certain that you are God, blessed throughout endless ages.

Yet our sighs—and the tears of my sinful soul—implore you to recount yet again what you have done for us. For when, recalling what you have done for me, I remember what I have done to you, my spirit quakes, my soul is deeply troubled, and I am wounded, pierced through with boundless grief.[154] And no wonder! I weigh what the servant has done to his Master—and the numberless torments the Master bore to atone for his servant. My conscience, Lord Jesus, bears witness of what I have done to you. Your cross bears witness of what you have done for me! You are God; I am but man. Yet for me, God, you became a man. You are the Creator; I but a creature. Yet creature you deigned for my sake to become. You are Master; we your servants. And for your servants you became a servant; for us pilgrims you became a pilgrim, for us exiles an exile, poor in our poverty, humbled for our lowliness. For us you became mortal: you died not by any natural death, but by a harsh and

[154] While the vocabulary here is scriptural, the combinations elude direct citation; *anima conturbatur* recalls Ps 41:7 *(anima mea conturbata est),* while *vulneror* points to Is 53:5 *(vulneratus est propter iniquitates nostras)* as the source and scope of Ogier's wounding grief.

bitterly shameful death on a cross. These are your works, my God. I ponder them and tremble. I recognize in them that you are merciful; and so, revived, I find my trust in you. Above all else I love you. From the depths of my being I long for you.

These works, brothers, are the cause of Christ's love; let each of us examine our love for Jesus. What more ought he have done, and did not do?[155] How could he have loved more than he did? Greater love for us he could not have, than to have laid down his life for us in death. As blessed Truth himself is witness, *No one can have greater love than to lay down his life for his friends.*[156] Never let that love lessen, brothers! Never let Christ's love grow bitter to you. Christ's love is wholly sweet and delightful. It does not torment its possessor, it delights! It does not weary, it strengthens: it drives away all earthly things and grasps the things of heaven. It requires Christ's commandments and makes us strive with all our might to keep them. Then it brings us with springing steps from observing his precepts to the reception of perfect joy. At last we rejoice with him for whom we have so often sighed with desire in this vale of tears.[157]

Thus quite rightly he says, *'I have told you these things so that my own joy may be in you and your joy be complete.* I instruct and admonish you to keep my teachings and remain in my love, so that my joy may fill you, and that I

[155] From the *Improperia* of the Holy Friday liturgy (*GR* 176), based ultimately on Micah 6:2.

[156] Jn 15:13, out of sequence here (see n. 36).

[157] Cf. Ps 83:7 as in the Marian antiphon for Compline, *Salve Regina*.

have cause to rejoice over your love for me. Then you can experience and possess the joy the elect receive at the bestowing of rewards.' All who from the depths of their hearts embrace Christ in the arms of love—all who bind themselves to Christ, purely, unstintingly, unflaggingly, in the bosom of lovingkindness—may count Christ's joy as their own. Theirs is the joy Christ received from the Father when he rose again, ascended into heaven, and took his place at his Father's side; they shall have greater joy in that than in the joy to be received from Christ on judgment day. Therefore, dearest brothers, may Christ's joy abide in you whether actively or passively, whether as lover or as loved one, whether the joy with which Christ rejoices in us, or that joy with which we rejoice in him. Let us keep Christ's commands so that he might rejoice in us and we in him. May the joy of his blessedness remain in us, not only that joy with which he blesses and gladdens those who rejoice in him, but even that joy by which he is glorified by his Father. May we be found worthy to reign through the same Jesus Christ our Lord,

who with the Father and the
Holy Spirit lives and reigns,
one God, blessed through endless ages.
Amen.

XIV

FOURTEENTH HOMILY

This is my commandment, that you love one another as I have loved you. You are my friends if you do what I have commanded of you.

John 15:12, 14

IN PRAISE OF OUR REDEEMER let not our tongues be mute, lest we find ourselves suddenly among those who are silent concerning him.[158] In this regard it is as urgent that we avoid becoming perfunctory in our day-to-day conversing about the Lord as it is for us to curb our tongues from idle talk, lest the sentence of dire damnation befall us. Let us everywhere condemn to perpetual exclusion all idle talk—all that neither resounds of Christ nor befits the gravity of monastic observance. Rather let us tune our lyres to the sweet speech overflowing from the Father's Word. Let the tongue be the plectrum of the mind, and to our Saviour let our voices' magistral trumpet intone those sweet words that flowed forth from his honeyed lips.[159]

[158] Cf. Ps 113:17, especially in Jerome *(Psalmi iuxta Hebraicum): Non mortui laudabunt Dominum nec omnes qui descendunt in silentium.*

[159] *. . . ad dulcia eloquia a Verbo Patris eructata cithara nostra suas chordas extendat, et plectrum mentis lingua vocis magistra tuba insonet salvatori, quæ de ore mellifluo Christi*

Over what I mean to set before you here let no shadow of base advantage fall; undarkened by disdain, and closely bound in love, let it sparkle for you more brightly than any jewel! May it taste more sweetly on the palate of your hearts than any honeycomb. The author of sweetness himself, whose every wish prospers and whose will all things obey, is capable of what appears impossible: may he bring such sweetness to your hearts that you ever delight to hear of him—and may he teach me deeper wisdom of all that concerns him. May he enable the lance of my tongue to wound and pierce the foe of mankind who expends such force to make Christ's words worthless in our hearing, and what we preach and teach a sentence of damnation to ourselves and others. May Jesus ever help us, he who loved us and washed us from our sins in his blood. May he protect and defend us from the devil, instructing us by his word, and molding us by his example. May he establish his decree and ratify his rule. O sweet decree, O rule of life: decree of love and rule of loving-kindness! May Christ establish and fulfill it; may he ratify and perfect it in himself and in us!

Love one another as I have loved you. This is the commandment Jesus gave his disciples:[160] the commandment of loving-kindness, the rule of love. Our sweet exquisite Lord sets forth this charge; how sweet and exquisite it is, for

---

profluxere dulcia eloquia vitæ. The passage is rich in allusions principally to the Psalms (e.g. 44:2, 118:103, 150:3); the striking image of *plectrum mentis* recalls Prudentius (*Cathemerion* IX), as *ore mellifluo* does Bernard.

[160] See Homily V, where the commandment is first enunciated (Jn 13:34), and n. 152.

love itself enticingly decrees it. All difficulty disappears where there is loving-kindness. Where love is true it is not toil to love. To love's command all gladly hearken; to love's yoke all willingly bend their neck, according to their desire: the wayward pursue wayward love and the lewd their lust, but the saintly devote themselves to holy love and the chaste to chastity. Therefore the Lord gives his commandment of love, his rule of loving-kindness, that all might obey it and hasten to subject the neck of their pride to the yoke of his humility. So, brothers, as good disciples of Christ, be ready to hear Christ's command as the trumpet of the Gospel intones it. Embrace it. Everywhere and in everything fulfill it. Through love return to him from whom your swollen pride drew you away.

Now let your love attend to what true love commands: exquisite love, unheard-of love, dutiful love, godly love, love altogether sweet and delightful. Love is the beauteous bridegroom, the comely one, shining white and ruby red. He is the one chosen out of a thousand, Christ the judge of the age to come, the Prince of Peace, the Lord of life. The Lord Jesus, throughout all time blessed, tells us, *This is my commandment: love one another just as I have loved you*. How light, how exquisite, how sweet the command! Light to bear, exquisite to embrace, sweet and delightful to cling to: what could be lighter, sweeter, more exquisite, than to love? All of us, well or ill, rich or poor, foolish or wise, noble or base, slave or freeman—all of us can do this. Let no one make excuses or beg off. All without exception are capable of love. And it is to love one another that the Lord commands us.

Of course many love others—but not with godly love. They love with a love that blasphemes the Lord, with a love that is merely
Job 2:4 that of one body for another—*skin for skin.* Their love conceives sorrow and gives birth
Cf. Ps 7:15 to iniquity. With spurs of wickedness and evil, blind lust drives on its bolting mount[161] of promiscuous desire until it careers headlong into the pit of hell. It is there such love resides —there to which it inescapably impels. Against all such love Christ adds: *just as I have loved you.* How has Christ loved us? We have already recalled how Christ gave himself for us, but I would once again engage your own awareness of it. In your love, in your holy faith, you know that Christ's body and blood, sacrificed and received at the altar, bears witness to you of how he loved us. Savor that love whenever you defer to your neighbor the advantage you yourself might have enjoyed. And should your holiness require yet another Christlike love, seek its cause in the temporal goods you have from him.

Mark well that Christ's love is twofold: one aspect is temporal and universal,[162] the

[161] *Equuleum suum:* in both classical and Patristic usage, *equuleus* (or *eculeus*) represents an instrument of torture, the rack; its non-figurative sense ('foal, pony'), evident here in Ogier's extended image, is best known from Varro *(Menippeæ): neque furentem eculeum . . . insanus equiso . . . educet* 'nor let an unsound stable boy lead out a mad pony'. In the phrase *ad impetiginem calcaribus . . . ire compellit,* Ogier's use of *impetigo* (as in English the name of a pustular disease of the skin) is similarly influenced by etymology—as if a play on *impetus,* (see also n. 132).

[162] *Temporalis* also refers (e.g. in Augustine) more distinctively to the season of earthly existence; this is understood by Ogier as creation's common boon, enjoyed irrespective of individual merit.

other spiritual and particular. The temporal is meted out to all—to the just and the unjust alike—through the loving-kindness of the Creator. The spiritual or particular is reserved for those who lead righteous and devout lives. This latter love is bestowed in two ways: in the conferring of virtues; and in the reward of merit. It is by the first of these that he strengthens us with virtues against the missiles of the enemy most foul. By the other he heaps the riches of everlasting glory on us when we rightly triumph over our tyrant. Christ's own affectionate love bestowed both forms of love on us when, for that love, he washed us in his blood from every defilement of flesh and spirit. And just as Christ loved us with a two-fold love, so he bids us burn with love—for him, and for our neighbor. When our love for God and for our fellows flows from a pure heart, a good conscience, and genuine faith, sin is easily resisted. For then we abound in every goodness; casting aside the world's wan charms, and all that our human frailty finds difficult and arduous we can accomplish with love, so long as we love God with our whole heart and soul, with that perfect loving-kindness that is ours from him. If we love him with all our heart, there will be nothing left that could lead us to sinful desires.

To love God is to occupy ourselves with him alone, to conceive the state of enjoying the sight of him. It is to hate sin and to loathe the world. And it is to love our neighbor, with respect to whom the worth of our loving is reckoned. It is to maintain a rightful measure within that love, not to abuse that love's established order. Love's order is abused, and its measure neglected, whenever we love the world, which we ought to disdain, or love our bodies beyond the bounds of reasonable care; whenever we do not love our neighbor as ourselves—or perchance we do not love God more than we love ourselves. We ought indeed to love our bodies to the extent that we maintain them in good health, and recognize their weaknesses; for then their movements are fit to serve the spirit, in harmony with both soul and reason. And, too, it is in our bodies that we shall rise on the day of resurrection to live for ever with the Lord in blissful glory.

We love our neighbor as ourselves when it is to no advantage of ours to do so, nor for any hoped-for gain or return, nor from ties of kinship or affinity, but for this alone: that we share a common nature.[163] Let us then love all our neighbors with genuine solicitude for their well-being. Let us promote in them the godly life that leads to life eternal, just as we strive towards this end ourselves. To the extent that we are able to do so, we ought to provide them with what they need. We love God with all our heart when we fully exert ourselves to please him alone: when he alone is our desire, our hope, our end, the totality of our love and loving-kindness. Otherwise our love for him is imperfect, and, without loving-kindness, we are no longer God's own. However much we

[163] *Proximos nostros tunc diligimus . . .*: the line is taken (by Mabillon, and so by Migne) as the incipit of Sermo XV (see Introduction on the numbering of the homilies); at some point in the transmission, a scribe was led to interpret the previous sentence *(. . . ut in die resurrectionis gloria felici perenniter cum Domino vivat)* as a closing doxology.

toil, God will not reward us hereafter if during our wretched solitude[164] we fail to hold true to the straight path of loving-kindness. That path is this: to love not only those who love us, but also those who hate us, and to hold these no less dear than we do ourselves. This is a straight and narrow path; few travel it.[165] Those who do disdain themselves for Christ's sake, apart from whom all things are base and worthless. When, on that path of love, they come upon devilish brambles meant to waylay them, these travelers bound over them like leaping stags, running swiftly and powerfully; it is the love of their heavenly home that spurs and guides them. That same devil, who prompts hatred among us brothers, those travelers dash to naught. When insults and injuries wreak stirrings of the mind that drive us wild to rail against our brothers, those followers of love's path rein in such stirrings and dash them against Christ. So as to gain all for Christ, they lay down their lives, those who in loving-kindness prostrate themselves before friends and enemies alike. Whoever obeys Christ's commands by devoting himself to him in mutual loving-kindness, is truly a friend of Christ. Let him rejoice who for Christ's sake hates himself and loves Christ above all else. In loving-kindness he embraces all that is loveless.

[164] *Ærumnosa solitudine* echoes the classics (e.g. Persius: see n. 167), but cf. Mk 4:19 *(ærumnæ sæculi et deceptio divitiarum),* Jesus' explanation of the Parable of the Sowing of Seeds.

[165] *Stricta et angusta est semita ista, et pauci vadunt per eam,* paraphrasing Mt 7:14 *(quam angusta porta et arcta via est quæ ducit ad vitam, et pauci sunt qui inveniant eam).*

Such a one is truly a monk. Anyone else, be he cowled or in rags, smooth shaven or tonsured, let him possess what he will, be what he will, bear the very image and likeness of a monk: this is no monk. I am referring in particular here to that disgraceful kind of madness whereby such a person—and there are many who suffer that malady—is prone to anger, easily provoked, quick to hate. They bear the itching of their prurient hearts on their scratchy tongues and scabby skin.[166] Their minds are corrupted: they are unsettled, shiftless, unable to give a straight answer. Prone to muttering, given to grumbling and jealousy; they are conceited and cocky. Fastidious at table, yet not one word of gratitude for all God's bounty passes their lips. Naked they stand, in the hide of deceitful Adam, without that garment of salvation which befits a creature fashioned in God's likeness in holy truth and justice.

Their foreheads smoothly groomed, they keep their rough old skins:
Beneath their raging breast a cunning fox![167]

Let all such monks' foreheads blush: *let them*
Ps 6:11 *swiftly be confounded and utterly ashamed*. Let them confess and be healed. Let them change their disposition and guide their steps in the path that leads to eternity, the way of love most chaste, the glorious road of loving-kindness. Brothers, let mutual loving-kindness be our

[166] *Scabiem cutis,* cf. n. 18.

[167] Persius, *Saturæ* (5.116); Ogier has changed the person of the verbs from second person singular to third plural. .

rule: let us love God above all, laying down our lives for love of him, obeying his commands in everything and towards all. Thus may we be found worthy to be called—and to be—Christ's friends.

You are my friends if you do what I have commanded of you. O what great honor, O abundance of inestimable loving-kindness. O deeply rooted goodness, O inexplicable solicitude! Our condition as servants makes us unworthy; yet he has deigned to call us and have us as his friends. The lavisher of sweetness, the lover of loving-kindness—indeed, loving-kindness himself, blessed delight, delightful serenity, untroubled tranquillity, happy eternity, eternal happiness: the Lord, Jesus Christ, wholly desirable, wholly lovable, our incomparable treasure, our pearl of great price, the life of the living, the hope of the dying, the eternal bliss of all who for his love have forgone happiness in this world. How happy the friend of Christ! How happy the one who for love of Christ accepts his own wretchedness! Truly worthy of eternal happiness are all who despise themselves, in whom they find no pleasure, so as to please their Creator. But let the haughty know, the conceited, the apostate,[168] mangy under their luxurious furs, perverted of conscience, self-satisfied, puffed up with pride: let them know that no one will be pleasing to his Creator until and unless their error leads him to displeasure with themselves. Let it displease

[168] *In Galgalis vitiorum fœdatus,*: in league with the Gilgal of vices—cf. Hos 9:15: *omnis nequitiæ eorum in Galgal;* Am 4:4: *venite . . . ad Galgalam et multiplicate prævaricationem.*

us as well, brothers, we who used to be wicked (and who perhaps are still). Let our pleasure be this: that, though we are far from our goal, we shall—may it please our Lord—be made perfect in the keeping of his commandments and so, from being his enemies, become his friends. *You are my friends,* he told the disciples, *if you do what I command of you.*

It is still to you, monk of Benedict, that I am speaking. Yes, brother, you. How quickly you come to table, how slow to the oratory; a healthy guzzler, but a sickly singer. You are alert to gossip, but sleepy at Vigils; all mouth to speak, you lose your tongue at psalmody; ever ready to slander and rant, but slow to prayer. Reproaching others, you indulge yourself: prompt to note the *mote*, unaware of the
Lk 6:41 *beam*. Do you not see, lover of envy, persecutor of Christ, inventor of wickedness, destroyer of discipline, friend of vice, virtues' foe? These are the very faults that blind our eyes and separate us from God! These are the vices that pervert the *conversus*[169] and make a monk a demon.

When from the depths of my heart I consider the state of well-being the Saviour has granted me (how rare that is God knows, yet knows as well how dear)—when I consider with what fervent loving-kindness towards the beloved the true Lover loves whom he has ransomed with his lovingly shed blood; then how dismayed within me I am with myself. Dismayed, perplexed, indeed I would

[169] 'Lay brother'; the pun *quæ conversum faciunt perversum* is paralleled by the play on assonances of *monachum dæmoniacum*, referring to the choir monks.

despair altogether, had not the Word become flesh and dwelt among us, had he not given himself as propitiation for our sins, and, ascending into heaven, taken up again his place beside his Father. Yet even to me, sunk of dismay and feverish in my faults—even to me, from his regal seat[170] he stretches out his hand and says, *'Come to me, you who labor* in the labor of sin *and are burdened* with its heavy weight, *and I will refresh you* by sparing you and showering the grace of my love upon you. For *you will be my friend if you do what I have commanded you to do.'*

Surely it is the same with you. Are you not dismayed as well? Let all Christ's enemies be dismayed, *let them turn back and quickly be ashamed;* then they too will be Christ's friends. *Ps 6:11* We are his friends if we love him with all our hearts. No friend of his could love him less than wholly. For if we are partly chaste and partly proud, let us recall that *God resists the proud and grants grace to the lowly*. So let us love *Jas 4:6* him in every part, let us cling to him with all our hearts; therein lies safety, therein lies salvation. To cling to him means this: to found our hope on him, to love nothing beside him, and so disdaining everything for him, to hate and scorn and count all passing things as naught. What is good and delightful is to love the *Cf. Ps 132:1* Lord Jesus Christ utterly. All who do so are his friends.

Let us reflect, brothers, on the greatness of our Redeemer's mercy. We are unworthy

[170] *De sua sede regali . . . extendit*, a recollection of Wis 18:15, *omnipotens sermo tuus de cælo a regalibus sedibus . . . prosilivit.*

to be reckoned his servants, yet we are called his friends—and we are his friends so long as we abide in his love. Let us then keep the commandments of the Lord, our one true friend, the Creator of all, so as to be found worthy not only to be reckoned among his friends, but to enjoy as well our inheritance as his children. For this we must deny ourselves for the sake of Christ who *emptied himself* and for our salvation *took on the form of a*
Phil 2:7 *servant*.[171] In that condition he released what he had not seized, giving himself willing to be scourged and sacrificed, slain on the cross. This is why Christ should be loved—and this is how, if we deny ourselves for him, he will be our Lord. Happy the denial and contempt by which a sinner is made just, an enemy a friend, a servant a son, and—greatest of all—by which a servant of the devil is made a child of God.

Therefore, O monk of Christ, despiser of yourself as well as the world. The reward of such contempt is great beyond measure: inestimable the multitude of sweetness, happiness, and eternal glory Christ gives to those who love him. It is his very self! Nothing is dearer, nothing is sweeter or more precious, nothing is more lovely than Christ.[172]

[171] Developing the allusion, Ogier's *solvit quæ non rapuit* recalls Paul's *non rapinam arbitratus est esse se æqualem Deo* of the preceding verse.

[172] *Nil carius, nil dulcius, nil preciosius, nil speciosius Christo;* cf. *Nil canitur suavius, nil auditur iucundius, nil cogitatur dulcius quam Iesus Dei Filius,* from the hymn *Iesu dulcis memoria* (see n. 89). If the hymn's attribution to Bernard of Clairvaux was already current by the early 1200s, its paraphrase here may well constitute a concluding homage to Ogier's spiritual guide and father.

He is health that knows no ailment,
he is life that knows no death,
he is joy that knows no mourning,
he is brightness without shadow,
sweetness without bitterness.

Such is the prize of all who deny themselves on his account.

May Christ grant himself as our reward:
he who lives and reigns without end,
God, blessed for ever and ever.
Amen.

Index of Sources

E = *Expositio, On the Lord's Words to His Disciples at the Last Supper*
IN = Translator's Introduction,
T = *Tractatus, In Praise of the Lord's Holy Mother*

Scriptural citations identified in marginal notes are listed by Homily number only. Citations occur in Vulgate order and enumeration.

B. EXTRA-BIBLICAL SOURCES

Bibliography

Adriani, Giovanni Battista. *Beati Oglerii . . . Opera quæ supersunt.* Turin, 1873.

Barré, Henri. 'Le *Planctus Mariæ* attribué à Saint Bernard', *Revue d'ascétique et de mystique* 28 (1962).

Bauer, Erika ed. *Zisterzienser-Predigten (Homiliæ 9 et 13 expositionis super Evangelium in Cena Domini Oglerii de Trino) in der Übertragung des Heinrich Haller O.Carth.* Munich, 1969.

Bell, David. 'Lists and Records in English Cistercian Libraries', in *Analecta Cisterciensia* 43 (1987).

———. *An Index of Authors and Works in Cistercian Libraries in Great Britain.* London, 1992.

Guenée, Bernard. *Histoire et culture historique dans l'Occident médiéval.* Paris, 1980.

James, M. R. *The Apocryphal New Testament.* Oxford, 1955.

Marx, C.W. 'The *Quis dabit* of Oglerius de Tridino, Monk and Abbot of Locedio', *The Journal of Medieval Latin* 4 (1994).

Mikkers, Edmund. 'Ogier de Locedio', *Dictionnaire de Spiritualité,* 11:733–736.

Smid, H.R. *Protoevangelium Jacobi: A Commentary* (Assen 1966).

Sticca, Sandro (tr. J.R. Berrigan). *The Planctus Mariæ in the Dramatic Tradition of the Middle Ages* (Athens GA, 1988).

Testuz, Michel. *Papyrus Bodmer V: Nativité de Marie.* Geneva, 1958.

CISTERCIAN PUBLICATIONS

Texts and Studies in the Monastic Tradition

Texts in English translation:

- Monastic insights from the desert, and from christian monks and nuns East and West
- Cistercian homilies and treatises from the formative twelfth and thirteenth centuries

Studies of the monastic tradition:

- Its history, customs, architecture, liturgy, and influence, from desert beginnings through the Middle Ages and into the present day
- Reflections on prayer and the christian vocation by contemporary contemplatives
- Audio and video resources on monasticism as well as books published abroad and not readily available in North America

All books are available singly or by series standing order. Standing order customers automatically receive new titles as they appear at a 25% discount from the list price

Series:

- Cistercian Fathers
- Monastic Wisdom
- Cistercian Studies
- Cistercian Liturgy

Editorial Offices

Cistercian Publications • WMU Station
1903 West Michigan Avenue • Kalamazoo, MI 49008-5415 USA
tel 269 387 8920 fax 269 387 8390
e-mail cistpub@wmich.edu

Customer Service—North America: USA and Canada

Cistercian Publications at Liturgical Press
Saint John's Abbey • Collegeville, MN 56321-7500 USA
tel 800 436 8431 fax 320 363 3299
e-mail sales@litpress.org

Customer Service—Europe: UK, Ireland, and Europe

Cistercian Publications at Columba Book Service
55A Spruce Avenue • Stillorgan Industrial Park
Blackrock, Co. Dublin, Ireland
tel 353 1 294 2560 fax 353 1 294 2564
e-mail sales@columba.ie

To explore the range of titles offered by Cistercian Publications, please request our free complete catalogue from one of the customer service offices or visit our website at **www.cistercianpublications.org**